Cognitive Interfaces

Cognitive Interfaces

Constraints on Linking Cognitive Information

Edited by

EMILE VAN DER ZEE
and URPO NIKANNE

OXFORD

UNIVERSITY PRESS

OXFORD
UNIVERSITY PRESS

Great Clarendon Street, Oxford OX2 6DP
Oxford University Press is a department of the University of Oxford.
It furthers the University's objective of excellence in research, scholarship,
and education by publishing worldwide in

Oxford New York

Athens Auckland Bangkok Bogotá Buenos Aires Calcutta Cape Town
Chennai Dar es Salaam Delhi Florence Hong Kong Istanbul Karachi
Kuala Lumpur Madrid Melbourne Mexico City Mumbai Nairobi
Paris São Paulo Shanghai Singapore Taipei Tokyo Toronto Warsaw
with associated companies in Berlin Ibadan

Oxford is a registered trade mark of Oxford University Press
in the UK and in certain other countries

Published in the United States
by Oxford University Press Inc., New York

© Editorial matter and organization: Emile van der Zee and Urpo Nikanne 2000;
© Individual chapters their authors 2000

British Library Cataloguing in Publication Data
Data available

Library of Congress Cataloging in Publication Data
Data applied for

ISBN 0–19–829961–3
ISBN 0–19–829962–1 (Pbk.)

10 9 8 7 6 5 4 3 2 1

Typeset in Minion
by Peter Kahrel, Lancaster
Printed in Great Britain
on acid-free paper by
Biddles Ltd., Guildford and King's Lynn

Contents

Preface

Cognitive science has evolved to a point where cognitive scientists have some good insights in different areas of cognition such as language, visual perception, and motoric tasks. Although theory formation in each of these areas has by no means come to an end, the level of theory formation increasingly allows us to consider cognitive behaviour that requires a linking between different kinds of cognitive information. In all traditions in cognitive science—whether symbolic, modular, non-symbolic, or non-modular—the human mind is considered as more than a set of separate pieces of information. The mind is considered as a system that functions as an integrated whole, carrying out tasks on the basis of different kinds of available information. This means that the linking of cognitive information and constraints on such linking is becoming an increasingly interesting and challenging object of study. In this book we have brought together several kinds of research that consider some aspect of cognitive information-linking. In the introduction to this book we try to point out the consequences of each chapter for our understanding of the constraints on linking cognitive information.

We would like to express our gratitude to Ray Jackendoff, who has been an inspirational source for many aspects of our work. Jackendovian insights can be seen in our introductory chapter, and in the way in which the chapters are organized in this volume, even though the chapters themselves represent different schools of thought.

We would also like to thank John Davey, editor in linguistics at Oxford University Press, and several anonymnous reviewers, for their support and guidance with the editing process.

We hope that the book is interesting for all students and researchers in cognitive science who are interested in issues relating to cognitive information representation, or in issues relating to cognitive interfaces. We also hope that the chapters in this volume not only inspire those who work in the classical cognitive tradition, but also students and researchers in the non-symbolic and non-modular cognitive science traditions.

Lincoln and Oslo, October 1999

Emile van der Zee
Urpo Nikanne

Abbreviations

CS	conceptual structure
DAT	dative
DEF	definite
DF	discourse form
DO	direct object
ELA	elative
EPP	Extended Projection Principle
GEN	genitive
GF	grammatical form
IEPS	inferred eventual position or state
IO	indirect object
LCS	lexical conceptual structure
LF	logical form
LSS	lexical spatial structure
MOU	micro-object unit
MRU	micro-relation unit
MSe	mean standard error
NOM	nominative
n.s.	not significant
OBJ	object
PF	phonetic form
PL	plural
PST	past tense
QR	Quantifier Raising
REFL	reflexive
RS	Referential Structure
RT	response time
SG	singular
SR	spatial structure
SUBJ	subject
TF	thematic form

List of Figures

1

Introducing Cognitive Interfaces and Constraints on Linking Cognitive Information

EMILE VAN DER ZEE and URPO NIKANNE

Cognitive science considers the human mind as an information-processing device which processes spatial information, linguistic information, motoric information, etc. (Posner 1989; Wilson and Keil 1999). Our minds are able to link together these different kinds of information in order to make it possible, for example, to talk about what we see or to act upon what we hear. All chapters in this book consider the linking between different kinds of cognitive information. More specifically, each chapter looks at some of the constraints that play a role in linking different kinds of cognitive information to each other. Why is it possible for English speakers to say, for example—when they link visual information to linguistic information—*The bike is next to the building*, but not *The building is next to the bike* (Talmy 1983; Landau and Jackendoff 1993)? This chapter looks at some general constraints on linking different kinds of cognitive information, and also shows how the different chapters in this book that address specific constraints fit into this more general picture.

Cognitive science is an area with many conflicting theoretical frameworks and ideas. However, it seems fair to say that most cognitive scientists would agree on the sketch of the cognitive architecture of the human mind as shown in Figure 1.1.

This cognitive architecture captures the idea that different sensory systems provide our mind with some information input, that our minds deliver an information output in terms of body movement or speech, and that there are different cognitive structures that are responsible for converting the information input in a particular output. Solid arrows in Figure 1.1 represent mapping relations between different kinds of cognitive information. Such mapping relations are carried out by cognitive interfaces. Interface 1 maps spatial information to linguistic information and vice versa. This mapping relation explains, among other things, our ability to talk about what we see and our ability to imagine ourselves what we read. Interface 2 maps linguistic information to motoric information,

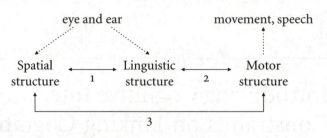

FIGURE 1.1. A sketch of some basic kinds of information that
are represented in the human mind

and the other way around. This explains, for example, our ability to speak about
what we want to communicate using language, and our ability to formulate into
language what we do. Interface 3 maps spatial information into motoric information and vice versa. This explains, among other things, our ability to do the
things that we imagine ourselves doing or to imagine what we can do. Cognitive
interfaces are thus important elements in our cognitive architecture. They make
it possible to carry out tasks that require more than one kind of cognitive information.

The major goal of this book is to bring together new research on cognitive
interfaces. The chapters are from such different areas as psychology, linguistics,
and computer science. And, what is more, they not only show that interfaces are
an important research object for the more classical symbolic or modular theories
in cognition, but also for more recent non-symbolic or non-modular approaches
in cognitive science. We will come back to this latter issue in more detail below.

The human mind also represesents concepts or categories on the basis of
which we categorize, for example, different kinds of sensory information, so that
we can generalize over many perceived instances in our behaviour. Many cognitive scientists assume that categorical information is represented in a separate
cognitive system (Fodor 1983; Jackendoff 1983, 1987*a*, 1997). Such a system makes
it possible for us to think or have beliefs about the perceived spatial layout,
about language, about our motor system or about any other kind of cognitive
information. The assumption is, thus, that there is a central level of information
representation at which all kinds of cognitive information are compatible. Figure 1.2 accounts for this possibility, while at the same time zooming in on some
of the details of the language faculty.

Figure 1.2 describes our cognitive architecture in terms of different modules
of information representation (Chomsky 1965, 1981, 1986*b*, 1995; Jackendoff 1983,
1987*a*, 1992, 1996*a*, 1997; Marr 1982). Such modules represent different kinds of
cognitive information in terms of autonomous information structures. This
means, for example, that the grammar and the spatial representations that generate spatial structures is different from the grammar and syntactic representations

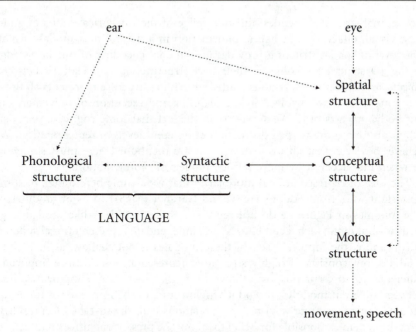

FIGURE 1.2. The cognitive architecture of the human mind in terms of different levels of information representation

that generate syntactic structures. Figure 1.2 is no longer representative of the different ideas in the cognitive science community about the human mind. Cognitive scientists differ as to whether they favour a modular cognitive architecture, as to what modules represent, and as to what the different modules are that can be assumed (Garfield 1987). We assume the cognitive architecture in Figure 1.2, however, for heuristic reasons, as it enables us to discuss the different kinds of mapping relations in the human mind in more detail than in Figure 1.1. We therefore ask those who do not agree with the model in Figure 1.2 to suspend their disbelief and bear with us for the moment. It is our belief that even if one would not agree with the exact nature of the mapping relations that we discuss here, those mapping relations must somehow be present in any cognitive architecture of the human mind. In this chapter we only discuss those mapping relations that are represented by solid arrows.

Let us, before we discuss the cognitive interfaces in more detail, briefly go into the properties of the different representational modules in Figure 1.2. The language faculty in this figure is described in terms of phonological structure and syntactic structure; respectively, levels of representation that represent our knowledge of linguistic sound patterns and our knowledge of linguistic form.

Conceptual structure encodes our knowledge of the categorical status of auditory, visual, olfactory, and haptic information in a neutral or a-modal format. The level of spatial structure provides an a-modal encoding of our knowledge of the 3D structure of objects, their part structure, spatial relations between objects, and object parts, regions, paths, etc. Motor structure represents all those components that are involved in the planning and execution of movements of our body, or parts of it. We are aware of the fact that some cognitive scientists favour an even more refined distinction of different levels of representation. We believe, however, that all distinctions that are mentioned here must somehow be taken into account by more refined models of representation.

The idea of representational modularity that we assume here differs in some important ways from Fodor's (1983) and Gardner's (1983) ideas of modularity. The modules in Figure 1.2 do not represent entire faculties—like the language faculty—but refine such faculties to several independent representational systems. Furthermore, the input to each of these modules is not shallow, as in Fodor's modules, but consists of highly structured representations. A more important difference for present purposes, however, is that there are mapping relations between different modules. In Fodor's architecture of the mind, for example, all modules only have (one way) mapping relations with the so-called Central System; the system responsible for belief fixation. The present cognitive architecture, however, also allows for interfaces between different kinds of modules. As we have seen this assumption is necessary in order to account for carrying out cognitive tasks that involve several kinds of cognitive information. Just like Fodor's modules, however, interface modules are domain specific and informationally encapsulated (Jackendoff 1997).

This book is divided into four parts. The first two parts discuss the properties of the conceptual-to-syntactic-structure interface and the conceptual-to-spatial-structure interface. The conceptual-to-motor-structure interface is not addressed in this book in detail, but is briefly alluded to by Bryant, Tversky, and Lanca. We therefore devote minor attention to the conceptual-to-motor-structure interface in this introduction. Part Three is concerned with interface properties in word representations. This means that it will look at interface properties at more than two different levels of information representation, because word representations carry more than two kinds of cognitive information. Part Four considers mapping relations between different kinds of cognitive information from a connectionist perspective. Researchers working within this perspective consider mapping relations between different kinds of cognitive information from a neuronal level of processing (Elman 1996). The chapters in Part Five do not necessarily agree with the idea of representational modularity as depicted in Figure 1.2.

Let us now consider some of the more general properties of cognitive interfaces, before going into the details of the specific interfaces that are addressed in this book. Before we can describe general interface properties we need to address the way in which information is represented in each of the representational modules that interface with each other. The most interesting way in which information may be represented in representational modules is in terms of headed hierarchies (see Jackendoff 1987a: 249–51 for a discussion of non-hierarchical and non-headed hierarchical representations as well). Let us look at some examples. Although theories of syntax may differ considerably from each other, all syntactic theories assume that syntactic information is represented hierarchically. Theories that are based on constituent structure assume that each sentence is composed of phrases and phrases of words. Words belong to different syntactic categories or 'parts of speech', and the category determines the syntactic behaviour of the word. These syntactic categories (verb, noun, adjective, adverb, etc.) are assumed to be primitives on the level of syntactic structure. Constituent structure helps us to explain, for example, why certain sets of words seem to behave as a unit when it comes to word-order and coreference relations. In English, for instance, it is possible to topicalize a whole noun phrase: [NP *This red convertible*] *I have never seen before.* However, it is not possible to topicalize any single part of a noun phrase: **Red I have never seen this convertible before* or **Convertible I have never seen this red before.* In addition, one can refer to a whole noun phrase with a single pronoun: *I bought* [*a nice red Italian convertible*]i *and I like it*i *very much.* The pronoun *it* is coreferential here with the whole noun phrase *a nice red Italian convertible.*

The idea of headedness explains why the syntactic behaviour of a phrase is determined by the syntactic category of its head. For instance, a noun like *ice cream* is in object position in a sentence like *John likes ice cream* in the same way that a noun phrase *the ice cream that was bought at the fair* is in object position in *John likes ice cream that was bought at the fair.* Assuming that the noun phrase is a projection of the head noun, it is understandable that the category of the head determines the syntactic behaviour of the entire phrase. In other words, syntactic representations are hierarchical in nature and possess the property of headedness.

The headedness of syntactic phrases leads to another concept, namely, 'dependency'. So far we have only discussed constituency, which is based on inclusion. For instance, the noun phrase (NP) *red convertible* includes the head noun (N) *convertible* and the adjective phrase (AP) *red*, which only includes the head adjective (A):

(1)

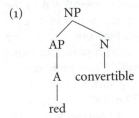

Another way to approach the relation between the above adjective and noun is in terms of dependency. In the NP *red convertible* the adjective *red* is dependent on the head noun *convertible*. This is illustrated in (2).

(2)

There are different kinds of dependency relations. Some modifiers are obligatory and some are optional. For instance, the subject and object of a transitive verb are obligatory; they are said to be selected by the verb. On the other hand, in our example, the adjective *red* is not an obligatory modifier of the noun *convertible.*

There are grammars whose syntax is based on constituency. For example, traditional Immediate Constituent analysis (starting from Bloomfield 1933), or, for instance, the 1960s versions of transformational grammar (see Chomsky 1957, 1965). And there are dependency grammars (starting from Tesnière 1959) in which the syntactic structure is based on dependency. In order for us to understand syntax, it is necessary to include both constituency and dependency in the description of the syntactic structure. One possibility is to try to develop a theory of a single structure in which both dependency and constiuency are integrated, as is the case with the so called X-bar structures in generative grammar (since Chomsky 1970). Another possibility would be to understand constituent structures and dependency structures to be separate layers ('tiers') of the syntactic representation, both of which express one different side of the entire representation.

Spatial, motoric, and conceptual representations also seem to be headed hierarchical structures. Let us briefly consider spatial representations of objects in terms of Marr and Nishihara (1978) and Biederman (1987). Marr and Nishihara claim that at the coarsest level of spatial representation objects are represented as generalized cones; cones that are represented by sweeping a contour along a main axis. This means, for example, that for the purpose of locating a human body, that body can be represented in terms of the main axis of the cone representing the entire body. However, for the purpose of specifying the position of an arm with respect to the trunk, a hand in relation to an arm, or a finger in relation to a hand, we need to zoom in at spatial elements lower down in the spatial hierarchy. The axes of each of the cones making up an object can be considered as the heads of each of these spatial structures. In the same way that we can determine the position of a human body in relation to other objects in terms of the main axis of this body, we can determine the position of a body part in relation to another body part in terms of the main axis of such a body part.

There is also evidence that motoric representations are headed hierarchies. For example, the central nervous system appears to consider a grasping movement in terms of a sequence of equilibrium positions of the hand, resulting in a fine-tuning of the hand by taking into account relevant environmental factors (Bizzi *et al.* 1984). The fact that the planning of grasping takes place in terms of hand motion planning (Flash and Hogan 1985) seems to show that the involved motoric representations are headed structures, in which the hand is the head of a 'movement phrase'. Pending further evidence we assume here that motoric representations fall in the same scheme as other central representations, since similar planning structures could be imagined for *kicking*, for instance.

Different theoretical frameworks of conceptual or semantic information representation assume that these representations, too, are headed hierarchical structures. Let us illustrate our point by considering a situation in which somebody describes or sees Tommy throwing a ball to Chuckie. We tend to categorize such a situation in terms of an action or an event. This action or event consists of Tommy causing a ball to go to Chuckie by the act of throwing. This example illustrates that at its highest level of representation a conceptual representation may consist of an event, that at a lower level of representation this event consists of an object moving from one location to another, and that at a still lower level of conceptual representation this event is encoded as being brought about by throwing. The idea that manner is specified at the lowest level of representation accounts for the idea that the same event could have been brought about by an act of rolling, sending, etc. Conceptual structures are headed by functions or operators that map conceptual representations into, for example, an action or a manner. In other words, all representational modules that we consider here seem to generate headed hierarchical structures.

In trying to determine general interface properties we need to determine whether constituent structure, headedness, or hierarchical structure plays any role in linking cognitive information. Let us consider the simple example of categorizing a perceived **arm** as an ARM (in this book, spatial entities are represented in bold and concepts in capitals). In order to establish a link between an **arm** representation and an ARM representation we need to know which level of spatial or conceptual representation must be accessed. Accessing the wrong level of representation may result in categorizing a perceived **body** or a **finger** as an ARM. What follows from this example is that the hierarchical structure of the involved representations is important, as well as the constituent structure, but that headedness is not. Let us consider each of these claims in turn. **Arm** forms a constituent at the level of spatial representation and ARM forms a constituent at the level of conceptual representation. We are thus looking at a linking between constituents, depending on their place in the hierarchy at a particular level of information representation. However, the mapping relation between two constituents does not necessarily have anything to do with the heads that are involved in generating those constituents at their level of information representation. For example, for the purpose of categorizing **arm** as an ARM, not only the axis generating an **arm** is important at spatial structure, but also the **contour** that is swept along it, the **texture** that is part of an **arm**, etc. This latter example also shows that information may be lost in mapping it from one level of representation to information at another level of representation. If there would be a complete mapping of elements from one structure to another, representational structures would only be notational variants of each other.

Having established some very general properties of cognitive interfaces, we now consider the properties of the conceptual-to-spatial-structure interface, followed by the properties of the conceptual-to-syntactic-structure interface.

It must be noted at this point that the properties of any interface depend—obviously—on assumptions about the cognitive archtitecture involved. We have assumed here that there is only a single interface between conceptual and spatial structure, and between conceptual and syntactic structure. Whether these assumptions are correct is an empirical question. For example, there could be seperate interfaces between conceptual and syntactic structure, and between syntactic and conceptual structure. Other authors, stressing other kinds of empirical evidence, have come to other conclusions about the number of interfaces or their properties. In relation to the conceptual-to-spatial-structure interface there are authors that assume, for instance, intermediate representations or processes between perceptual and conceptual representations. For example, Logan and Sadler (1996: 497), and, according to Shallice (1996), also Bub *et al.* (1988) and Chertkow and Bub (1990), seem to have such views. In relation to the conceptual-to-syntactic-structure interface, Bierwisch and Lang (1989) and Wunderlich (1991), among others, assume a level of representation in between conceptual and syntactic structure: a level of semantic form. Obviously, having other ideas about representational levels between the levels that we assume here has consequences for the properties of the involved interfaces. However, no matter whether one has more fine-grained views of the involved interfaces than we have here, we feel that those properties that we will mention here must be instantiated somehow by any possible alternative.

The properties of the conceptual-to-spatial-structure interface have been extensively discussed by Jackendoff (1987a: ch. 10, 1987b, 1996a, 1997). Our discussion of these properties will therefore rely heavily on this work—while at the same time extending it.

The following list gives an overview of some of the entities and relations that are represented both at the level of spatial and conceptual structure:

(1) object and object part
(2) location and region
(3) extrinsic movement (movement along a path)
(4) intrinsic movement (object deformation)
(5) count–mass distinction
(6) reference frame representation
(7) object and path axes
(8) object contours

(9) object texture

(10) distance

(11) part–whole structure

Given the general constraints on linking that we discussed before, the spatial-to-conceptual-structure linking of the above entities or relations could be thought of as rather straightforward. However, it appears that the involved interface also functions as a 'filtering mechanism' in that not all the richness of spatial structure is preserved for conceptual structure, and that not all the richness of conceptual structure is preserved for spatial structure. Let us consider some examples. As shown by Landau and Jackendoff (1993), not all aspects of the spatial representation of an object are represented for all parts of language equally. Even though we need much spatial detail for the relation between perceived people and names, or between perceived objects and English nouns, we tend to abstract objects to their axial structure or contour structure if such objects play a role in a spatial relation. For example, in order to know whether *The stick is lying along the kerb* we only need to know whether the main axis generating the stick representation is parallel to and some distance away from the main axis generating a kerb representation. The conceptual-structure representation of the preposition *along* only seems to have access to axial information and distance information. As is clear from Carlson's chapter, however, it is also the case that prepositions like *above* pick out functional information of the objects that are involved in describing such spatial relations. *Above the toothbrush*, for instance, picks out another region than *above the piggy bank* if the objects above them are—respectively—a toothpaste tube and a coin. Although the functional properties of the involved objects are clearly instrumental in representing a region at spatial structure, the functional features on the basis of which those regions are represented cannot themselves be available at spatial structure; these features are not part of the grammar at this level of representation.

The following list contains some constraints on linking conceptual-to-spatial structure representations (but there are many more of these):

1. Conceptual structure represents functional features of objects and object parts, whereas spatial structure does not (see Carlson, this volume).
2. Conceptual structure represents negation, whereas Spatial Structure does not.
3. Conceptual structure represents modal and social predicates, whereas spatial structure does not.
4. Spatial structure represents all path features, whereas conceptual structure can make a selection of all path features at this level of representation (see Nikanne, this volume).
5. Spatial structure represents all possible curvature values, whereas lexical conceptual structure does not (see van der Zee, this volume).
6. Spatial structure represents height in a non-ambiguous manner, whereas conceptual structure does not (see Gasser *et al.*, this volume).

The constraints on the spatial-to-conceptual-structure interface discussed so far follow from some general architectural constraints; that is, they follow from what is represented at spatial structure and what is represented at conceptual structure. However, there are also constraints on the linking between two levels of information representation that follow from the way mapping relations develop in a system. Two such constraints follow from the particular language environment a child grows up in, and the particular cultural environment the childs finds itself in. For example, it appears that English verbs of rotation do not make a distinction between rotation around vertical and horizontal axes, whereas most Dutch verbs do (see van der Zee in this volume). The questions that need to be answered in relation to such a difference are, for instance, whether different languages make different selections among the available set of mappings, whether certain mappings are unique to certain languages, etc. (see also Gasser *et al.*, this volume). The influence of a particular cultural environment may determine even finer constraints on information linking. For example, even though in American English and Dutch all major cities are part of the vocabulary, as well as all cardinal directions (North, South, East, and West), major direction is specified in terms of major cities in the Netherlands, but in terms of cardinal directions in the US. We can thus conclude that constraints on spatial-to-conceptual-structure linking not only follow from the available cognitive architecture at birth, but also from the development of the cognitive system in a particular environment.

Let us now consider the properties of the conceptual-to-syntactic-structure interface. The most striking similarity between the level of syntactic structure and conceptual structure is that both levels of representation are based on selection (and other kinds of dependency relations between heads and modifiers; see the discussion of the term 'dependency' above). A word needs to be accompanied by one or more other syntactic elements in order for a sentence to be grammatical. For instance the transitive verbs *send*, *kiss*, and *buy* must be accompanied by two noun phrases that encode the subject and the object of the verb. These transitive verbs can thus be said to select two noun phrases. Conceptual structure, as understood in conceptual semantics, is based on semantic relations, or functions, like CAUSE (encoding causation) (see e.g. Nikanne's and van der Zee's chapters). These relations must be accompanied by other elements. For instance CAUSE selects the causer and the caused situation. The relation GO (change/move), on the other hand, selects the element that is moving or changing, plus the path along which the movement takes place (change is understood as an abstract kind of movement). For example, the verb *send* means roughly 'cause to go'. It must therefore be accompanied by a Causer, a Theme, and a PATH (where the head of a PATH is PATH function). These arguments must be expressed in linguistic representations, and, in addition, the linking between these linguistic representations and conceptual structures must be somehow transparant. Figure 1.3 shows the syntactico-conceptual linking between the syntactic and semantic representations of the verb *send* and its complements.

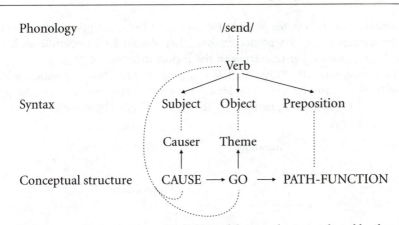

Phonology   /send/

FIGURE 1.3. Syntactico-semantic linking of the complements selected by the verb *send*. Arrows indicate selection and dotted lines indicate linking

In addition to the linking of words and their semantic structure, the syntactic-to-conceptual-structure interface also explains the linking between morphemes and their semantic structure. Morphemes are traditionally defined as the 'smallest items carrying meaning' (i.e. word stems, suffixes, prefixes, etc.). This is a slightly misleading characterization, as there are morphemes that do not seem to carry any particular meaning or that are only there to indicate relations to other syntactic elements (e.g. genitive case often only indicates a particular relation between the head and the modifier). However, the traditional definition of morpheme is based on the quite correct observation that many—or perhaps most—morphemes carry a meaning and, thus, that there is a morphological–conceptual interface. For instance, the past-tense suffix expresses a particular temporal concept. Also, the derivational suffix *-able* (e.g. *read-able*, *understand-able*, etc.) expresses a certain meaning such that *V-able* means 'possible to V'.

One major part of research on the syntactico-semantic interface is to determine which part of syntactic structure corresponds to which part of conceptual structure. There are, for instance, the following restrictions (see Nikanne 1995, 1997*a*, 1998; Jackendoff 1977, 1983, 1990):

(*a*) Syntactic predicates (verbs, prepositions, etc.) are linked to conceptual functions (CAUSE, GO, TO, etc.)
(*b*) Syntactic arguments (SUBJ, OBJ, etc.) are linked to conceptual arguments (Causer, Theme, Goal, etc.)
(*c*) The leftmost conceptual argument of the lexical conceptual strucure of a verb is linked to SUBJ.

In order to illustrate these constraints, we can take a simple example and analyze the sentence *Mary sent the letter to Bill.* We need the descriptions of the words of that sentence and a sentence analysis that should be compatible with the lexical descriptions. Let us start with the lexical structure of *to*.

The lexical syntactic category of *to* is a preposition. This preposition selects a noun as its complement.[1] The lexical conceptual strucure of *to* is the path function TO, whose complement has the role of Goal (Figure 1.4).

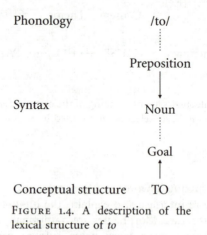

Phonology   /to/

                                   Preposition

Syntax   Noun

                                   Goal

Conceptual structure   TO

FIGURE 1.4. A description of the lexical structure of *to*

The lexical structures of the words *Bill, letter,* and *Mary* are as illustrated in Figure 1.5. They are all nouns, whose lexical conceptual structure is THING. (On THING and other conceptual categories see Jackendoff 1983, 1990, 1991.)

Figure 1.6 illustrates the linking between the phonological, syntactic, and conceptual representations of the sentence *Bill sent the letter to Mary*. The phonological representation is not analysed in any detail as we are concentrating on the syntactico-semantic linking. It must be noted that the correspondences between the lexical structures in Figures 1.3–1.5 can be recovered in the analysis in Figure 1.6.

The syntactico-semantic linking in our example obeys the constraints given in (*a*)–(*c*) above. On the syntactic level, the verb *send* selects three elements: the subject noun, the object noun, and a prepositional phrase. The preposition *to* selects a noun as its complement. Syntactic elements that select other elements as their complements, like verbs and prepositions, are syntactic predicates. Syn-

---

[1] This description is slightly simplified, as it is the case for many other lexical items that we discuss below. E.g., the complement of the preposition *to* is not always a noun, as is illustrated in a sentence like *John came here to play*, where the complement of *to* is a verb. Similar simplifications play a role in considering proper names and the article *the* further on in this chapter. However, our purpose here is not to go into all the details of syntactic theory, but only to illustrate some general properties of the syntactic-to-conceptual-structure interface.

Phonology	/mary/	/letter/	/bill/
Syntax	Noun	Noun	Noun
Conceptual structure	THING	THING	THING

FIGURE 1.5. A description of the lexical structure of the nouns *Bill, Mary,* and *letter*

tactic predicates are linked to functions like CAUSE, GO, and TO, which are predicates at the level of conceptual structure. Arguments at syntactic structure and conceptual structure are also linked to each other. In addition, the leftmost argument of the verb *send* is linked to the subject (see also Figure 1.3).

The general ideas on the linking of cognitive information and the constraints on linking such information can be found in each of the chapters in this book. Each of the chapters, however, looks at some of the interface properties that we have considered here in more detail. In the remainder of this introduction we will consider the contribution of each of the chapters in this book in relation to the issue of constraints on cognitive interfaces. We will discuss each of the chapters briefly within each of the different parts of the book.

Part One presents constraints on the conceptual-to-syntactic-structure interface. The two chapters in this part discuss central topics of representation-based and cognitively oriented linguistics, whose roots are in Generative Grammar (Chomsky 1957).[2] The conceptual-to-syntactic-structure interface has become one of the most crucial parts of Generative Grammar in the past few years, especially within the so-called Minimalist program (Chomsky 1995). According to this program there are two kinds of syntactic representation: one that is relevant to the interface between syntax and phonology and one that is relevant for the

---

[2] There is another major school of thought within theoretical linguistics, aiming to integrate language to other cognitive domains. This school calls itself Cognitive Linguistics (see for instance Langacker 1990 and Lakoff 1990). Cognitive Linguistics differs from the work in some of the chapters in this volume in that it is not based on representations and in that it does not assume the existence of (an autonomous) syntax. However, the goal of the more formal cognitively based linguistics and Cognitive Linguistics is the same: to come up with a theory of language that is integrated in a general cognitive theory.

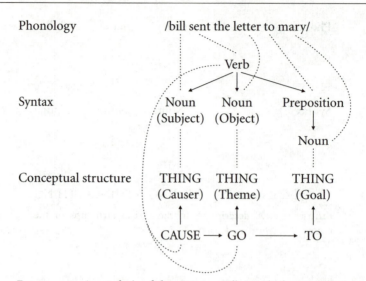

FIGURE 1.6. An analysis of the sentence *Bill sent the letter to Mary*

syntactic-to-conceptual-structure interface. The chapters by Christer Platzack and Lars Hellan discuss some original ideas about the nature and properties of the syntactic-to-conceptual-structure interface.

Drawing on examples from Norwegian, Swedish, German, Italian, French, English, and Finnish, Platzack discusses the linking between syntactic structure and the system of 'thought'. In the current Minimalist program in linguistics (Chomsky 1995, 1998) it is generally postulated that there is only one interface between syntactic structure on the one side, and all systems of thought on the other side. Platzack takes issue with this idea and argues for a model where the systems of thought access multiple interface levels. It is claimed that there are three such levels: Thematic Form, Grammatical Form, and Discourse Form. The information exchanged at these levels pertains to the information assembled at the V-domain, the I-domain and the C-domain, respectively. Conceptual evidence—deriving from the way the computational system works at all three levels—and empirical evidence is presented for this idea. Platzack's work thus shows that both conceptual and empirical material constrain the structure of the cognitive interface.

On the basis of examples from Norwegian, German, Oryia, and English, Hellan argues that one formal device of indexing between conceptual structure and syntactic structure is able to account for both 'track keeping' and the indication of discourse referent/binding. That is, the formal device for syntactic to conceptual binding can also be used for 'pure' syntactic binding. Hellan interprets his formal indexing device as a true semantic device, thus explaining syntactic binding as a result of syntactic to conceptual structure binding. Hellan's work thus shows how the properties of a cognitive interface may explain information representation properties at a particular level of information representation.

Part Two presents constraints on the conceptual-to-spatial-structure interface. The two chapters in this part show that both theoretical linguistics and experimental psychological research contribute to our insights in the properties of this interface. In recent years the properties of this interface have received increasing attention (see P. Bloom *et al.* 1996), after an initial formulation of the details of this problem (Miller and Johnson-Laird 1976).

Urpo Nikanne discusses linguistic expressions that refer to spatial movement. He looks in particular at Finnish descriptions of Figure movement along a path. Nikanne shows how constraints at the level of conceptual structure determine a linking with representations at spatial structure. He also discusses asymmetries between the spatial and conceptual encoding of paths. From this latter observation he concludes that although conceptual structure representations constrain the properties of the conceptual-to-spatial-structure interface, that each level of information representation still has its own distinctions to contribute to this particular interface.

Carlson takes issue with the idea that only spatial features play a role in the description of spatial relations, as implicitly assumed in P. Bloom *et al.* (1996). She argues for and, on the basis of experimental evidence, shows that the functional relation between two objects determines how we describe a spatial relation between those two objects. It is shown that two objects in a functional relation elicit more intrinsic descriptions, and that two objects in a non-functional relation elicit more relative/absolute descriptions. Carlson argues that mental models are interface representations between conceptual structure, encoding functional relationships, and spatial structure, encoding different possible reference frames. The selection of a particular reference frame depends on the relative prominence of functional and spatial features that are present in a mental model. This work shows that taking into account functional information—in addition to spatial information—gives another interpretation of mental models than in the case of David Bryant *et al.* (see below).

Bryant *et al.* present experimental evidence which shows that a verbal triggering of memory about the spatial layout of a scene cannot be explained by assuming memory of a mental image of a scene (as assumed in classical mental imagery research), but only by assuming memory of a mental model of a scene. These authors also present evidence for the use of mental imagery if subjects have to describe the layout of a scene while observing a scene. On the basis of their research Bryant *et al.* conclude that mental models are not intermediary representations between linguistic and spatial information representation, but interface representations between motoric and spatial information representation.

They see mental models as part of a control system to simulate the environment, generate goal directions, and monitor progress towards goals. Bryant *et al.* thus show how the logic of an experimental set up can constrain our ideas on the cognitive status of interface representations.

Part Three discusses constraints on the lexical interface. The constraints discussed in the chapter by van der Zee draw on two interfaces that seem necessary for the representation of words that refer to spatial entities: the syntactic-to-conceptual-structure interface and the spatial-to-conceptual-structure interface. This chapter follows the tradition of conceptual semantics (Jackendoff 1983, 1990, 1997; Nikanne 1990), while building especially on a paper by Jackendoff (1987*b*), in which Jackendoff points out for the first time the need for considering at least these levels of information representation for representing words that refer to spatial entities.

Van der Zee argues that the lexical structure of Dutch nouns, verbs, adjectives, and adverbs that refer to path curvature, object curvature, and surface curvature (e.g. *a kink, to zigzag, bent,* and *circling*) contain both conceptual and spatial-information distinctions. In particular, he shows (1) that part of the meaning of Dutch curvature words must be described by spatial features encoding axis and contour curvature, (2) that curvature words preferably refer to focal curvature values, and (3) that there is a systematic link between conceptual and spatial representations in the lexical structure of Dutch curvature words. In addition, he shows that there is a systematic linking between the conceptual and syntactic representations of Dutch curvature words, in the sense that the derivation of Dutch verbs, adjectives, and adverbs that refer to curvature distinctions is constrained by some general conceptual features and by the conceptual structure of Dutch nouns that refer to curvature distinctions.

Part Four discusses constraints on 'interfaces' from a connectionist perspective. We put 'interfaces' in quotes here, because from a connectionist perspective it does not neccesarily make sense to talk about interfaces (because of the implicit connotation that symbolic mapping relations may be involved). However, both chapters show in an interesting way how the neural architecture of the brain constrains mapping relations between different kinds of cognitive information. Michael Gasser, Eliana Colunga, and Linda Smith use a model of the neural architecture of the brain to illustrate their point, whereas John Slack's chapter shows what the consequences of some of the properties of neurons are in terms of constraints on representations and interfaces from a more theoretical point of view.

Gasser *et al.* consider how relational concepts like ABOVE and NEXT TO may develop in our brains. On the basis of a review of the literature they conclude that relational concepts must be similarity-based and must be influenced by the specific developmental history and the language environment the organism lives in. They present a connectionist model (Playpen) which takes into account the biological and empirical constraints on learning relational concepts. They show that this model is able to learn such concepts, given the above constraints. Their approach assumes one single interface between language and vision: a module of 'spatial concepts'. They argue that in the adult cognitive system this module consists of '. . . multiple sublayers each performing some form of transformation on the patterns it receives from above or below, each connected to its neighbours by an interface in the form of a simple pattern of connectivity' (p. 213). The work of Gasser *et al.* thus shows that although the question of interfaces is hardly ever discussed in connectionism, the connectionist framework does provide a handle for discussing cognitive interfaces.

Slack's chapter looks more closely at the problem of encoding relational structures on neural networks. He begins by assuming that the brain employs a common currency of representations based on distributed patterns, or vectors, and then focuses on how to differentiate the arguments of an asymmetric relationship like SUCCESSOR_OF in terms of such representational tokens. His chapter concentrates on the compositional operation, Merge, assumed in the Minimalist approach in linguistics to account for combining two categories into one at the level of syntactic structure (Chomsky 1995, 1998), and argues that such operations implemented as neural networks are applied to types rather than to tokens. This means that the arguments of an asymmetric relational structure must be differentiated by their type. Slack shows that some of the structural properties of language, and, in particular, the constraints on X-bar structure, derive from the fact that there is a limited set of types that can be employed to differentiate the components of synchronic representations based on vectors. Furthermore, he shows that the two language interfaces, Phonetic Form and Logical Form, require structures to be encoded that differ in terms of the distributions of synchronic and diachronic components they employ. According to this theory, X-bar structures reflect the constraints resulting from accommodating the Logical Form interface on neural networks. Slack's work shows that constraints on cognitive representations may derive from biological constraints inherent to the human brain. The kinds of constraint that apply to representations also apply to 'interfaces' between representations.

PART ONE

Constraints on the Conceptual-Structure-
to-Syntactic-Structure Interface

2

Multiple Interfaces

CHRISTER PLATZACK

Within present-day generative grammar (the Minimalist program, Chomsky 1995, 1998), it is generally postulated that autonomous syntax (I-language) provides information to two kinds of performance systems—sensori-motor systems and systems of thought. These systems are taken to be indivisible and unitary; that is, all sensori-motor systems access one interface-level, and all systems of thought access a distinct interface-level. This assumption is at issue in the present chapter, which opts for a model where the systems of thought access multiple interface-levels. It is claimed that there are three such levels— Thematic Form, Grammatical Form, and Discourse Form—and that the information exchanged at these levels pertains to the information assembled at the V-domain, the I-domain, and the C-domain, respectively. A conceptual argument for the idea that these three syntactic domains exchange information with the systems of thought via designated interfaces is based on the way the computational system works at these three domains. In addition, a handful of empirical arguments are presented, many of which are related to the concept of 'chain', which must be interpreted differently from what is standardly assumed in a model with multiple interfaces to the systems of thought.

2.1. Introduction

2.1.1. *The Organization of Grammar*

In this chapter, written within the Principles-and-Parameters approach to generative grammar, I will argue for a closer connection than is usually assumed between the derivation of the clause and its semantic interpretation. I will pursue the hypothesis that the structure is assembled by a computational system in three steps, and that each step has its own interface to meaning.

It is an underlying assumption of the Principles-and-Parameters approach (see for instance Chomsky 1995) that there is a component of the human mind/brain dedicated to language, that is uniform to all human beings. Under the influence

The work on this chapter was supported in part by grants from Humanistisk-samhällsvetenskapliga forskningsrådet and from the Bank of Sweden Tercentenary Foundation. Thanks to Ute Bohnacker, Lars-Olof Delsing, Cecilia Falk, Kleanthes Grohmann, Gunlög Josefsson, Urpo Nikanne, and Henrik Rosenkvist for reading and criticizing a preliminar version of this chapter, and to Inger Rosengren for thought-provoking discussions. These scholars are in no way responsible for my use of their comments. I also like to thank Urpo Nikanne for inviting me to participate in this volume.

of the environment, this state undergoes changes during the first 30–40 months of life, resulting in an attained state called the *internal language* (I-language) of a natural human language. I-language is considered a way of computing the connection between form (*PF*, phonetic form) and meaning (*LF*, logical form): the point of connection is called *Spell-out*, and the part of the computational system assembling structure prior to Spell-out is known as *overt syntax*. Roughly speaking, the computational system selects elements from the mental lexicon and generates a structure which undergoes certain reformulations. The result of the computational process provides input to the sensori-motor systems and the systems of thought; PF and LF are interface levels between the computational system and other cognitive faculties. The organization of I-language can be illustrated by the diagram in (1), where the lines represent the computational system.

(1)   Mental lexicon

Recently, the minimal assumption behind (1)—that I-language has two interface levels to other cognitive faculties—has been questioned. From a purely theoretical point of view, Uriagereka (1998) explores the possibility of multiple spell-outs at the PF side. Here I will mainly be concerned with the exchange of information between I-language and the systems of thought. The standard model in (1) just offers one interface with this property, namely LF, which leads to problems with the fact that syntax expresses, simultaneously, both the propositional content of the sentence, including the speaker's view of this content, and the way the sentence contributes to discourse interpretation. Consider for instance the following English examples:

(2)   (*a*)   Mary saw John.
      (*b*)   John Mary saw.
      (*c*)   John saw Mary.
      (*d*)   Mary John saw.

The word order of (2*a*) and (2*b*) tells us that Mary is the subject, the person seeing somebody, and that John is the object, the person being seen. Likewise, the word order of (2*c*) and (2*d*) tells us that the roles of Mary and John are reversed. Simultaneously, (2*a*) and (2*b*), and (2*c*) and (2*d*), respectively, differ in how they say what they say about the world.

There are several ways of capturing the dual function of syntax in a grammar of the form in (1): there might be a particular interface to discourse, as suggested by Vallduví (1992) and Holmberg (1999), or the contribution to discourse interpretation must be relevant at LF, as the model in (1) suggests. Engdahl (1998) has shown, however, that the latter strategy has severe drawbacks. In this chapter I will explore a more radical solution, inspired by Uriagereka (1998), arguing that there is no single Spell-out point as in (1), but dynamic access to the systems of thought. I will investigate a specific implementation of this idea, namely that the interpretative mechanisms are fed at particular points in the computation as the derivation unfolds, and that the systems of thought interpreting these interfaces are designed to do different things, partly reflected by the derivational history of the clause at different stages in the derivation.[1]

To be more concrete, I will argue that there is a close correspondence between the dynamic access to LF and the layout of the clause, which, according to the currently prevailing view within the Minimalist program, consists of three phrases—the VP, the IP, and the CP, organized as in (3).

(3)

Today the general view is that these phrases stand for different domains, each containing several different projections. The VP is often assumed to be composed of different VP-shells (e.g. Larson 1988; Chomsky 1995), the IP of at least a Tense Phrase (TP) and an Agreement Phrase (AgrP) (e.g. Pollock 1989), and the CP of functional projections like Fin(ite)P(hrase) and ForceP(hrase) (Rizzi 1997).

As I will argue, there is a connection between the composition of the clause in (3) and the type of information expressed at each domain, suggesting that different interpretative mechanisms have access to the assemblance of the V-domain, the I-domain, and the C-domain, respectively. See Rosenkvist (1995) for a suggestion along these lines, and Grohmann (in progress) for a detailed discussion of a closely related idea. Roughly speaking, the information present at the VP-level concerns the predicate–argument structure (theta-structure) of the clause, the information present at IP concerns the purely grammatical aspects of the clause, and the C-domain contains information that links the propositional content of the clause to discourse. This model is illustrated in (4).

(4)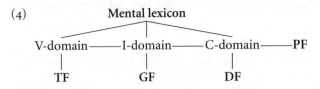

---

[1] This resembles early versions of the Extended Standard Theory of Generative Grammar, like Chomsky (1972) and Jackendoff (1972), where systems with multiple interface levels between syntax and semantics were assumed.

The parts of (4) which are not in bold face represent the computational system, the outline of which will be presented in Section 2.2. Essentially, this system works as is assumed in (1). Lexical entities (more precisely, bundles of phonological, grammatical, and semantic features[2]) are selected from the mental lexicon and merged into a phrase structure (the V-domain). This structure is expanded into the I-domain by merging functional projections that attract the elements of the V-domain; the dual input from the lexicon and from the V-domain is indicated in (4). Finally, the I-domain is expanded into the C-domain, once again by dual input, this time from the I-domain and the lexicon. The V-domain, the I-domain, and the C-domain represent different steps in the computational process.

The interfaces to other cognitive systems are given in bold face in (4). TF stands for 'thematic form', GF for 'grammatical form', DF for 'discourse form', and PF for 'phonetic form'. To illustrate, if for instance a *wh*-phrase is overtly raised from its merged position in VP to Spec-AgroP in the I-domain and then to Spec-CP, it is pronounced in the last position, marked as the direct object in the second one, and interpreted for its specific role in the event in the first one.[3]

I assume the same stepwise exchange of information to the systems of thought and the sensori-motor systems from the various sub-parts of the extended noun phrase, preposition phrase, and adjective phrase; at least for the extended projection of the noun, there is a close correspondence to the extended projection of the verb, as has often been noticed (see especially Chomsky 1970). When these structures have been assembled and the information provided by the internal grammar has been exchanged at the various interfaces, these phrases participate in the build-up of other structures as unanalysed wholes, where the parts are linearly, but not hierarchically ordered. See Uriagereka (1998) for a discussion of some consequences, and also the end of Section 2.5.1.

My chapter is organized in the following way. In the last part of this introduction, I will clarify how to interpret the interface levels TF, GF, and DF. Section 2.2 contains a brief presentation of the computational system. Section 2.3 outlines a conceptual argument for the hypothesis that the most economic model, with a single spell-out point (see (1)), cannot be maintained, but is preferably replaced by a model with multiple interfaces. The empirical arguments of Sections 2.4 and 2.5 highlight various phenomena that are problematic for a

---

[2] 'Semantic' is used in a broad sense here. A lexical entity may lack phonological and/or semantic features: an element without phonological features has no influence on PF, and an element without semantic features has no influence on TF, GF, and DF.

[3] Multiple information of this kind concealed in a single phrase or word led to the introduction of *chains* in Chomsky (1981) as a way to relate different positions through which a particular element had moved. In later versions of the theory, the concept of chain gained importance—from being a notational convenience, chains have come to be considered proper syntactic entities. This assumption is not readily compatible with (4), as discussed in section 2.4. See also Hornstein (1998).

model like (1) but easy to account for in (4). Section 2.6 contains a concluding discussion.

2.1.2. *The Interfaces to the Systems of Thought*

Like LF in (1), TF, GF, and DF in (4) are syntactic structures that constitute interfaces between the I-language and various systems of thought. Consider first TF. At this interface, the structural information available in the V-domain is exchanged with semantic information that can be formulated in (something close to) predicate logic, or maybe represented as an image schema (see Langacker 1986) or a conceptual structure *à la* Jackendoff (1997). At this interface, the external and internal arguments of the verb are expressed in X-bar terms: the internal argument is the complement of the lowest instance of V, whereas the external argument is the specifier of V. Additional information available at the V-domain, modifying the predicate in various ways (time, place, manner), is expressed by circumstantial adverbials in specifiers of higher VP-shells (Larson 1988; Josefsson and Platzack 1998). Applied to the examples in (2), it is at TF that *Mary* will be interpreted as the experiencer in (2*a*, *b*) and as the perceived object in (2*b*, *d*).

Turning to GF, this is the interface where I-language and the systems of thought exchange information concerning *grammatical meaning*, i.e. the type of information contained in the choice of mood, voice, aspect, etc., as well as the choice of subject and object. The semantic role of the latter choice is illustrated in the embedded clauses of (5*a*) and (5*b*), where the subject corresponds to the object of the related active verb in (5*a*), to the indirect object in (5*b*):

(5) (*a*) Han väntade sig   *att en belöning skulle tilldelas henne av staten.*
            he   expected REFL that a   reward   should be-given her   by state-the
            'He expected a reward to be given to her by the state.'
     (*b*) Han väntade sig   *att hon skulle tilldelas en belöning av staten.*
            he   expected REFL that she should be-given a   reward   by state-the
            'He expected her to be given a reward by the state.'

Since the word order variation is within an embedded clause, pragmatic influences are minimized.

Other types of information exchanged at GF regard the specification of the aspect of the sentence and information about the modal value of the sentence. This type of information is always present as soon as we utter a sentence.

Consider finally DF. At this interface, information is exchanged concerning the anchoring and evaluation of the proposition in the actual context (the speaker's here and now). As an illustration, consider the so called 'Verum focus' in (6), which was first described by Höhle (1988); capital letters indicate the element in focus.

(6) (*a*) Ich weiss DASS er kommt.
        I   know that he comes
        'I know that he will come.'
    (*b*) Peter HAT sie geliebt.
        Peter has she loved
        'Peter has been in love with her.'

In (6*a*) the complementizer is in focus, in (6*b*) the finite verb; both elements are in the same position C°, given the standard account of verb second (den Besten 1983). Stressing the element in C° has the effect that only the truth value of the clause is put in focus—this follows as an effect of C° bearing the finiteness feature, which anchors the proposition to the here and now of the speaker, thus making an evaluation of its truth-value possible (see Section 2.5).

2.2. The Computational System

In this section I will briefly present the computational system of the Minimalist program, as it emerges in Kayne (1994), Chomsky (1995), Cinque (1997) and Rizzi (1997). Chomsky (1995) proposes that the computational system makes use of the three generalized transformations *Select, Merge,* and *Attract.* Select enumerates lexical items, i.e. more or less conventionalized bundles of phonological, grammatical and semantic features, from the mental lexicon. These feature bundles are brought together in a binary branching X-bar structure by Merge. Attract, finally, targets two identical grammatical features in a chain, forcing the c-commanded[4] feature to raise to the position of the c-commanding one. When attraction takes place prior to Spell-out, it must involve phonological features: in such a case the attracting feature is said to be strong. Weak attraction, which does not involve phonological features, takes place between Spell-out and LF.

    Consider a numeration like {John, Mary, saw} which can be merged in two different ways:

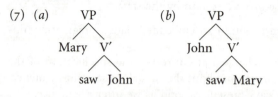

(7) (*a*)   VP   (*b*)   VP
       Mary V'   John V'
          saw John   saw Mary

---

    [4] The structural relation c-**command** picks out a domain of the structure which is in the scope of a particular element. More precisely, in a structure like (7*a*), *Mary* c-commands V', *saw* and *John*, V' c-commands *Mary*, and *saw* and *John* mutually c-command each other. Kayne (1994) argues that c-command should be restricted to *asymmetric c-command*, meaning that the c-commanded element must precede the c-commanded element(s). According to this definition, the c-command relations in (7) are the ones mentioned above, with the exception that V' does not c-command *Mary*, and *John* does not c-command *saw*.

Example (7a) corresponds to the sentences in (2a, b), whereas (7b) corresponds to (2c, d). The two local relations available in the diagrams, the Spec–Head relation and the Head–complement relation, respectively, are used to represent the thematic relations involved; in this case the DP interpreted as the person seeing somebody carries the external role and the DP interpreted as the person being seen carries the internal role. In addition to the thematic roles, the structures in (7) also represent the tense value (through inflection), and the word order of (2a, c).

The sentences in (2) have grammatical properties that are not structurally represented in (7), presuming that a local relation can only represent a single grammatical property. It is obvious that the word orders of (2b, d) are not represented, and there is no structural correlate to the fact that the sentences in (2) are declaratives with particular values for tense and aspect. Furthermore, the structures in (7) do not reveal the epistemic and deontic modalities of (2), viz. that there is no doubt in the mind of the speaker regarding the truth of the sentences, and the speaker's conviction that the subject is able to see the object. Within the Minimalist program, grammatical properties like these are represented in the extended projection of the verb, that is, the IP and the CP; see (3).

One-to-one correspondence between local relations and grammatical meanings can be obtained by the functional projections on top of the VP, the featural composition of which attracts features of the verb and its argument(s). Attraction is obligatory, hence when a functional projection hosts a feature that is also found in a position c-commanded by it, attraction must take place. When two identical features are brought together in a functional projection by attraction, they are eliminated from the computational system. Formally, attraction is forced to take place, since no grammatical features are allowed to be present at LF, where only chains (the derivational history, so to speak, of a feature bundle selected from the mental lexicon) are available to the interpreting systems. Hence grammatical features are just a formal device to drive the computation,[5] what matters is the two-dimensional assembly of chains that we call 'phrase structure'.

Grammatical features are of two kinds, verbal and nominal (Chomsky 1995). Verbal features attract verbal heads,[6] nominal features attract extended nominal projections, that is, DPs. To account for cross-linguistic word order variation, features are furthermore assumed to be either strong or weak, as mentioned above. Strong features must be eliminated at the latest at Spell-out, hence their presence in a numeration has consequences for visible word order. It is commonly taken for granted that strong features can only be a property of functional projections. Strong verbal features trigger the raising of V in overt syntax

---

[5] In addition to grammatical features there are semantic features, which are not eliminated. Hence such features are interpretable at LF; see Chomsky (1995: 277 ff.). Since the distinction between interpretable and non-interpretable features is fuzzy, I will not dwell on these matters here.

[6] Since head attraction also takes place within the extended projections of nouns, adjectives, and prepositions, *head feature* is a better name. I here follow contemporary practice.

to the head of a functional projection, and strong nominal features trigger the raising of a DP in overt syntax to the specifier of a functional projection.

Since strong features trigger visible movement, it is the distribution of strong features that determines the word order of a language. A language with a strong nominal feature for the subject, for example, will realize the subject in a particular position at the left periphery or close to the left periphery of the sentence. English is a language of this type, whereas Italian, in which the nominal feature for the subject is weak, allows the subject to remain at the right periphery at Spell-out, as in the following example from Burzio (1986: 21).

(8) Esamineranno il   caso molti esperti.[7]
      will-examine   the case many experts
      'Many experts will examine the case.'

As indicated in (3), the I-domain is embedded under CP. In the words of Rizzi (1997: 283), the C-domain is 'the interaction between a propositional content (expressed by the IP) and the superordinate structure (a higher clause or, possibly, the articulation of discourse, if we consider a root clause)'. Elements of the C-domain express sentence type (declarative, interrogative, imperative), reflect certain properties of the verbal system of the clause (finiteness), and make explicit various pragmatic systems (topic-comment, focus-presupposition).[8] A simplified structure at Spell-out of the sentence (9) is given in (10).

(9) John, Mary probably hates.

In (10) the topicalized phrase *John* is adjoined to CP.[9] From this position it heads a chain, the tail of which is in Spec-AgroP. The trace in this position has the same index as the topic. Spec-AgroP is also the head of a chain, which includes the complement of V; both links in this chain are empty (traces with index i). The second chain expresses the information that the internal argument of the verb is the object.

Consider next the subject, *Mary*, which is overt in Spec-CP, heading a chain with its tail in Spec-AgrsP.[10] Spec-AgrsP is simultaneously the head of

---

[7] The analysis implies that the object is overtly raised across the subject to the I-domain. Note that the subject may remain sentence final also after circumstantial adverbials:

(i) Ha letto tutto bene Gianni.
      has read all   well Gianni
      'Gianni has read everything well.'

[8] This does not exclude the possibility that certain aspects of the I-domain (see section 2.4.2), and even the V-domain (see section 2.4.5), may have relevance for discourse interpretation. What is claimed, however, is that these aspects are not read off until the C-domain is assembled, i.e. at DF.

[9] A more careful account of topicalization is given in section 2.5.

[10] The description is simplified and will be extended below. As noted by Cecilia Falk (p.c.), the division of labour indicated makes it easy to account for oblique subjects in a language like Icelandic. Consider the following example:

(10)

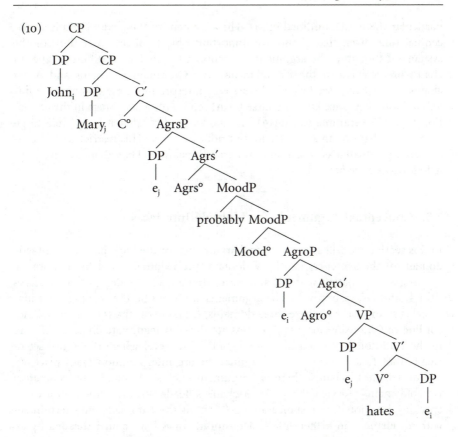

a chain with its tail in Spec-VP. This chain reveals an agreement relation between the verb and *Mary*, which might be taken as an expression for (abstract) nominative case.

Regard finally the head chain. Since the tail of the chain is a verb, we have an extended V-chain, revealing the grammatical relations that the verb takes part in. The head of the chain, C°, expresses the finiteness feature, Agrs° subject–verb agreement, Mood° the speaker's evaluation of the probability of the event expressed by the verb, Agro° object–verb agreement, and V° the particular event.

In the following sections we consider arguments for multiple interfaces, in

(i) Mér   líkuðu   hestarnir.
   me.DAT liked-3PL horses-the.NOM
   'I liked the horses.'

As is well known (see for instance Sigurðsson 1988: 204), oblique subjects like *mér* in (i) share many syntactic properties with nominative subjects, especially positional ones, but they do not (overtly) agree with the tensed verb (see Boeckx 1998 for a discussion). Hypothetically, one might account for these facts by assuming that oblique subjects are attracted to Spec-CP but not to Spec-AgrsP.

particular the model outlined in (4). The argument of the next section is a conceptual one: given that chains are important objects of interpretation for the systems of thought,[11] the argument of Section 2.3 is that since different types of chains are relevant at the I-domain and the C-domain (A-chains and A-bar chains, respectively, see below), the systems interpreting these domains are different. Note that since DF (discourse form) represents a later stage in the derivation than GF (grammatical form), the model predicts that it is possible to go from an A-chain to an A-bar chain, but not vice versa. This restriction has usually been postulated as an axiom in the traditional model based on (1); given (4), it follows as a theorem.[12]

2.3. Conceptual Arguments for Multiple Interfaces

In this section we will give conceptual arguments for the idea that each syntactic domain of the sentence, i.e. the V-domain, the I-domain, and the C-domain, exchanges information with the systems of thought via the designated interfaces TF, GF, and DF, respectively. The arguments are based on the way the computational system works in these three domains, focusing on the role of chains. According to Chomsky (1995: 194), chains are the only legitimate object at LF, and in the traditional Minimalist program, LF is the level where the entire set of chains that feed interpretation is unified before interpretation takes place. In addition to head chains, there are argument chains (A-chains) and operator-variable chains (A-bar chains). An A-chain is headed by an element in a Case-checking position (for instance an AgrP within the I-domain) and terminates with an element in a theta-marked position. An A-bar chain is headed by an element in an A-bar position (for instance the topic position) and terminates with an element in a Case-checking position (AgrP). Note that the Agr-position thus can be part both of an A-chain and an A-bar chain.

Since A-chains and A-bar chains have different properties, there must be some way at LF to distinguish them. In my proposal, the A/A-bar distinction is derived from (4) as a result of multiple access to the systems of thought: information carried by A-bar chains is exchanged at DF, information carried by A-chains at GF. In Section 2.4 I will discuss the status of chains in a grammar organized as in (4), arguing that the chain is not a proper element of such a grammar.

---

[11] The argument given here is independent of the question whether or not chains are proper grammatical objects, see the discussion in section 2.4.

[12] Delsing (1993: 109 ff.) points out that there is a similar restriction on head movement: a lexical head may move to another lexical head position, or to a functional head position, and a functional head may move to another functional head position, but movement from a functional head to a lexical head seems to be excluded. As Delsing (p.c.) notices, this observation follows directly from the model in (4).

From the assumption (see Section 2.2) that the attracting features of the I-domain are either verbal or nominal follows another important difference between the I-domain and the other two domains: only DPs and Vs can be moved around in the I-domain, whereas there is no such restriction connected with the other two domains. This suggests that only DPs and Vs may have grammatical functions that are positionally determined, whereas all kinds of phrases (including embedded clauses) can have positionally determined thematic and pragmatic functions. To the best of my knowledge, this is a correct prediction. Consider for instance the fact that all types of phrases (including CPs) may be topicalized, and that CPs and PPs, in addition to DPs, may have thematic roles. That CP objects and PP objects are distributed differently from DP objects is shown in the next subsection.[13] It is also well known that the distribution of CP subjects differs from the distribution of DP subjects: in V2-languages, a DP-subject, but not a CP-subject, inverts with the tensed verb, as shown in (11):[14]

(11) (a) *Numera   har *att   man kommer för sent* inte någon betydelse.
         nowadays has that you   come   too late not any   importance
     (b) Numera   har <u>det</u> *att   man kommer för sent* inte någon betydelse.[15]
         nowadays has it   that you   come   too late not any   importance
         'Nowadays it does not matter that you are late.'

We will now consider each domain in turn, starting with the I-domain.

---

[13] As Henrik Rosenkvist (p.c.) has remarked, this will explain why the indirect DP object usually has a position higher than the indirect PP object. Consider also the fact that many languages, including English and Mainland Scandinavian, have the inflected genitive in front of the head noun, whereas a prepositional possessive follows the noun:

(i) (a) What is *the ship's* name?
    (b) What is the name *of the ship*?

Thanks to Lars-Olof Delsing (p.c.) for reminding me of this fact.

[14] As Cecilia Falk (p.c.) points out, there are cases with CP subjects where inversion is not as bad as expected. One example of this type is given in (i):

(i) Ska *att jag bor på landet*   behöva innebära sämre service?
    shall that I   live in country-the need   mean   worse service
    'Is it necessary that my living in the country results in worse service?'

[15] The following word order is not possible either, as Henrik Rosenkvist (p.c.) has remarked:

(i) *Numera har det inte *att man kommer försent* någon betydelse.
    nowadays has it not that you come too late any importance

It could be argued that my account predicts the well-formedness of (i), where the CP subject remains in its VP position. However, as we will see below, Swedish (like English) has a strong feature in IP attracting a DP object (Josefsson and Platzack 1998), hence the object must raise to a position in front of the base position of the subject, as in (ii):

(ii) Numera har det inte någon betydelse *att man kommer försent.*
     nowadays has it not any importance that you come too late

2.3.1. *The I-Domain and the GF Interface*

According to the model in (4), GF is the interface where information concerning grammatical meaning is exchanged, i.e. the type of information contained in the choice of mood, voice, aspect, etc. In a recent book, Cinque (1997) argues that all human languages have the same hierarchy of functional projections within the I-domain, basing his arguments on a cross-linguistic study of the order of sentence adverbials, affixes and auxiliaries. Cinque's hypothesis offers an explanation of the fact that, cross-linguistically, categories like tense, mood, and aspect typically are expressed by these grammatical means, and that, cross-linguistically, there is a remarkable similarity regarding the order in which these categories occur, independent of form. The projections that Cinque recognizes usually have specifiers containing adverbials, and heads hosting auxiliaries, affixes, particles, or serving as intermediate steps for the main verb when this is attracted to some higher position. The hierarchy proposed by Cinque is given in (12):

(12) [Mood$_{\text{speech act}}$ [Mood$_{\text{evaluative}}$ [Mood$_{\text{evidential}}$ [Mood$_{\text{epistemic}}$ [T$_{\text{past}}$ [T$_{\text{future}}$ [Mood$_{\text{irrealis}}$ [Mood$_{\text{necessity}}$ [Mood$_{\text{possibility}}$ [Mood$_{\text{volitional}}$ [Mood$_{\text{obligation}}$ [Mood$_{\text{ability/permission}}$ [Asp$_{\text{habitual}}$ [Asp$_{\text{repetitive}}$ [Asp$_{\text{frequentative}}$ [Asp$_{\text{celerative}}$ [T$_{\text{anterior}}$ [Asp$_{\text{terminative}}$ [Asp$_{\text{continuative}}$ [Asp$_{\text{perfect}}$ [Asp$_{\text{retrospective}}$ [Asp$_{\text{proximative}}$ [Asp$_{\text{durative}}$ [Asp$_{\text{generic/progressive}}$ [Asp$_{\text{prospective}}$ [Asp$_{\text{completive}}$ [Voice [Asp$_{\text{celerative}}$ [Asp$_{\text{completive}}$ [Asp$_{\text{repetitive}}$ [Asp$_{\text{frequentative}}$ $\cdots$

According to Cinque the hierarchy in (12) is universal, and it is present in all finite clauses in all languages, even in a simple sentence like *John saw Mary*, where only past tense is morphologically indicated. Consider for instance the fact that the absence of any expression for epistemic modality forces the interpretation that there is no doubt in the mind of the speaker regarding the truth of the sentence, and that the absence of an expression for ability modality (a kind of deontic modality) signals the speaker's conviction that the subject is able to perform the action. Note also that the event is always given a value with respect to telicity (Aspect).

In addition to the hierarchy in (12), the I-domain contains a NegP[16] and Agr phrases where the subject and the object are checked. As Cinque (1997: 224) notes, 'it is possible to interpret the different (or multiple) positioning of negation and agreement as stemming from a "spell-out" difference: whether a language expresses overtly a lower or higher Agr or Neg (or more than one)'. Hence, sticking to Cinque's conception of the I-domain, all human languages have the same hierarchy of functional projections in this domain, and for the cases where cross-linguistic word-order variation is attested, a description in terms of strong and weak grammatical features appears to be feasible.[17]

---

[16] Presumably there are several different Neg phrases, interspersed among the higher adverb-related projections; see Cinque (1997: 203) and Zanuttini (1997).

[17] As Urpo Nikanne (p.c.) points out, this presupposes a very strong one-to-one relation between

It should be noted that if Cinque is right, the I-domain is identical for all languages at GF, the interface where the I-domain exchanges information with the systems of thought: all languages share a predetermined hierarchy of functional projections for grammatical categories of various kinds. This means that the systems of thought interacting with this hierarchy do not need to possess any language-specific properties: the same local relation universally expresses the same grammatical meaning.[18,19]

2.3.2. *The C-Domain and the DF Interface*

According to the model in (4), information concerning the particular context in which a sentence can be used is exchanged at DF, the interface between the C-domain and the systems of thought. This includes speech-act systems as well as focus/background and topic/comment information. Movement designated to express such information is usually taken to result in A-bar chains; *wh* movement (13) is a typical example. Note that there are two A-bar chains in (13), one involving *who*, the other one *did*.

(13) $[_{CP}$ Who$_i$ did$_v$ $[_{IP}$ Mary t$_v$ $[_{VP}$ call t$_i$]]]?

Whereas A-movement is feasibly described in terms of attraction and strong/weak features, it has proved much harder to account for A-bar movement with this mechanism. Although *wh*-movement per se does not seem to be problematic (we may assume a strong WH-feature in C in languages with *wh*-words at the left periphery), other instances of A-bar movement are not as easily handled. Consider for instance the obligatory raising of *did* in (13), which seems to indicate the presence of a strong V-feature in the C-domain. But such a description would erroneously predict *do*-insertion also in cases like (14) where the subject is the *wh*-word of the clause:

(14)   (*a*) *Who did call?
        (*b*) Who called?

Consistency forbids us to claim that there is a strong feature forcing *did* to be in C° in (13) but not in (14). As we will see in Section 2.5, the difference between (13) and (14) with regard to *do*-insertion is better accounted for in terms of

syntax and semantics at this point. Since the thesis that syntax is an autonomous system entails no claim whatsoever about the closeness of the fit between form and meaning, the demonstration of such a fit neither supports nor defeats the autonomy thesis. See Newmeyer (1998: 44 f.) for discussion.

[18] At this level, only the structural relations are of importance; categories such as adverbial and auxiliary (or to be more precise, the structural correspondences to these notions) are relevant only for the computational system.

[19] Naturally, it is impossible to prove that the interpretation given here of Cinque's hierarchy is correct. Among other things, it predicts universality of grammatical categories, an idea widely held in generative circles, but often disputed by linguists of other persuasions.

a general constraint of movement (Shortest Move; see Chomsky 1995: 181 ff.).[20]

Chomsky (1995: 324 f.) notes a problem with A-bar operations such as extraposition, right-node raising, VP-adjunction, scrambling, etc., suggesting that these constructions 'may not really belong to the system we are discussing here as we keep closely to [. . .] movement driven by feature checking within the $N \rightarrow \lambda$ computation', where N is the numeration and λ is LF. However, to follow Chomsky would mean that we give up all attempts to account for the important aspect of human language to express different types of information within a single hierarchy. To my mind it is better to give up the model in (1) and replace it with the model in (4), as I argue in this chapter. Since the typical instance of movement driven by feature checking takes place within the I-domain, it might be fruitful to investigate the consequences of restricting feature-checking to this domain.

It is obvious that the form of the interface between the C-domain and the systems of thought is heavily dependent on our assumptions of the C-domain. Currently, there are widely diverging opinions within the Minimalist program, ranging from Cinque (1997: 227), who suggests a C-domain more or less of the same type as the I-domain, i.e. composed of different projections functionally specialized,[21] to Platzack (1998), according to whom the C-domain is universally characterized by a Visibility Condition, but otherwise may differ profoundly between languages. Here, we will stick to the assumption that the C-domain differs from the I-domain in not being identically structured in all languages. It follows that the systems of thought that exchange information with the C-domain at the DF interface cannot rely on a simple inspection of the hierarchical structure, as was possible at GF. Hence, we conclude that the system interpreting the interface DF of (4) is not identical to the system interpreting the interface based on the I-structure, i.e. GF. In Section 2.5 we return to a more detailed discussion of the C-domain.

2.3.3. *The V-Domain and the TF Interface*

The V-domain (the lexical domain of the extended V-projection) is the domain that results from merging a (main) verb with its argument phrase(s); this domain is also assumed to contain circumstantial adverbials, i.e., adverbials that in the words of Cinque (1997: 40) differ from the adverbials of the I-domain 'in not being rigidly ordered with respect to each other'.

---

[20] It would not help to claim that *did* is absent from the numeration underlying (14), since the strong V-feature in C would then attract the tensed verb, producing the ungrammatical (i*a*):

(i) (*a*) *Who called just?
   (*b*)   Who just called?

CP must be present, otherwise we erroneously predict that *who* is not a proper subject.

[21] Even if Cinque does not suggest a *universal* hierarchy in this domain, such a thought has been expressed at least by Michal Starke (p.c.). Note that this is incompatible with Hornstein's (1995) proposal that the C-domain is only being targeted by visible movement.

From a semantic point of view, the argument closest to the verb is proto-typically the argument corresponding to the object, as shown by Marantz (1984: ch. 2). Among other things, Marantz (1984: 24) notes that the choice of this argument (the *internal* argument) may affect the semantic value of the subject (the *external* argument), but not vice versa. It is also well known that idioms are often formed by verb and internal argument, very seldom by verb and external argument.

Since the selection of arguments determines the event or state articulated by the clause, this information should be unambiguously expressed by syntax. This motivates that the arguments have predetermined positions in the V-domain, positions which, depending on the particular verb, are linked to particular thematic roles by the systems of thought.[22] One way to implement this idea is to assign the status 'internal argument' to the DP merged with the verb, hence given the numeration underlying the examples in (7), i.e. {John, Mary, saw}, the internal argument is *John* in (7a) but *Mary* in (7b). The remaining argument, merged as specifier to V' (*saw John* or *saw Mary*), is interpreted as the external argument; if two arguments are given external status, as in a numeration like {John, Mary, flowers, bought}, yielding either *John bought Mary flowers* or *Mary bought John flowers*, the argument not merged with verb + internal argument must be merged as specifier to a higher VP shell. For *John bought Mary flowers* we get the structure in (15).

(15)

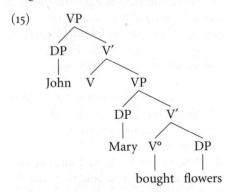

The higher V is usually taken to contain an invisible 'light' verb,[23] present in the numeration (without phonological features) as Cause or something similar, and the DP in local relation with this verb is the agent or originator of the event.

---

[22] This is not logically necessary. Borer (1993) and Arad (1996), for example, have argued that the internal argument is the 'event measurer', and that this argument is represented by the phrase in local relation to an aspect phrase or a telicity phrase in the I-domain. Given this account, VP may be seen as an unordered set of elements. This hypothesis is not compatible with the assumption of a particular interface between VP and the systems of thought that I am arguing for in this chapter.

[23] Light verbs are visible in many languages, see for instance Grimshaw and Mester (1988) and Baker (1996: 353 ff.).

Note furthermore that unless the lower verb is attracted to the I-domain, it must be raised to the light verb to yield the correct word order.

As mentioned above, the V-domain also contains circumstantial adverbials, merged in specifiers of higher VPs, as argued in Josefsson and Platzack (1998). Thus, the V-domain of sentence (16*a*) is given the structure in (16*b*):

(16) (*a*)   Mary hated John tremendously

(*b*)

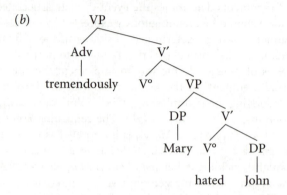

Since (16*b*) does not conform to the word order of (16*a*), there must be strong features in IP, below the negation, attracting both the verb and its arguments.[24] This has been proposed for English by Johnson (1991) and Koizumi (1993), and for Swedish by Josefsson and Platzack (1998); see these papers for arguments (an additional argument was given in footnote 15). Here we will just highlight two obvious facts, involving a comparison between internal arguments that are DPs and internal arguments that are PPs and CPs.

The assumption that there is a strong nominal feature above VP, attracting the internal argument, immediately predicts that internal arguments that are PPs or CPs are not attracted, since they are not nominal in nature. Such arguments should therefore behave differently from an internal argument-DP. This is correct, as shown by the following Swedish examples, taken from Josefsson and Platzack (1998) (in the examples the internal arguments are in bold face, and the circumstantial adverbials in italics):

(17) (*a*) Han hade studerat **förslaget**   *länge.*
              he   had   studied suggestion-the long
              'He had studied the suggestion for a long time.'
        (*b*) *Han hade studerat *länge* **förslaget**.
              he   had   studied long   suggestion-the

---

[24] Cinque (1997: 41f.) assumes successive movement of the lower VPs to higher specifiers within the VP shells to handle discrepancies like (16*a*, *b*). Given such raising there is no c-command relation between the object and the circumstantial adverbials, hence this description fails to account for the binding facts associated with the sentence *jag ställde stolen, på sin, plats* 'I put chair-the on its.REFL place', where the possessive anaphor is bound by the object. See the discussion of example (24).

(18) (*a*) Han hade tänkt **på förslaget** *länge.*
he had thought of suggestion-the long
'He had thought about the suggestion for a long time.'
(*b*) Han hade tänkt *länge* **på förslaget.**
he had thought long of suggestion-the

(19) (*a*) ??Han hade avslöjat **att de var gifta** *för henne på bussen.*
he had revealed that they were married for her on bus-the
'He had revealed for her on the bus that they were married.'
(*b*) Han hade avslöjat *för henne på bussen* **att de var gifta.**
he had revealed for her on bus-the that they were married

The ungrammaticality of (17*b*) shows that an internal argument-DP must precede circumstantial adverbials. PPs may be either in front of or following such adverbials, and CPs prefer to follow. The obligatory raising in (17) follows immediately from the assumption that there is a strong nominal feature in the I-domain. Below I will discuss cases with Heavy NP Shift, which seem to contradict this description.

The word-order variation in (18) is interesting in the present context, since it cannot depend on a strong feature—if our assumptions are correct. This indicates that there are different triggers of movement for the I-domain (strong and weak features) and the V-domain. As a matter of fact, Josefsson and Platzack (1998) suggest a general freedom of scrambling within lexical shells, including VPs. This freedom is indicated by the various possibilities to order circumstantial adverbials, illustrated in (20).

(20) (*a*) Vi plockade blåbär i skogen i lördags.
we picked blueberries in forest-the in saturday
'We picked blueberries in the forest last Saturday.'
(*b*) Vi plockade blåbär i lördags i skogen.
we picked blueberries in saturday in forest-the
'We picked blueberries last Saturday in the forest.'

Consider now the implications of these observations for the interfaces. To interpret the I-domain, i.e. the interface GF in (4), the systems of thought need to read off the hierarchical structure of the I-domain, which immediately provides the information relevant at this interface. For the V-domain, the TF interface in (4) only partially functions in the same way: the interpreting systems must be able to determine which argument is the internal one and which the external one. The additional elements of the V-domain may come in any order, theoretically, which suggests that there is no underlying universal hierarchy. Hence the information provided by these elements—mainly circumstantial adverbials—must be possible to get, simply by inspecting the relative position of each phrase. This indicates that the systems interpreting GF and TF are different.

2.3.4. *Conclusion*

As a conceptual argument for my hypothesis—that the interpretative mechanisms are fed after the assemblance of the V-domain, the I-domain, and the
C-domain, respectively—I have demonstrated in this section that these three
domains are partly different, although they are all X-bar structures. My claim is
that there is a clear connection between the composition of a domain and the
type of information expressed by each domain, suggesting that the systems of
thought interpreting the interfaces of each domain must be different. At TF the
thematic information is exchanged, as well as information about the modification of the event, expressed by circumstantial adverbials. At GF, information
about grammatical meanings is exchanged. Chains are relevant at this interface,
since an element may be related to several points in the hierarchy. At DF, the
information exchanged concerns pragmatic information and information regarding sentence type. Phonological information is only exchanged with the sensori-
motor systems at the C-domain (PF).

Due to the assumed organization of I-language with several interfaces to the
systems of thought, chains cannot be taken as proper objects of the interfaces,
as will be shown in the next section. Before turning to this discussion, we will
mention here a related consequence of (4), having to do with the connection
between the three domains, the V-domain, the I-domain, and the C-domain.
Presuming that there is a way to keep track of which element is associated with
a particular θ-role or a particular event (this is not necessarily a task for the
computational system), information about which elements are present in the
derivation must be transported from one domain to the next. When passing
from the V-domain to the I-domain, for example, we do not need the hierarchical structure of the V-domain: the information expressed by this hierarchy is
exchanged with the systems of thougth at TF. What must be preserved is the
elements merged at the V-domain, hence the V-domain can be seen as a numeration for the computational system building up the I-domain. This numeration
is linearly, but not hierarchically ordered. In the same way, the information
concerning the hierarchical structure of the I-domain is not necessarily preserved
when passing from the I-domain to the C-domain. The linear order of visible
elements at the I-domain provides the numeration for the computational system
building up the C-domain. A consequence of this loss of structure will be that
the only hierarchical information present at PF is the one at the left periphery,
the one assembled at the C-domain.

2.4. Chains

According to the Chain Condition (Chomsky 1995: 46), argument chains must
be headed by a Case position and terminate in a θ-position. When an argument
is raised successive-cyclically in several steps, not every pair of links fulfill the

Chain Condition. Thus, it is a technical problem for the Minimalist program that chains may contain intermediate traces that are neither Case positions nor θ-positions. A case at hand is the derivation outlined in (21):

(21) The car$_i$ seemed t$_1$ to be fixed t$_2$.

Here *the car* is in a Case-checking position at the left periphery of the clause, and the trace t$_2$ is in a theta-marked position, but the intermediate trace t$_1$ is neither in a Case position nor a θ-position. Discussing cases like this, Chomsky (1995: 301) comes to the conclusion that the intermediate traces are invisible at LF: the only legitimate chain in this case involves *the car* and t$_2$, which is obtained when formal features of the intermediate trace(s) are erased. See also Kitahara (1997) and Hornstein (1998).

It is obvious that legitimate objects at the semantic interfaces in (4) cannot be chains of the type just discussed. With information about θ-roles exchanged at TF, there is no reason to assume that the computational system at work within the I-domain has access to any structure of the V-domain: that would be highly redundant. Chains are established at the I-domain and enter GF, but these chains differ from the type mentioned above in not having the tail in a theta-marked position. What I claim is that the legitimate object at GF is the universal structure postulated for this level, consisting of the Cinque hierarchy and additional positions (Agr positions, etc.). The chains at this level are connecting certain points of this universal hierarchy, saying that particular subsets of grammatical meanings are combined in a single chain, for instance, subject and event measurer, as *three litres of water* in *Three litres of water poured out*. Notice that this description provides for the possibility that the chain does not contain any link with phonological features: in the model in (1), this would correspond to the case where there is no strong feature in the I-domain.

Trace erasure cannot be a part of the system just described, since that would mean that information about a particular grammatical meaning was erased. Hence, the theoretical apparatus of the system does not need to contain a mechanism for trace erasure, which we take to be a desirable result. As mentioned, there must be a way to relate the elements of the I-domain and the C-domain to the θ-roles at TF, but it is not obvious that this is a task for the computational system. For the computational system building up the I-domain, the elements of the V-domain can be seen as a linearly but not hierarchically ordered numeration, as mentioned above.[25]

Consider next the C-domain. The information exchanged between I-language and the systems of thought at DF is dependent on the linear configuration of

---

[25] As mentioned in the introduction, I assume the same stepwise exchange of information to the systems of thought and the sensori-motor systems from the various subparts of the extended noun phrase, preposition phrase, and adjective phrase. As a consequence, these phrases partake in the numeration as unanalysed wholes. The only head in this numeration which is not concealed within a phrase is V, the head of VP.

phonological features at this interface. It is preferable to assume that the computational system of the internal grammar is not burdened with relating these features to a particular chain at the I-domain and a particular θ-role at the V-domain: in the system outlined here, this linking is extralinguistic, taken care of by the systems of thought.

2.4.1. *Reconstruction*

In a grammar like (1), with a single interface to the systems of thought, interpretation does not take place until all chains are assembled, A-chains as well as A-bar chains. For such a grammar, cases where a phrase appears to occur at LF in a position lower than its PF position are anomalies. In a grammar like (4), on the other hand, with multiple interfaces, such cases are expected, since there is nothing that would prohibit a phrase from being interpreted in its A-position at GF and in its A-bar position at DF. The various phenomena that are assembled under the label 'reconstruction effects' are exactly like this. Consider the standard account of an example like (22):

(22) [Which pictures of himself]$_i$ did John like t$_i$?

As indicated by the trace, a sentence like (22) is derived by movement of the *wh*-phrase *which pictures of himself* to the left periphery of the clause. An effect of this movement is that the anaphor *himself* occurs in a position higher than its antecedent *John*, leaving a trace in an A-position c-commanded by the antecedent. Since an anaphor must be A-bound by its antecedent at LF (the antecedent, co-indexed with the anaphor, must c-command the anaphor from an A-position), it must obviously operate on the antecedent and its trace in a case like (22). But the trace is a trace of the whole *wh*-phrase, not of the anaphor, hence it is not clear that the anaphor is visible at the position of the trace. To bypass this problem, the standard solution within earlier Principles-and-Parameters grammar was to appeal to reconstruction, according to which the fronted phrase was moved back into the position of the trace, prior to interpretation. The ad hoc character of this operation is obvious.

Another solution to the reconstruction problem is attempted within the Minimalist program. According to Chomsky (1995), movement consists of copying and subsequent deletion. The sentence in (22) is derived by movement of *which pictures of himself*, which leaves a copy behind. At LF the *wh*-phrase separates into the quantifier *which x* and its associate *x pictures of himself*. The well-formedness condition *Full Interpretation*, which applies to all interfaces according to Chomsky (1995), requires one of the two copies of both the quantifier and the associate to delete. The *wh*-quantifier must be interpreted in Spec-CP, hence it is the copy in the A-position that must be deleted. There is no restriction of this type on the associate, thus if the copy in Spec-CP is deleted, the associate will be interpreted in the A-position, and the anaphor is bound by the antecedent.

This account is summarized in (23), where the deleted parts are crossed out.

(23) Which ~~pictures of himself~~ did John like ~~which~~ pictures of himself

As Brody (1995: 131 ff.) has shown, there are several problems with an approach to reconstruction where the quantifier and its associate are separate at LF, both empirical and conceptual ones. In a grammar of the type argued for in the present chapter, with separate interfaces to the systems of thought, the reconstruction problem disappears. Since binding operates on A-chains, the relation between the antecedent and the anaphor may be determined already at TF, where *John* c-commands the phrase *which pictures of himself*, since *John* is the external argument, and the *wh*-phrase the internal argument. The fronting of the *wh*-phrase takes place at the I-domain (attraction to Spec-AgroP) and at the C-domain (raising to Spec-CP), and the quantificational part of the interpretation is read off at DF. With a model like (4), there is thus no need for reconstruction, and no need for copies or for the division of the fronted phrase in a quantifier and an associate.

There is an interesting piece of support for the account of binding suggested here, where the configuration at TF is the relevant one.[26] Consider the examples in (24).

(24) (*a*) Jag la   flickan$_i$ i sin$_i$ säng.
        I   put girl-the in her (REFL) bed
      (*b*) *Jag la   flickan$_i$ i sängen trots   sina$_i$ protester.
        I   put girl-the in bed-the despite her (REFL) protests

In both (24*a*) and (24*b*) the direct object is the antecedent of a reflexive possessive in a circumstantial adverbial. However, only (24*a*) is well-formed, and only in (24*a*) is the reflexive possessive part of an adverbial which is strictly subcategorized by the verb. Assuming the V-domain order to be Free circumstantial adverbial(s) > Direct Object > Strictly subcategorized adverbial, we immediately account for the binding facts of (24). Note that the direct object is in front of both adverbials at PF, since it is attracted by a strong feature in AgroP (as mentioned in Section 2.3.3) and that the order between the adverbials is more or less free, as witnessed by the well-formedness of both (25*a*) and (25*b*).

(25) (*a*) Jag la   flickan$_i$ i sin$_i$ säng trots   hennes protester.
        I   put girl-the in her (REFL) bed despite her   protests
      (*b*) Jag la   flickan$_i$, trots   hennes protester, i sin$_i$ säng.
        I   put girl-the, despite her   protests, in her (REFL) bed

2.4.2. *Object Shift*

Since the model in (1) is dependent on the concept of chain, whereas this is not the case with the model in (4), cases where descriptions based on chains lead to

---

[26] This was pointed out to me by Cecilia Falk (p.c.).

peculiar or unwanted results can be taken as indirect support for (4). The particular word-order properties of weak pronouns in the Scandinavian languages, known as Object Shift, is a case at hand—see Holmberg (1984, 1999), Cardinaletti and Starke (1999), and Hellan and Platzack (1999) for details. Generally speaking, when the main verb has been raised out of VP to a position in front of the negation, weak pronouns and clitic pronouns tend to appear in positions different from the strong pronouns or full DPs. This is illustrated by the Norwegian examples in (26), taken from Hellan and Platzack (1999).

(26) (a) *Ola ga   ikke Marit appelsinen.*
        Ola gave not Marit orange-the
     (b) *Ola ga   henne ikke appelsinen.*
        Ola gave her   not orange-the
     (c) *Ola ga   henne den ikke.*
        Ola gave her   it   not
        'Ola didn't give it to her.'

In the present framework, object shift is interesting both from a rhetoric–pragmatic point of view and from the point of view of word order. The technicalities of deriving the word order of Object Shift is of less importance here; see Johnson (1991) and Holmberg (1999) for some suggestions. For our purposes it is enough to notice that object shift involves overt movement across sentence adverbials to a position that cannot be analysed as strong; if it were strong, this movement should involve all types of DP. Furthermore, it differs from most other movements in being parasitic on V-movement. Pragmatically, Object Shift has roughly the effect of indicating that the weak object is not the focus—in SVO-languages like the Scandinavian ones, the object is in focus in the unmarked case, but not when it has been shifted to the left. See Diesing and Jelinek (1993) for an attempt to implement this observation in a syntactic description.

   Of particular importance to our discussion is that the combination of properties accompanying object shift makes it an anomaly in a system distinguishing between A-chains and A-bar chains. Holmberg and Platzack (1995: 145 ff.) notice, for example, that it is neither A-movement nor A-bar movement: like A-movement, object shift is clause-bounded (see (27a)), does not license a parasitic gap, as in (27b) and is insensitive to cross-over (27c), whereas it differs from standard cases of A-movement in not inducing a Relativized Minimality violation, shown in (27d) and not binding an anaphor, see (27e); the examples are taken from Holmberg and Platzack (1995: 146–7):

(27) (a) *Hon ansåg   han$_i$ tydligen   [t$_i$ var oduglig] (Clause bounded)
         she considered he   apparently   was incompetent
     (b) *Jag kastade den$_i$ inte t$_i$ innan jag hade läst e. (Parasitic gap)
         I   threw   it   not   before I   had read

(c) Dom tilldelade honom$_i$ i hans$_j$ frånvaro t$_i$ priset. (Cross-over)
they awarded him   in his   absence   the prize

(d) Läste studenterna$_j$ den$_i$ inte t$_i$ alla t$_j$? (Relative minimality violation)
read students-the it   not   all

(e) Han ansåg   dem$_i$ till deras$_j$/*sin$_i$ besvikelse   t$_i$
he considered them to their/possessive REFL disappointment

vara lika bra. (Binding)
be equally good

Since chains are not proper objects for the model in (4), a 'mixture' of A- and A-bar properties as illustrated in (27) should not be excluded; hence (27) is not an anomaly for the model advocated here. Regarding the interpretation of cases with Object Shift, we notice that the shifted object must be visible in a position higher than the position where it is interpreted by the systems of thought interacting with GF, which presumably is Spec-AgroP. At the C-domain it is realized in front of the sentence adverbials. The particular pragmatic information expressed by the shifted object (see Diesing and Jelinek 1993) must be signalled to the systems of thought exchanging information with I-language at the interface DF by its occurrence in this position.

2.4.3. *Quantificational Scope*

As mentioned above, it follows from the multiple interface hypothesis (4) that chains should not be thought of as proper syntactic elements. It is important to stress that this may have unwanted empirical consequences, hence this move must be supported by a demonstration that our account can handle the facts that were accounted for by chains. Among such facts are scope ambiguities like the one in (28):

(28) Someone attended every seminar.

Both the reading where *someone* has scope over *every*, and the reading where *every* has scope over *someone*, are available. The standard approach to this ambiguity within Principles-and-Parameters theory is to apply an operation called Quantifier Raising (QR)—see May (1985)—whereby the quantifier with wide scope raises to a position where it c-commands the other quantifier. As Hornstein (1995) has shown, QR is a problematic operation, and he therefore proposes a reanalysis of quantifier scope ambiguities without recourse to movement rules like QR.

Hornstein's (1998) solution to the scope-ambiguity problem presupposes that reconstruction is possible in A-chains. However, given the theory in (4) with multiple interfaces to the systems of thought, even reconstruction can (and must) be dispensed with (see Section 2.4.1). As mentioned in the introduction to Section 2.4, it follows from (4) that the elements of the V-domain can be taken as the numeration for the computational system building up the I-domain. If we assume that quantificational scope is determined at each interface to the systems of thought, that is, TF, GF, and DF, and that only phrases with phonological features are relevant, the ambiguity in (28) is accounted for. At TF, *some* > *every*,[27] since *some* is part of the external argument, and *every* is part of the internal argument. At GF, *every* > *some*; as mentioned above, the direct object is attracted to a strong position within the I-domain (Spec-AgroP), and there is no strong position attracting the subject (EPP is a matter for the C-domain, as argued in Platzack 1998 and further discussed in Section 2.5). At DF, finally, *some* > *every*. Hence, both orders are present to the systems of thought, resulting in quantificational scope ambiguity.

It is important to note that this description crucially depends on the assumption that the object, but not the subject, is overtly raised to the I-domain in English. For a language without overt raising of the object to the I-domain, my description thus predicts the absence of the discussed quantificational scope ambiguity; the same prediction pertains to languages where the subject is overtly raised to Spec-AgrsP. To determine whether or not these predictions are correct will be the subject of future work.

2.4.4. *Clause Boundedness of QR*

It has long been known (Farkas 1981) that QR is clause-bounded. Hence, for example, the quantifier-scope ambiguity found in (29*a*) is absent from (29*b*):

(29) (*a*) Someone hates everybody.
       (*b*) Someone believes that John hates everybody.

The clause-boundedness of QR is an embarrasement for the QR analysis, since it requires positing different locality restrictions for QR and what has been believed to be LF *wh*-movement. In the present system, the clause-boundedness illustrated in (29*b*) follows as a theorem, as will be demonstrated below.

In Section 2.4.3 we argued that quantifier scope is established by inspecting the orders of quantifiers at TF, GF, and DF. Hence, (29*a*) displays ambiguous scope, since both *some* > *every* and *every* > *some* are attested, as was shown in Section 2.4.3.

Consider now (29*b*). Deriving this sentence, only the order *some* > *every* is attested, the reason being that the embedded clause is not raised to Spec-AgroP at GF: the corresponding raising of the DP object was the prerequisite for including the scope *every* > *some* in the interpretation of (29*a*). The absence of CP-raising is a consequence of CPs lacking f-features to be checked in Agr phrases, as argued, for instance, in Josefsson and Platzack (1998). Hence, our account of quantifier scope ambiguity, which is heavily dependent on the model

---

[27] In this context, the notation 'x > y' means 'x has scope over y'.

in (4), does not force the introduction of an ad hoc constraint to be compatible with data, as is necessary when these facts are described in terms of the QR approach based on (1).

2.4.5. *Heavy DP Shift*

Consider the following examples (the internal arguments are in italics).

(30) (*a*) I would like to introduce *Bill* to Mary.
(*b*) *I would like to introduce to Mary *Bill*.[28]
(*c*) I would like to introduce *all the teenagers who can play the drums* to Mary.
(*d*) I would like to introduce to Mary *all the teenagers who can play the drums*.

As mentioned, English is assumed to have a strong nominal feature within the I-domain for attracting objects, which is why we expect (30*a, c*) but not (30*b, d*). The exceptional (30*d*) is a case of Heavy DP Shift, where a complex DP appears at the right periphery of the clause, in spite of the presence of the attracting nominal feature. Structures with an unchecked strong feature are ruled out, according to Chomsky (1995: 198): 'if a strong feature remains after Spell-out, the derivation crashes'. As the ungrammaticality of (30*b*) indicates, this is also the case in normal situations. For cases like (30*d*) to be acceptable, the DP at the right periphery must be 'heavy' or complex in some badly understood way; notice also that Heavy DP Shift is never obligatory, as shown by the well-formedness of (30*c*), despite the heavy object.

Given the theory outlined in this chapter, there seems to be a simple account of Heavy DP Shift: what we have is a reorganization of the linear order of the numeration (the linearization of the I-domain and the V-domain; see above). Hence we assume that the strong-object feature in Spec-AgroP has attracted the object, pied piping the phonological features, so avoiding a derivational crash at PF. As a consequence, the numeration constituting the input to the computational system building up the C-domain has the order illustrated in (30*c*). At the C-domain, any part of this numeration may be reordered and placed in final position, where it receives focal stress; in (30*d*), it is the object that has been postponed.

Support for the description outlined here is provided by the quantificational scope properties of cases with Heavy DP Shift. Consider the Swedish examples in (31):

(31) (*a*) Jag har *tre studenter med utländsk bakgrund* på alla mina lektioner.
I have three students with foreign background at all my lessons

---

[28] With stress on *Bill*, the example is acceptable.

(*b*) Jag har på alla mina lektioner *tre studenter med utländsk bakgrund.*
   I have at all my lessons three students with foreign background

Example (31*a*) displays a quantificational scope ambiguity, expected on the basis of my account in Section 4.3. At TF, *alla* > *tre*, since circumstantial adverbials are merged above the internal argument, see Section 2.3.3. At GF, *tre* > *alla*, since the object has been attracted to Spec-AgroP. Now, if Heavy DP Shift (31*b*) is (roughly speaking) a reordering of (31*a*), we correctly predict it to have the same quantificational scope ambiguity. On the other hand, a description where Heavy DP Shift is analysed as the absence of raising to Spec-AgroP, as suggested by Kayne (1994), would not provide us with an account of the scope properties: given this description, *alla* has scope over *tre* at all interfaces, wrongly predicting no scope ambiguity.

2.5. The Left Periphery

In this section we will illustrate some consequences for the C-domain of a grammar organized as in (4). As was reported in Section 2.3.2, there is presently no consensus among linguists working within the Minimalist program with respect to the organization of the C-domain. In the following discussion I will stick to the account presented in Platzack (1998) when I have to depart from what is generally assumed.

With Rizzi (1997: 283; see also Branigan 1996, Platzack and Rosengren 1998, and Section 2.2) I take the C-domain to have at least two parts, one facing outwards and the other inwards. The outward facing part, called ForceP by Rizzi (1997), is a sentence type or clause type projection where the head contains information about the type of the clause.

The inward facing part of the C-domain, which Rizzi calls FinP, has a head with the feature [finite], which relates this phrase to tense and mood. Enveloped between ForceP and FinP are projections for topic and focus, according to Rizzi (1997), who stresses that 'the topic–focus system is present in a structure only if "needed", i.e. when a constituent bears topic or focus features to be sanctioned by a spec–head criterion'.

Finiteness, in my conception, expresses the localization of a predication in time and space, giving it the value of the speech act. Whereas tense introduces a time aspect in the clause, relating the predication to a time line, finiteness determines the precise value of this time line by identifying the speech time with the here and now of the speaker at the moment of speech. Without this anchoring of the time line associated with the predication, no truth value can be determined, hence finiteness can be said to make a proposition out of a predication. FinP is also the projection where EPP is established—that is, the specific subject–predicate relation which constitutes the proposition. Following Alexiadou and

Anagnostopoulou (1998) I opt for a parametrization of EPP, according to which EPP is checked in FinP either by move/merge XP or move/merge X°. In the first case we have an overt subject, in the second case we have overt subject–verb agreement.[29]

We will first consider *wh*-fronting, which has already been alluded to in the discussion of example (13). We will then turn to topicalization, which is not movement but insertion at the left periphery of an element drawn from the Mental Lexicon. Finally, we will briefly discuss Topic drop (including Diary drop) which turns out to be a case of late deletion.

2.5.1. *Wh-movement*

Consider *wh*-movement in English:

(32) (*a*) Who called?
     (*b*) *Who did call?
     (*c*) *Who she called?
     (*d*) Who did she call?

According to the discussion in Section 2.3, the input for the computational system building up the C-domain is the linear order of bundles of phonological features assembled at the V-domain and the I-domain;[30] we will refer to this order of phonologically visible elements as the numeration, using this term in a slightly different way than Chomsky (1995) does. For (32*a*) this numeration is given in (33*a*), and for (32*d*) it is given in (33*b*). Notice that there is no *do* present.

(33) (*a*) {called, who}
     (*b*) {called, who, she}[31]

The computational system working at the C-domain picks the feature [finite] from the lexicon and merges it as Fin° on top of the numerations in (33); since English has strong EPP, the subject must raise to Spec-FinP in both cases, yielding (34*a*, *b*).

(34) (*a*) $[_{\text{FinP}}$ who$_i$ $[_{\text{Fin}°}$ e $]$ {called, t$_i$}$]$
     (*b*) $[_{\text{FinP}}$ she$_i$ $[_{\text{Fin}°}$ e $]$ {called, who, t$_i$}$]$

---

[29] Alexiadou and Anagnostopoulou (1998) relate EPP to a feature in Agr, whereas I claim that a feature in Fin° is involved, following Branigan (1996).

[30] Note that lexical insertion of visible elements is also possible in the C-domain, as is mentioned in the discussion of (4).

[31] Recall that the object is attracted to Spec-AgroP in overt syntax, as mentioned earlier, and the verb is subsequently raised to a head position below NegP but above AgroP; see Josefsson and Platzack (1998) for details. Hence, in languages where the subject is not overtly raised to the I-domain, the numeration has the order verb–object–subject.

Since a single *wh*-element must be sentence-initial in English, *who* in (34*b*) must raise. This raising would, however, lead to a violation of a general constraint on computation, Shortest Move or the Minimal Link Condition (Chomsky 1995), that roughly speaking states that movement must take place stepwise; in (34*b*), stepwise raising is blocked by the presence of *she* in Spec-FinP. According to Richards (1998), the Principle of Minimal Compliance offers two ways to ignore such an obstacle. One possibility is to expand the structure by merging a new head above the obstacle; in English, the dummy auxiliary *do* is used for this purpose (see Arnold 1995 for a detailed discussion). Hence, after having picked *do* from the lexicon and merged it on top of FinP, the computational system allows *who* to be fronted, yielding the structure (35):

(35) [Who$_j$ [did [$_{FinP}$ she$_i$ [$_{Fin°}$ e] {called, t$_j$, t$_i$}]]]^{32}

In a verb-second language like Swedish, no *do*-support is necessary: here the finite verb is merged on top of the obstacle. Corresponding to (35) we thus have (36):

(36) [Vem$_j$ ringde$_v$ [$_{FinP}$ hon$_i$ [$_{Fin°}$ t$_v$] {t$_v$, t$_j$, t$_i$}]]
        who   called   she

Italian, which is neither a verb-second language nor a language with *do*-support, uses a third strategy. Being a null–subject language, Italian has the possibility to check EPP without raising the subject to Spec-FinP; corresponding to (32*d*) we have (37), where the pronoun is replaced by a full noun for the subject position to be visible:

(37) [$_{FinP}$ Chi$_j$ [$_{Fin°}$ telefona$_v$, {t$_v$, t$_j$, Maria}]]]
        who   called   Mary

The second way to ignore the obstacle, given the Principle of Minimal Compliance, is to involve the obstacle itself in a movement that obeys Shortest Move; see Richards (1998: 620). This strategy seems to be used in Finnish, where an example like (38*a*) has the structure (38*b*), in which the subject is raised to an obligatory Topic position within the C-domain; see Holmberg and Nikanne (to appear).^{33}

(38) (*a*) Ketä   Marja rakastaa?
              who-PARTIT Mary loves
        (*b*) [ketä$_j$ e [Marja$_i$ e [$_{FinP}$ t$_i$ [$_{Fin°}$ rakastaa$_v$] {t$_v$, t$_j$, t$_i$}]]]
              who   Mary   loves

Having outlined how my account handles cross-linguistic variation in languages

---

^{32} Note that the main verb must be enumerated without tense affix to yield (32*d*).
^{33} Thanks to Urpo Nikanne (p.c.) for bringing the Finnish facts to my attention.

where the *wh*-phrase must be clause initial,[34] there are some other issues concerning *wh*-fronting that should be mentioned. Since Chomsky (1977) it is well known that the relation between the *wh*-phrase and the gap with which it is associated is independent on the construction type (question, relative clause, pseudo-cleft, etc.), and much research tried to account for this relation. Since these accounts have been expressed in terms of chains, there is reason to outline how the *wh*-phrase is related to its gap in the present model. I will restrict myself to three cases where the gap is within another constituent:

(39) (*a*) Which folder$_i$ does he keep the letter [$_{PP}$ in t$_i$]?
      (*b*) Who$_i$ did he find [$_{DP}$ a picture [$_{PP}$ of t$_i$]]?
      (*c*) Who is he [$_{AP}$ superior [$_{PP}$ to t$_i$]]?
      (*d*) Which car$_i$ did John say [$_{CP}$ that Bill fixed t$_i$]

Consider the numerations which constitute the inputs to the computational system building up the C-domains in these four cases. In (39*a*), this numeration contains the PP *in which folder*, in (39*b*) the DP *a picture of who*, in (39*c*) the AP *superior to who*, and in (39*d*) the embedded clause *that Bill fixed which car*. Structures like these participate in the build-up of other structures as unanalysed wholes, where the parts are linearly, but not hierarchically ordered.

As mentioned above, PPs, APs, and DPs are supposed to have been assembled stepwise in the same way as clauses. Extending the parallelism, since the highest domain in the case of clauses (the C-domain) is able to communicate with the context, we will assume the same function for the highest domains of PPs, APs, and DPs. It follows that we expect to find escape hatches in the highest domain not only for clauses, but also for PPs, DPs, and APs; with respect to PPs, this was already argued for in van Riemsdijk (1978: 226 ff.), and for DPs by Szabolcsi (1983) and many others. Prior to the build-up of the C-domains of (39) therefore, the *wh*-phrases have moved to the left peripheries of the PP, DP, AP, and CP, respectively, from which they are available to the computational system building up higher projections. Proper characterizations of these phrases for the inputs to the C-domains of (39) will thus look like (40):

(40) (*a*) [which folder$_i$ {in t$_i$}]
      (*b*) [who$_i$ {a picture of t$_i$}]
      (*c*) [who$_i$ {superior to t$_i$}]
      (*d*) [which car$_i$ {Bill fixed t$_i$}]

Although the proposed model does not use chains of the traditional type, the mechanism outlined to account for the relation between a *wh*-phrase and its gap is similar, and should therefore provide the same results as an account in terms of chains.

---

[34] I will not discuss languages with multiple *wh*-fronting, such as many Slavic languages.

2.5.2. *Topicalization*

In this subsection we will discuss examples like (41), in which the object is interpreted as the topic of the sentence. In (41*b*) it is the second sentence that is relevant.

(41) (*a*) John, Mary saw.

     (*b*) Certain persons resisted his military regime; those persons he called 'pseudointernationalists'.[35]

These examples appear to violate Shortest Move. However, several linguists, including Weerman (1989), Kosmeijer (1993), Branigan (1996), Chomsky (1997), and Rizzi (1997), have provided support for the hypothesis that a topicalized DP is not *moved* to initial position but generated there, related to the gap in VP (actually in Spec-AgroP) by an invisible operator. Adopting this description, (41*a*) can be assigned the structure in (42), where the initial DP and the operator Op are inserted as parts of the derivation of the C-domain, and the object trace is bound by the invisible operator, which in its turn is bound by the topic:[36]

(42) $[\text{John}_j \text{ e } [_{FinP} \text{ Mary}_i \text{ } [_{Fin°} \text{ e }] \text{ Op}_j \{\text{saw, t}_j, \text{t}_i\}]]]$

The Italian counterpart to (42) is (43), where the operator is a visible clitic:

(43) $[\text{Giovanni}_j \text{ e } [_{FinP} \text{ Maria}_i \text{ } [_{Fin°} \text{ e }] \text{ lo}_j \{\text{ha visto t}_j\}]]]$
    John   Mary   him has seen

In both cases the operator is adjoined to the left periphery of the remnant IP/VP, here indicated by curly brackets. In a verb-second language like Swedish, there is no visible difference between *wh*-fronting and topicalization; see (44) and compare with (36). The finite verb is raised above the subject also in the topicalization case.

(44) $[\text{John}_j \text{ e } [\text{ringde}_v \text{ } [_{FinP} \text{ hon}_i \text{ } [_{Fin°} \text{ t}_v \text{ }] \text{ Op}_j\{\text{t}_v, \text{t}_j, \text{t}_i\}]]]$[37]
    John   called   she

---

[35] The example is from Whitehall (1964).

[36] The invisible feature bundle merged as the object of the verb, and interpreted for theta-role at TF, must be attracted to the I-domain, to make sure that the grammatical meanings related to the object are available at GF (Grohmann, p.c.). Note that this description involves overt raising of invisible features, given the presence of a strong nominal feature in AgroP, as argued above. This is a consequence of the base-generation account of topicalization, and would be avoided if topicalization was described as movement.

[37] Note that the raising of the finite verb to a head position in front of FinP makes available a specifier position that can be filled by a personal pronoun (Left Dislocation):

(i) Johan, *honom* ringde hon.
    Johan him   called she

It is possible that this pronoun, like the clitic in (43), is a visible instance of the operator.

Like Swedish, Finnish has the same word order in clauses with a topicalized element as in clauses with a *wh*-fronted element; compare (45) with (38*b*).

(45) [Jussia$_j$ e [Marja$_i$ e [$_{FinP}$ t$_i$ [$_{Fin^o}$ rakastaa$_v$] Op$_j${t$_v$, t$_j$, t$_i$}]]]
     Jussia   Mary   loves

Note that we assume the same analysis in terms of escape hatches as for *wh*-fronting when relating a topic to a gap inside a PP, DP, AP, or CP; in the case of topicalization it is the operator that has moved to the left periphery of these constituents before raising.

At this point it is important to note that the insertion of a phonologically realized topic is necessary in cases like (42), (44), and (45). The numerations providing the input to the computational system in these cases all contain a strong nominal feature (AgroP) that has attracted an operator without phonological features. This operator is bound by the realized topic, which obviously is enough for preventing the derivation from crashing at PF. For the Italian example in (43), as for the Swedish left dislocation case in note 37, the situation is different, since the operator is phonologically realized.

2.5.3. *Topic Drop and Diary Drop in Swedish*

As noticed already by Ross (1968) and further developed in Huang (1984), it is possible in many languages to leave out a contextually prominent subject or object in sentence-initial position, but not in other positions. Consider the Topic-drop example in (46*a*), and the Diary-drop example (Haegeman 1990) in (46*b*).

(46) (*a*) Var är boken? (Den) Är på bordet./ (Jag) tror den är på
        where is book-the it   is on table-the/ I   think it   is on
        bordet.
        table-the
    (*b*) (Jag) Träffade Erik igår.
        I   met   Erik yesterday

There are several aspects of constructions with null topics that are of interest to a theory with multiple Spell-out as (4). Cardinaletti (1990) lists many properties of object null-topic constructions that indicate that an A-bar-type fronting is involved. For such cases we assume an account in terms of escape hatches, as in Section 2.5.1.

We will here consider another aspect of null-topics, having to do with the PF interface. As mentioned in Section 2.5.2, the insertion of a phonologically realized topic in cases with topicalization can be seen as preventing a crash at PF, since there is no other element with phonological features to take care of the strong N-feature in AgroP. In cases with null topics, there is no visible element, however, and we have to ask ourselves why the structure is allowed. The logical solution is to assume that the topic is inserted just as in the cases with overt topic, but deleted prior to PF. Taking recoverability to be a condition of successful deletion, we conclude that the deleted topic must have the same reading as the contextually prominent topic. This is also the case, as far as I know. We can topicalize the head of a non-restrictive relative clause (47), but Topic drop is not possible (48a); compare (48b), which shows that Topic-drop is possible if there is no relative clause involved:

(47)   Sven träffade jag igår,   som förresten   just har rest   till Paris.
        Sven met   I   yesterday, that by the way just has gone to Paris

(48) (a) *Sven, säger du. Träffade jag igår   som förresten   just har rest
          Sven, you. say. Met   I   yesterday that by the way just has gone
          till Paris.
          to Paris
      (b) Sven, säger du. Träffade jag igår.
          Sven, say you, Met   I   yesterday.
          'Sven, you say! I met him yesterday.'

See Platzack (1999) for an account of extraposed relative clauses in Swedish where it is shown that the head of a relative clause must be in a particular structural relation to the relative complementizer. This property, which we quite arbitrarily may indicate as $Sven_R$ in (47), is not part of the contextually given information. Recoverability is therefore blocked in (48a), and Topic drop is not allowed.

2.6. Concluding Discussion

In this chapter I have presented a model of I-language (4) where the systems of thought access multiple interface levels. A clear difference between (4) and other models, including (1), is the presumed correspondence between the interface levels and the derivational history of the clause (the assembling of the V-domain, I-domain, and C-domain, respectively), as well as the assumption that invisible movement (or its correspondence in a representational framework) is allowed to take place between the point where the I-domain is entering the numeration of the C-domain and where the I-domain exchanges information with the systems of thought, that is, GF.

    If the arguments outlined here for distinguishing between different systems of thought for thematic structure, grammatical structure, and discourse structure are accepted, it would still be logically possible to retain the model in (1), with three different systems of thought working on LF. Such a model would be less economical than (4), however. First of all, we would have to distinguish A-chains from A-bar chains, something which is not necessary in the present model, where (the remnants of) these chains belong to different domains. Secondly, since such a system would have a single LF, it would be natural to see the interface LF as consisting solely of one type of element—compare Chomsky's (1995) assumption that the only legitimate object at LF is a chain. All kinds of semantic and pragmatic factors would have to be reducible to chains in one way or another. As Engdahl (1998) points out, this might lead us to postulate chains also for capturing for example the grammatical correspondences of sociolinguistic systems such as honorifics in Korean, quite an undesirable consequence.

Under the approach taken in this chapter, with multiple interfaces to the systems of thought, we are not forced to search for a common structural solution to all the aspects of interpretation that we manage to isolate. This freedom is both a virtue and a drawback. It increases our possibilities but leads to a less stringent theory, where relations between the various interfaces can be established not only on the syntactic side (the computational system) as in a model with a single Spell-out, but also on the semantic side. In this perspective it would be important to know how the systems interpreting TF, GF, and DF are related. I have said nothing of such relations in this chapter.

3

Constituent Linking Between Conceptual Structure and Syntactic Structure

LARS HELLAN

Accepting Jackendoff's (1987c, 1990) proposal that the semantic correlate of an NP-occurrence is not a single thematic role (as claimed in Chomsky's 1981 'Theta-criterion'), but a set of co-indexed argument positions in conceptual structure (the 'Revised theta-criterion'), this chapter seeks to establish a non-arbitrary basis for this type of co-indexation (called 'conceptual indexing'). It is proposed that, on the one hand, the presence or absence of conceptual co-indexing reflects lexical meaning, and on the other, a difference in compositional semantics according to whether, when two predicative items (such as a verb and a directional adverb) combine, one item fits into the semantic structure of the other (called 'conservative combination'), or the two items fit into a structure inherent in neither of them ('radical combination'). Conceptual indexing is distinguished from referential indexing (relevant in discourse structure) and from 'binding indexing' (relevant in the syntactic representation of anaphora).

3.1. Introduction

The *Theta criterion* (Chomsky 1981), according to which a given occurrence of an NP can represent only one theta-role, and a given role can be expressed by at most one NP,[1] may be seen as ultimately giving an answer to the following question:

Versions of, and aspects of, this chapter have been presented at the 16th Conference on Scandinavian Linguistics (Turku, 1996), at Sinn und Bedeutung (Tübingen, 1996), at the Deutsche Gesellschaft für Sprachwissenschaft (Düsseldorf, 1997), at a Workshop on the Syntax–Semantics interface (Trondheim, 1997; at FASSL II, Sofia, 1997 Legon, Accra, 1997; Tilburg 1997; an HPSG seminar in Trondheim 1999; and in a Workshop on Conceptual Semantics, Trondheim, 1999). I am grateful to the audiences in all these places for valuable comments, and likewise, to the editors of this volume. Particular thanks go to Dorothee Beermann, Jon Atle Gulla, and Mila Vulchanova.

[1] Cf. Chomsky (1981: 36): 'Each argument bears one and only one theta-role, and each theta-role is assigned to one and only one argument'. In a footnote (p. 139) commenting on this formulation, Chomsky acknowledges the possible correctness of Jackendoff's position, to be mentioned shortly (but deems this not to be crucial to the points developed in that work).

(i) In the accumulation of information concerning a given individual, under what circumstances does a distinct (i.e., *new*) token reference to that individual have to be made? That is, what provides the *occasion* for each new use of a token NP referring to the individual?

Jackendoff (1987c, 1990) discusses cases where a single NP occurrence in effect represents many roles.[2] For instance, in 'John bought the book from Peter', John may be seen as having the roles both as an agent, in giving money away, and inchoatively as a possessor (of the book), while Peter is inchoatively a non-possessor of the book, but at the same time a recipient of money. Jackendoff proposes that the Theta criterion be replaced by what he calls the *Linking Condition* (or *Neo-Theta criterion*),[3] in which a key construct is a *set of roles*, represented in a semantic argument structure through co-indexing between various argument positions. Such a set of positions, or roles, we will refer to as a *role complex*; the gist of this principle can be stated as in (ii) (from now on referred to as the *Neo-Theta criterion*):

(ii) The Neo-Theta criterion:
      A role complex can correspond to only one NP occurrence.

The main topic of this chapter is whether the notion of a *role complex* can be given a non-arbitrary delimitation, whereby the Neo-Theta criterion will in turn constitute a non-arbitrary answer to (1).

Technically speaking, the type of indexing used to represent membership in a role complex we will call 'conceptual indexing',[4] to be found at a level of representation that Jackendoff calls 'conceptual structure' (CS), a label we adopt as well. The overall question to be addressed in this chapter can then be phrased as in (iii):

(iii) Under what conditions will two or more semantic argument positions be subsumed under the same argument complex, that is, carry the same conceptual index?

It should be noted that even in the absence of a proper characterization of *role complex*, conceptual indexing could still serve as a notational device in CS to keep track of which role complexes correspond to which token NPs in the syntactic representation of the construction in question; some phenomena will be

---

[2] He also discusses instances where one role (complex) seems realized by many NPs, as in *the pocket has a hole in it*. Among grammatical patterns having the same property are constructions with resumptive pronouns and constructions with clitic reduplication ('doubling'). Although these constructions are all relevant to the validity of the Theta-criterion, they are not pertinent to the points to be developed here.

[3] Cf. Jackendoff (1987c).

[4] Jackendoff's own term for the relation expressed by this indexing is *argument binding*; this choice of term is partly motivated by his view of anaphoric binding as a relation between semantic arguments and not between syntactic constituents; see the discussion in n. 8.

mentioned in Section 3.3 which seem to necessitate such a device. The concern of question (iii) is rather whether this indexing is motivated in CS on purely semantic grounds.

Two types of motivation will be considered. In Section 3.1, we argue that lexical meaning in certain cases can be (partially) defined in terms of whether two roles have the same conceptual index or not. In Section 3.2, we consider a certain aspect of what may be called 'constructional meaning', namely, a distinction as to whether a combination of two items is semantically licensed by the meaning of one of the two items, or rather is constructionally motivated; we show that this distinction can again be represented in terms of sameness vs. distinctness of conceptual indexing.

Given that sameness vs. distinctness of conceptual indexing can be decided on a semantically non-arbitrary basis, what is suggested by the phenomena considered in Section 3.3 is then that in addition to its semantic function, conceptual indexing may conceivably also serve in a track-keeping role, thereby attaining an over-all *stitching* function with regard to the levels of syntactic and semantic representation.

Our discussion will not be embedded in any specific grammatical framework, and so our conclusions will not be confined to specific frameworks either.

3.2. Lexical Meaning as Reflected in Conceptual Indexing

3.2.1. *The Proposal*

The schema in (1) informally represents a conceptual schema of *ejection*, where someone/something—the Ejector—performs the ejection, where something—the Ejected—undergoes the ejection, and a Path represents the trajectory of the Ejected.

(1) Ejector—Ejected—Path

Both sentences in (2) can be seen as expressing this pattern; and in both, the roles of Ejector and Ejected are carried by the same individual:

(2) (*a*) John threw himself out of the window
     (*b*) John jumped out of the window

The verbs *throw* and *jump* both express ejection; however, with *throw*, it is possible, but not necessary, that what ejects is identical to what is ejected, whereas with *jump*, such identity is necessary.[5] Thus, it is a fact about the semantics of

---

[5] It may be argued that typical differences between occasions referred to by these verbs, such as the use of an arm vs. the use of legs, follow from this difference. In order for identity to obtain, the mechanism of the ejecting body which performs the ejection, must be one that in general supports the entire body, whereas in the case of non-identity, the body supports the ejection mechanism. For

these verbs that they both express the role-pattern in (1), but with different patterns of identity. These distinct identity patterns may be seen as what gets encoded by conceptual indices, such that the necessity of identity in *jump* is encoded through membership in the same role complex, and the lack of necessary identity in *throw* is encoded through membership of the roles in distinct complexes. It then follows by the Neo-Theta criterion that *jump* will have both of its roles Ejector and Ejected expressed through one and the same NP, whereas for *throw*, the lack of necessary identity will lead to the use of two NPs, one for each role. Thus, given a conceptual structure representation of $(2a, b)$ as in $(3a, b)$, —in the same style as (1)—respectively, where the subscripts represent conceptual indexing.[6]

(3) (a) Ejector$_i$—Ejected$_k$—Path   (*throw*)
     (b) Ejector$_i$—Ejected$_i$—Path   (*jump*)

The number of NP arguments in the frames of these verbs will have to be as indicated in (4), where the left subscripts function as syntactic *token-indices* of the NPs:

(4) (a) $_i$NP *throw* $_k$NP
     (b) $_i$NP *jump*

As the choice of conceptual indexing is made at a purely lexical level, there will be no implications as to what lexical content is assigned to each NP slot in $(4a)$; thus, even if, due to the reflexive in $(2a)$, it is actually one and the same individual which is referred to in the actual clause, it is the lexically encoded *lack* of necessary identity which prevails in the assignment of syntactic frame to the verb and leads to the syntactic pattern of two NPs associated with *throw*.

The next subsection accommodates the occurrence of the reflexive in $(2a)$ relative to this analysis. It also exploits a formal feature of the analysis anticipated in (3) and (4), namely, that the token-indices used in (4) are identical to the *conceptual* indices of the roles realized by the respective NPs shown in (3). We may refer to this as a *stitching* function of the indexing in question.

3.2.2. *Representing Anaphora*

When $_k$NP in (4) is lexically realized as *himself,* as in $(2a)$, this unambiguously establishes the Ejector and Ejected role in $(3a)$ as being carried by the same

---

upright-standing humans, this necessitates legs and arms as the respective mechanisms for jumping and throwing. For someone standing on his/her arms, though, the choice would be the reverse. Thus, (i) sounds plausible enough:

(i) Standing on his hands, John first threw the ball away with his feet, and then made a short jump with his hands.

[6] 'i', 'j', and 'k' will be used as variables over conceptual indices, the indices themselves being numerals (note that Jackendoff uses Greek letters in the variable function).

individual. The indexing in (3a) hardly serves to express such coreference, hence a distinct type of indexing has to be introduced for the purpose of representing *sameness of discourse referent*; we will refer to this type of indexing as *referential indexing*.

The introduction of referential indexing could be done in either of two ways:

(a) through the construction of a new level, which might be called 'referential structure' (RS); or

(b) through the assignment of a referential index to the role Ejected in (3), in *addition* to the conceptual index already present; both indices would be formally seen as features.

At the moment we have little basis for choosing between these options. In Section 3.3, we will argue that option (b) is preferable, but for informal descriptive purposes up to then, we will use a terminology reflecting option (a). Whatever is expressed in this terminology is readily translated into the format of option (b).

To induce the sameness of referential index in the referential structure of (2a), we assume a syntactic representation of (2a) which will include the information in (5), where the left subscripts still serve as token-indices, and the feature *bound-by:i* instantiates a feature *bound-by:X* lexically associated with any reflexive; X is here instantiated by the token-index of some NP present in the syntactic representation, namely, the binder:[7]

(5) $_i$NP   V $_k$NP   AdvP

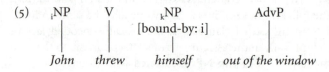

Here the feature *bound-by:i* represents *himself* as being bound by *John*. Granted that this is a licensed binding constellation, the following convention applies:

(6) Whenever an NP of the form

$_k$NP
[bound-by:i]

in a syntactic structure S is licensed, then, from the CS with which S is associated, derive a referential structure through replacing all occurrences of k as a conceptual index in CS with i.

---

[7] This formalism for expressing binding was first proposed in Higginbotham (1983), and is adopted in Hellan (1988). Aside from conceptually construing the notion of 'binding' in a more direct way than the more standardly used formalism of 'referential co-indexing', it also resolves a type of paradox which the latter notation, in conjunction with Binding Theory (Chomsky 1981) principles A and B, induces for sentences like (i).

(i) John has himself to consider. (cf. Hellan 1988: 56, n. 29)

When this replacement operation is applied to (3a), the result is an RS for (2a) with the role pattern Ejector$_i$—Ejected$_i$—Path.

Since RS is not the level of semantic structure from which syntactic structure is projected, at least as far as the Neo-Theta criterion is concerned, the indexation here obtained is not consequential for the number of NPs with which *throw* occurs.

Convention (6) exploits the identity between conceptual indices and syntactic token-indices.[8] It should be noted that this *stitching of levels* is compatible with a view of licensing conditions on reflexives as pertaining in part to syntactic factors, in part to semantic factors. An early example of relevant semantic factors —mentioned in Jackendoff (1990: 64–8)—is the contrast *John talked to Mary about herself* vs. **John talked about Mary to herself*; this contrast in acceptability may be seen as reflecting a general condition to the effect that the antecedent of a reflexive must be higher on a role hierarchy than the reflexive, a condition fulfilled in the first construction but not in the second (assuming that the *to* role is higher in the hierarchy than the *about* role).[9]

What we have presently shown is the need to keep two levels apart— conceptual structure and referential structure—where CS is the level for which the Neo-Theta criterion is defined; RS is the level where coreferentiality as induced by reflexive binding—by the rule (6)—is represented. This duality of representation is independent of how many and which levels of representation

---

[8] In Jackendoff (1990), the type of index-marking membership in a role complex—called 'argument binding'—is kept distinct from the type of indexing which serves to interlink role complex and syntactic token-constituent: the latter (which, in the absence of a particular label in Jackendoff op.cit., we may refer to as a 'linking index') is a syntactic token-index which also occurs as an index on the 'prominent' role in a role complex, that is, the role that determines the syntactic function (as subject, object, etc.) of the NP realizing the complex. Given that the linking index, like the stitching/ conceptual index, has a bi-level manifestation, and that the way in which the members of a role complex determine syntactic function can presumably be stated by reference being made to the set as such equally well as to a selected member of the set, plain economy of devices will seem to count in favour of the indexing system presently adopted.

[9] Jackendoff (1990) in fact proposes that anaphoric binding should not be represented in syntactic structure at all, but only in semantic structure. For arguments against such a proposal, see Hellan (1988) and Manning and Sag (1998). One type of example can be made on the basis of possessive reflexives in Norwegian. Due to constraints mentioned in section 3.3.1, the possessive reflexive *sin* in a construction like (i) is not licensed; however, in the passive 'counterpart' (ii), it is:

(i) *Jeg fortalte *Johan* en historie om   katten *sin*
     I   told   Johan a story   about cat   POSS-REFL
(ii) Johan ble fortalt en historie om katten *sin*
     Johan was told a story about cat POSS-REFL

It is unlikely that the CS's of (i) vs. (ii) would differentiate the constructions in the relevant respects, so as to predict the well-formedness of (ii) and the ill-formedness of (i). Another construction type that would probably be problematic to a purely CS-based account of these reflexives is the 'subject-to-subject-raising' construction exemplified in (iii):

(iii) Johan forekom   sine   venner å ha   skiftet   karakter fullstendig
      Johan appeared-to POSS-REFL friends to have changed character completely

the actual licensing conditions for reflexives will have to refer to.

Having shown that conceptual indexing can serve as part of the characterization of lexical meaning,[10] we next address an aspect of constructional meaning for the representation of which conceptual indexing can again be argued to be relevant.

3.3. Constructional Meaning as Reflected in Conceptual Indexing

3.3.1. *The Analysis*

Consider sentences (7a) from Norwegian and (7b) from German.

(7) (a) Jon løp ut
      Jon ran out
   (b) Johan ist an das andere Ufer geschwommen
      Johan is to the other bank swum
      'Johan swam to the other bank.'

Both sentences express the type of event in which someone is described as reaching the end point of a path: (7a) means that by the end of an activity of running, Jon was outside (of some area), at a point coinciding with the end point of the path projected by the running; (7b) means that Johan swam and thereby ended up on the other bank, as the end point of the path projected by the swimming. Jon and Johan are each presented in the following *two* roles: on the

---

[10] In order to focus on the principled aspects of the indexing, we have restricted the discussion to just the verbs *jump* and *run*. However, the empirical range can be appreciated not least when we look at verbs which express some kind of recursion, where types of recursion include iteration and 'cascades', with more or less definable 'cycles'. Dimensions of variation include

   (i) whether in each cycle there is a Mover (M) going from a location x to a location y;
   (ii) whether in each cycle there is a Conditioner (C);
   (iii) in case 'yes' to (i) and (ii), whether C is identical to or distinct from M;
   (iv) whether across cycles, the entity carrying the role of Mover is the same or not.

Some verbs can be distinguished according to criteria (iii) and (iv):

	(iii)	(iv)
run	identical	same entity
eat	distinct	distinct entity
spray	distinct	distinct entity
pull, push	distinct	same entity

In a conceptual structure describing the structure of these verbs, conceptual indexing will be necessary to express the properties mentioned.

It should be noted that not all 'argument' identity tied to lexical items is of a type that is captured by conceptual coindexing. A case in point is the 'obligatory control' imposed by the verb *try* between its subject and the understood subject of the infinitive complement: since various roles can be carried by the understood subject—cf. constructions such as *try to come, try to be elected, try to be given more responsibility*, the CS representation of this understood subject will not be coindexed with the CS representation of the matrix subject.

one hand in the role of what we may call *Mover*,[11] reflecting a role of performing a *monotonic* movement, and on the other hand the role of being located at a point coinciding with the end point of that monotonic movement, a role we may call *Path-end Located*. That there is still only one NP referring to Jon in (*a*) and to Johan in (*b*), follows from the Neo-Theta criterion if we assume a conceptual structure informally of the form (8) for the two sentences, with sameness of conceptual indices on the two roles.

(8) Mover$_i$ Path-end Located$_i$

In accordance with what we proposed in Section 3.1, such coindexing presupposes the *necessity* of a common bearer of the two roles in these cases. Unlike the situation in Section 3.1, the coindexing here cannot be held to reside exclusively in the meanings of *run* and *swim*, since the Path-end Located role would not be expressed in the absence of the directional constituents. Rather, in a monotonic movement with regard to location (i.e., one that projects a path), the Mover in the process is necessarily the same individual throughout the whole process and including the situation arising at the end, where the end point of the projected path is reached. Thus, if the verb expresses locational monotonic movement, and it combines with an adverbial element which can be understood as expressing an end point, then the construction constituted by this combination will have a conceptual structure including the identity shown in (8).

Semi-formally, we may think of this identity pattern as an abstract schema which is instantiated by given verbs and adverbials in combination. We will refer to this schema as the *schema of connected results* (for reasons which will become clear shortly). In order for a given verb to take part in an instantiation of this pattern, nothing more needs to be specified in its lexical definition than that it expresses monotonic development with regard to location. Similarly, in order for an adverbial (like *out*) to serve in an instantiation, its lexical specification needs only say that it can represent an end point. When a verb like *run* combines with an adverbial like *out*, their semantic specifications then merge into the schema of connected results, whereby the role-identity is induced (see Section 3.3.2 for a sketch of a formal mechanism accomplishing this). Construed this way, what induces the co-indexing in (8) is not the meaning of the verb per se or the meaning of the adverbial per se, but the merger of the two into the schema of connected result. One may therefore say that what induces the coindexing is a *constructional factor* rather than a purely lexical factor.

Both German and Norwegian provide near minimal pairs which can be analysed in terms of this analysis, and which corroborate it. In the Norwegian

[11] This notion is close to what is called 'Theme' in the tradition starting with Gruber (1965); however, although many authors, especially in the GB literature (cf. in particular Hoekstra and Mulder 1990), hold that an agentive role component is absent in such constructions, we assume that it is present, and for the moment our use of the notion 'Mover' is to be seen as compatible with an assumption of more or less agentivity residing in the entity carrying the role.

construction $(9b)^{12}$ the only syntactic difference from $(9a)$ is the presence of a reflexive object.

(9) (a) Jon løp ut. $(=(7a))$
         Jon ran out
     (b) Jon løp seg ut.
         Jon ran REFL out
         'Jon ran himself out.'

Semantically, the structure of $(9b)$ is one of *causation* where the situation caused is anything that could be causally related to the activity expressed by the verb, and not restricted to be a situation arising at the end of a path, as in $(9a)$. For instance, *out* in $(9b)$ can be understood relative to a prison, if Jon, for his good running, gets an early release as premium, or to a team,[13] when he runs so badly that he doesn't qualify for the team. We may refer to the resultativity expressed in this constellation as a *disconnected result*, as opposed to the *connected result* in $(7a/9a)$,[14] and to the role represented by the reflexive NP as *Disconnected Resultee*. The occurrence of a reflexive in $(9b)$ can be seen as a consequence of the Neo-Theta criterion in case we assume the following conceptual indexing in the case of a disconnected result, representing the *lack of necessary identity* between the bearers of the roles.

(10) $Mover_i$ Disconnected $Resultee_k$

This non-coindexing is well motivated. First, Norwegian provides considerable freedom in choosing other NPs than reflexives in this construction, as for instance in (11).

(11) Jon løp Mathias ut av laget.
     Jon ran Mathias out of the team

Secondly, even when a reflexive occurs, the semantic pattern instantiated is not one that *necessitates* the identity in question. This holds even in cases where anything other than a reflexive would seem odd in terms of physical plausibility, as in (12) (with (12c) as the extreme case).

(12) (a) Jon løp   seg   svett.
         Jon ran REFL himself sweaty

---

[12] While this type of construction has received much attention, especially based on English (for discussion, see for example Jackendoff 1990, section 10.4, Goldberg 1995, and references cited there), to my knowledge the point presently pursued has not been addressed much. Many factors of the construction type will be ignored here, such as its varying degrees of productivity.

[13] In the limiting case, the site of the caused situation may actually coincide with the end point of a path, as in *He drove himself into the ditch.*

[14] These notions 'connected' and 'disconnected result' were used in unpublished papers in 'Gestalt Grammar' by Vulchanova and Hellan in (1990).

   (*b*) Jon løp seg   trett.
        Jon ran REFL tired
   (*c*) Jon spiste seg   mett.
        Jon ate   himself full

The same reasoning applies to the German counterparts of the contrast in (9). Consider (13):[15]

(13) (*a*) Johan ist an das andere Ufer geschwommen. (= (7*b*))
            Johan is to the other   bank swum
            'Johan swam to the other bank.'
      (*b*) *Johan hat an das andere Ufer geschwommen.
            Johan has to the other   bank swum
      (*c*) Johan hat geschwommen.
            Johan has swum
            'Johan swam.'
      (*d*) *Johan ist sich aus dem   Rennen   geschwommen.
            Johan is REFL out of the competition swum
      (*e*) Johan hat sich aus   dem Rennen   geschwommen.
            Johan has REFL out of the   competition swum
            'Johan swam himself out of the competition.'

In German, the choice between *sein* ('be') and *haben* ('have') as auxiliary with verbs like 'swim' is generally assumed to follow a rule to the effect that if the construction expresses End of path, then *sein* is chosen, and if rather the activity as such is highlighted, the verb is *haben*; this is illustrated in (13*b*) vs. (13*c*). That the construction expresses End of path means that it instantiates the conceptual index identity of the *connected result* schema (8); by the Neo-theta criterion, we therefore predict that *sich* is impossible in such a construction, and hence that *sein* and *sich* cannot cooccur, hence the illformedness of (13*d*). For *sich* to occur, the role structure rather has to be that of disconnected result, as in (10), by which the activity as such is highlighted; in this case, we predict that the choice of auxiliary must be *haben*, which is confirmed by the wellformedness of (13*e*).

We thus see that both Norwegian and German have a consistent constructional pattern expressing *disconnected result*, partially described by (10), where two NPs can occur referring to the same individual. What necessitates these two NP positions, according to our analysis, is that by the meaning of this construction, there is no *necessity* that the roles expressed by these NPs be carried by the same individual. The opposite obtains for the type of construction given in (7). The use of conceptual indexing to represent whether, in these types of constructions, roles

---

[15] The literature on these constructions in German is quite rich, but I make no attempt to review it here; see Grewendorf (1989) for a thorough treatment in GB terms. Seibert (1993) is an approach close to that presented here. I am grateful to Anneliese Pitz, Anja Seibert, and Dorothee Beermann for discussion of the constructions addressed (the present examples are due to Dorothee Beermann).

are necessarily carried by the same individual or not, thus brings out a contrast which is clearly of a constructional nature. Serving as a representative of a meaning factor both at a lexical and a constructional level, the indexing as such confirms its role in conceptual structure.

3.3.2. *Implementing the Proposal*

To make the analysis more precise, we now offer a partial formalization of our construal of constructions as representing connected vs. disconnected result, and the role of conceptual indices in these construals. While, again, we are not employing the exact mechanisms of any available framework, the devices and procedures reflect rather common ideas and should be easily relatable to more concrete, existing analyses.

The formalization first focuses on the role of the *connected result schema*, in conjunction with the assumption that neither the verb, nor the adverbial constituent as such, embodies this schema. This can be seen to follow from a general assumption that we make, that in the Lexicon each sign will have a *minimal*, non-redundant, representation, abstracting away from all effects of combinations that are predictable from rules of grammar. This formal assumption matches another assumption: that the conceptual structure representation of a construction (down to a word in isolation) should reflect only what is directly expressed through that construction, and not what may be inferred by general reasoning, expected combinations, and so forth.[16] Thus, what need *not* be entered for an individual verb like *run* or *swim* are values such as beginning of path, end of path (i.e., the *connected result schema*), route of path, speed of traversal of path, etc. Such dimensions are *activated* only in so far as a verb, specified as expressing locational monotonic developments, combines with constituents which actually provide values for the parameters in question. Thus, the parameter end of path is activated only when the verb combines with an End-of-path constituent. Such activation now has to take place in the combinatorial process leading to (9a), giving the role structure (8), but not in the combinatorial process leading to (9b). Since the lexical elements in these constructions are basically the same, we need to posit two distinct procedures of combination. We will outline the procedure for connected result in some detail, and then point out in what respect that procedure contrasts with the procedure for disconnected result.

Conceptual structure will be visualized in terms of feature diagrams, where feature–value pairs are presented in tree form (the attribute dominating the

---

[16] Provisos must be made for 'implicit' arguments, i.e., roles that are expressible in principle, but can still be left out even though they are understood. For proposals concerning implicitations for verb arguments, see Hellan and Vulchanova (1995), where the licensing factor is proposed as also residing in CS, in the form of 'criteriality'. (This constraint on what is to be represented in CS may be seen to reflect a remark in Jackendoff 1996b: 307, to the effect that expressed telicity depends on what is 'on screen' in a sentence.)

value, which may in turn serve as an attribute).[17] Some of the main notions of the analysis proposed are illustrated in (14), representing the CS of *John ran out*.[18]

(14) Partial semantic structure of *John ran out*

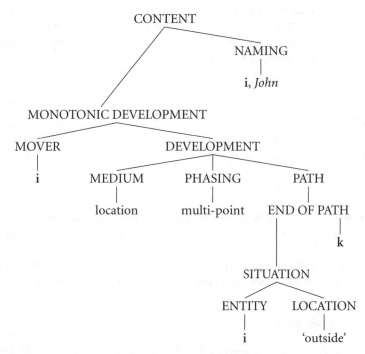

The specification of the monotonic development (that is, a development proceeding consistently in some direction or respect) makes a first distinction between the MOVER, marked for its conceptual index *i*, and the DEVELOPMENT. This in turn divides into three parameters: the MEDIUM specifies *with respect to what* the development takes place (other possible Mediums being size, quality, etc.), the PHASING specifies whether this is a gradual development or a two-point change (represented by the values *multi-point* and *two-point*), and PATH provides all possible specifications with regard to the path projected by the development. PATH (and likewise the attribute Mover) occurs as attribute only when MEDIUM is specified as location. In the present case, PATH has only one subspecification, namely END OF PATH, whose content-value is a specification of the situation obtaining at the end of the development. Here the conceptual

---

[17] Sort labels (see for instance Pollard and Sag 1987, 1994) are not included, but could be, and could then serve as basis for 'type declarations' of the type used in HPSG. Such devices could perhaps be used to regulate what we refer to below as possible 'downward expansions', but given the 'dynamic' nature of the latter, it is not clear how feasible the integration of this mechanism would be into the general HPSG format.

[18] The notions used in this analysis are introduced in works such as Hellan (1993), Pitz (1993), Gulla (1996), Hellan and Vulchanova (2000), and Vulchanova (1996).

index *i* occurs again, now as ENTITY (that is, the function labelled *Path-end Located* in (8)). The place itself we have informally encoded as 'outside'. In addition, the END OF PATH conceptual constituent carries an index (*k*) indicating (i) that it is in principle realizable syntactically, and (ii) that (14) can occur as the semantic specification of a clausal sign only in case there actually is in the syntactic structure of the sign a constituent with this same index, now as a token-index. In the syntactic representation of *John ran out*, this requirement is met, by a structure roughly of the form (15).

(15)

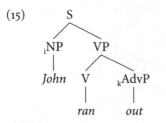

As we can see, the linking between (14) and (15) observes the Neo-Theta criterion in having just one NP realization corresponding to the two tokens of the conceptual index *i*.[19]

We now outline the sequence of combinatorial processes giving rise to the connected-result constructions. First, the *schema of connected results* will have the form (16).

(16) Schema of *connected result*

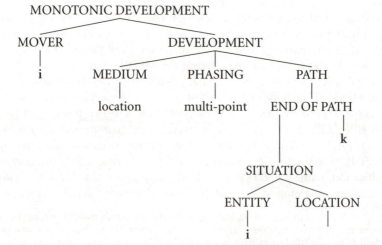

---

[19] This format for conceptual structure has in common with Jackendoff's (1990) format that it allows for treating thematic roles as derived constructs, definable in terms of more fine-grained structures (in the case of Jackendoff, function-argument structures). For more direct reconstructions of Jackendoff's system in feature-matrix terms, see for example Davis (1996) and Verspoor (1997).

Clearly, this is a substructure of (14), expandable into (14) through the specifications provided by *ran*, *out* and *John*.

Partial lexical *minimal* semantic structures of *run* (ignoring the tense factor) and *out* are given in (17*a, b*) (where 'j' in (17*b*) is possibly distinct from 'i' in (17*a*)):

(17) (*a*) Approximate, incomplete, minimal semantic structure of *run*

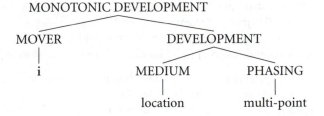

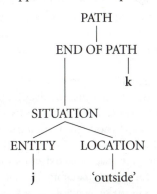

(*b*) Approximate, incomplete, minimal semantic structure of *out*

The combination of *run* and *out* now takes place in two steps. First, (16) is derived from (17*a*) through a process we may call a 'downward expansion' from (17*a*). This is a process of expanding down in the tree from nodes already present, where the new material, together with portions of the dominating material, matches some general schema or template on permissible attribute-value combinations. The schema in (16) is an example and serves as the place in this analysis where the necessity of identity between a Mover and a Path-end located is encoded.[20] Secondly, (17*b*) merges with (16), again giving a downward expansion, now with (16) as embryo, resulting in the structure (14).

---

[20] In the present case, the 'embryo' structure (17*a*) is properly contained in this template. However, a more correct minimal representation of *run* will also contain a part expressing the movements characteristic of running, and this part would not coincide when any part of (16). Formally, therefore, this expansion can be seen as an instance of what we will call 'conservative combination', here of the minimal 'run' structure and (16). It differs from the subsequent process of (16) combining with (17*b*) only in that the latter more directly reflects the combination between *run* and *out*, whereas the former is more like a preparatory step to the latter. One may well conceptualize these processes as merged together in *run* combining with *out*. The case may be seen as an instance of 'enriched composition' in the sense of Jackendoff (1997).

When two structures merge in such a way that one of them is exhaustively dominated by a single node X already present in the other structure, we call it a *conservative combination*, and the dominating structure (i.e., the one containing X) we call the *host* of the combination. In such combinations, index identity (here i from (17a) = j from (17b)) is induced by the following convention:

(18)   Given two structures A and B conservatively combining, with A as *host*, and with the substructure C in common, such that A contains the part C_A and B contains the part C_B, then, wherever C has the index x in a certain position where C_B has the index y, x uniformly replaces all occurrences of y in B. All other indices in B must be distinct from indices in A.

The mechanism of Conservative combination thus induces the indexing in (14) from the merger of (16) (as A), with (17b) (as B).

The above notion of conservative combination applies to *structures*. Derivatively, we say that two lexical signs X and Y combine conservatively, with X as host, in case the structure of X is a host for the structure of Y, or X hosts a structure M which in turn hosts the structure of Y. In the present case, by the latter clause, we can thus say that the sign of *run* combines conservatively with the sign of *out*, and that this relationship formally induces the conceptual coindexing.

The contrast with (9b) (the *disconnected* result), can now be seen to reside in a contrast between Conservative combination of the signs involved, and a combination to be called 'Radical combination', where neither of the two combinands, by themselves or through downwards expansion from the minimal representation of either, provides a slot into which the other can fit. Intuitively, this is again clear, since *run* hardly has any slot for disconnected consequences of events of running, and *out* has no slot for events causing the situation of outsideness in question. What the analysis will make available here is a template representing the disconnected result as such, into which the structures of *run* and *out* both fit, but such that neither of these fit into the other. This means that the conditions for index identification stated in (18) are not met. Adding to (18) that these conditions are the only circumstances under which indices of combining CS-structures can be identified, and that in all other cases indices from joining structures must be kept distinct, one derives a CS for the constructions (9b) and (13e) in which the relevant roles carry distinct conceptual indices, as in (10),[21] inducing the occurrence of distinct NPs in the syntax. (The interpre-

---

[21] Exactly what the CS of (9b) will be is a matter of some dispute; cf., e.g., discussion in Jackendoff (1990, sect. 10.4). The main alternatives addressed there are the structures (i) and (ii).

(i) Jon run CAUSE Jon out
(ii) Jon (GET) out BY Jon run

Due to constructions of the type *John gradually ran himself out of the team*, the structure in (ii) may seem preferable. Nothing in the above discussion, though, hinges on the choice.

tation of the reflexives in these cases then follows the same pattern as described in Section 3.1.)

3.3.3. *Summary*

Our proposal is that the use of one or two NPs in an otherwise similar environment consisting of a verb and a resultative complement expresses whether the combination between these signs is conservative or radical, reflecting the meaning difference between the connected and the disconnected result patterns. As the correspondence between the syntactic patterns and their semantics again is governed by the Neo-Theta criterion, the working of this principle makes crucial reference to the conceptual indexing in conceptual structure. Through (18), this indexing is a reflex of the distinction between conservative and radical combination, and is thus a derived construct. However, what the Neo-Theta criterion sees is a fully formed CS, where the indexing is now the only key to the history of the combination. So, even if derived, the indexing still is a proper holder of semantic information, and confirms its status as a legitimate part of CS.[22]

3.4. Track-keeping Indexing and its Relation to Conceptual Indexing

As noted above, the formal nature of conceptual indexing would make it apt for serving as a device whereby the referent of a token NP can be kept track of in semantic representation. Although we have established that conceptual indexing defends its place in CS in its own right, the possibility still remains that conceptual indexing could serve in this function as well. In this section, we first survey various cases showing the need for a track-keeping device; we then consider whether conceptual indexing can serve as such a device.

---

[22] As was the case in section 3.1, we kept the empirical ground rather limited through this exposition. A range of further instances of what we see as the contrast conservative vs. radical combination are constructions of adverbial modification discussed in Jackendoff (1990), viz. the construction types treated in chapters 8 and 9 there vs. those treated in chapter 10.

Another domain where the contrast can be seen is the serial-verb construction, in languages where some of the locative functions normally carried by prepositions in the European languages are carried by verbs. Examples are Kwa languages like Akan and Ewe. In a construction like (i) from Akan (from Sætherø and Hellan 1996) *kɔ* 'go' is such a 'prepositional' verb, with the final VP *kɔ-ɔ fie no mu* expressing the path of the ejected ball.

(i) Kofi fa-a   bɔɔl no **to**   kɔ-ɔ   fie   no   mu.
    K.   take-PST ball DEF **throw** go-PST house DEF inside
    'Kofi threw the ball into the house.'

Due to the necessary identity between what is affected by 'throw' and what is ejected (and moves), the present theory predicts that—to the extent that verb series may be 'broken up' through repetition of NPs expressed earlier in the sequence—one might in principle introduce a lexical NP before the second verb, but not before the final. This prediction appears to be borne out.

3.4.1. *Phenomena Whose Licensing Conditions Require a Track-keeping Device in Semantics*

The typical case to be considered is where the licensing conditions for an NP include conditions concerning semantic constellations in which the referent of the NP—identified as the *referent-on-that-token-use-of-the-NP*—takes part. Examples alluded to in Section 3.2.2 include the following conditions on reflexives, each instantiated in one or more languages:

(*a*) The reflexive must be *role-commanded* by its binder $=_{def}$
     The role or role complex realized by the reflexive must be lower on a role hierarchy than the role/role complex realized by the NP binding the reflexive.[23] (An example was given in Section 3.2.2; for more complex cases, cf. Hellan 1988: ch. 4.)

(*b*) The reflexive must be *predication-commanded* by its binder $=_{def}$
     The reflexive must be part of a constituent P such that P is understood as being predicated of the referent of the binder of the reflexive. This is exemplified in Norwegian (see for example Hellan 1988), in which, in order for NP *B* to serve as binder for an anaphor *A* of the form *seg* (*selv*)/*sin*, *A* must be contained in a constituent *P* standing in a predication relation to *B*. This requirement is illustrated in the following minimal pair (*A* and *B* in italics), using the third person possessive reflexive *sin*, with *Johan* as the only possible putative binder:

(19) (*a*) *Jeg fortalte *Johan* en historie om   katten *sin*.
          I   told   Johan a   story   about cat   POSS-REFL-3SG
          'I told Johan a story about his cat.'
      (*b*) Jeg gjorde *Johan* stolt   av katten *sin*.
          I   made Johan proud of cat   POSS-REFL-3SG
          'I made Johan proud of his cat.'

In (19*b*), *stolt av katten sin* is predicated of *Johan*, hence this construction is well formed, whereas in (19*a*), *en historie om katten sin* is not predicated of *Johan*, nor is any other constituent containing *sin*, hence (19*a*) is ill formed.

(*c*) The reflexive must be *perspective-commanded* by its binder $=_{def}$
     Relative to the putative binder *B*, the reflexive must be contained in a constituent *C* which represents a phrasing that can be attributed to the referent of *B*, i.e., which represents the referent of *B*'s perspective on the situation expressed. This is exemplified by the type of anaphors commonly called 'logophoric' (see among others Clements 1975; Sells 1987; Essegbey 1994).

---

[23] Davis and König (1998) give a general critique of the notion 'role hierarchy', and propose that grammatical constraints that seemingly involve such a construct are better construed in terms of event types related to verb types. Since the relevance of track-keeping would seem the same on either approach, we take no stand in the issue mentioned.

For these conditions to be implementable, track must be kept of both the reflexive and its binder in the relevant semantic representation, and also of the predicated complex *P* for the implementation of predication-command, and of the complex *C* for the implementation of perspective-command. For the role command factor, CS as conceived up to now will seem adequate as providing the necessary information, and it is possible that also the information needed to assess predication and perspective can be represented at this level; the track-keeping device is however needed no matter what the relevant levels of semantic representation may be.

Another type of construction whose representation necessitates track-keeping is the conditional type of *donkey anaphora,* as in (20), with the italicized pronoun being bound by the appropriate underlined NP:

(20) (*a*) If a man owns a donkey, *he* beats *it*
      (*b*) Wenn jemand eine Reise   tut, hat *er* was   zu erzählen
            when someone a journey does has he something to tell

In the absence of a syntactic c-command relation between binder and bindee, approaches such as Discourse Representation Theory (cf. Kamp and Reyle 1993; Asher 1994), Dynamic semantics (cf. for example Dekker 1997), or Heim (1982) seem to adopt the following licensing condition, however implemented (for example by extending the scope of an existential quantifier as the discourse proceeds):

(21) A binding relation between a pronominal *P* and an indefinite NP binder *B* is licensed if, in the appropriate type of logical/semantic representation, the variable representing *P* is bound by the same quantifier as the variable representing *B*.

Such a condition presupposes that at the logical level of representation, variables are annotated in such a way that one can keep track of which syntactic NP they represent.

In cases like (20), what is at stake is the licensing of a certain reading of the pronominal, and not grammaticality as such, as in the case of anaphora mentioned above. However, examples partly similar to (20) obtain where (21) is relevant for grammaticality, namely, so-called *correlative* constructions of a type found, for instance, in many Indo-Aryan languages, where a morphologically marked type of indefinites (introduced by *j-*) has as a grammaticality requirement that there be a consequent clause containing a pronominal bound by the *j*-element. An example from Oriya is given in (22) (coindexing of the underlined and italicized elements indicates the correlations):[24]

(22) Jeun   pua$_i$ jeun   jhiaku$_j$ dekhilaa *se*$_i$ *taaku*$_j$ pasanda kalaa.
      whichever boy whichever girl-ACC saw   he her   liked
      'Whichever boy saw whichever girl, he liked her.'

---

[24] From Sahoo and Hellan (1998). Srivastav (1991) deals with similar constructions in Hindi.

It is a grammaticality requirement here that *jeun pua* ('whichever boy') binds *se*, and *jeun jhiaku* binds *taaku*. Each binding relation is an instantiation of the schema in (23) (with *n* and *t* as token indices in the syntax),

(23) . . . $_n$NP . . . $_t$Pron$_{\text{bound-by-n}}$

What (21), then, posits as a licensing constellation in the logical representation is of the form (24), for some operator OP (such as *A* or *m*), with one instance of the schema for each binding relation (in this schema, *bound by k* is equivalent to a subscripted variable x_k in standard logical notation):

(24) $_k$OPx . . . x . . .   x
                 [bound by k]   [bound by k]
                 [track-keeping index: n]   [track-keeping index: t]

Clearly, thus, a track-keeping device is needed also when pronominals are bound across clauses, like in (20) and (22).

3.4.2. *Conceptual Indexing as a Track-keeping Device*

We now consider to what extent track-keeping indexing can be seen as formally equivalent to conceptual indexing. Let us first determine how the *bound-by* type of indexing used in (24) relates to conceptual indexing. It is obvious that in schema (24), when instantiated in a representation of example (22), the *x* tokens will correspond to distinct role complexes; these two types of indexing seem therefore distinct. The same holds for the simpler example (25):

(25) Every man admires himself.

Here *every man* and *himself* are linked to different conceptual indices, and yet, in a logical representation, the variable counterparts of the subject and object will be bound by the same universal quantifier, and hence be variables with the same *bound-by* index. Given that in Section 3.2.2, for a construction like *John admires himself*, we concluded that the identity expressed between the referents of *John* and *himself* should be represented in referential structure, rather than CS, by analogy of reasoning, the identity of variables with respect to the *bound-by* index in a representation of (25) should only be marked in RS. Thus, tentatively, the level of representation where *co-binding* of variables can be marked through identical *bound-by* indices will be RS.

Turning to the track-keeping indices, the analysis of the constructions in (20) and (22) seems to indicate that track-keeping indexing is necessary at a level where variables are represented as bound by quantifiers through the *bound-by* indexing. This would mean that track-keeping indexing has to be available in RS. Given that conceptual indexing is obliterated in RS, this should in turn mean that conceptual indexing and track-keeping indexing are after all different constructs.

However, at this point the terminology of CS and RS as distinct levels may be misleading. An alternative conclusion would be that the putative levels RS and CS are not distinct after all, but that elements at this (single) level are specified by features both for discourse referents (and binding by the same logical operators) and for role complexes—that is, conceptual index, where the latter also serves as a track-keeping index. Schematically, the semantic representation of (25) would thus include the specification shown in (26*b*), given (26*a*) as a partial syntactic index-annotated representation of (25).

(26) (*a*) $_i$NP   V $_j$NP
                  | | |
            every man   admires   himself

   (*b*) $_k$[... x   ...   →   ...   x   ...]
              BOUND-BY: k   BOUND-BY: k
              CONCEPTUAL IND: i   CONCEPTUAL IND: j

If we define REFERENTIAL INDEX as either an index for discourse referent or a *bound-by index* identifying a binding operator,[25] then (26*b*) can be restated as (27):

(27) $_k$[... x   ...   →   ...   x   ...]
          REFERENTIAL IND: k   REFERENTIAL IND: k
          CONCEPTUAL IND: i   CONCEPTUAL IND: j

We have now reached a position where it seems consistent to hold that the device of conceptual indexing, being a semantically motivated device in its own right, can at the same time serve as a device for track-keeping indexing.

To develop this construal, one obviously has to show that the formalisms for representing such diverse phenomena as quantificational variable-binding, predication, *responsibility for expression*, and discourse referents, are in fact compatible, and preferably unifiable, with whatever format one chooses for representing conceptual structures. This is not something we can substantiate now, but it will serve as a hypothesis to be explored.

3.5. Concluding Discussion

Postulating one and the same index to represent both a role complex in conceptual structure and an NP token in syntactic structure, implies a claim about identity of what is indexed on the respective occasions. Obviously, a role

---

[25] Given conventions determining which option is relevant in the given case.

complex and an NP are not identical entities as such; however, what they may *share*, to warrant coindexation, is belonging to the same sign. After all, signs are exactly this—combinations of conceptual structures and morpho-syntactic/ phonological forms.

The sign which is represented by an index in the CS of a verb (or verb construction), is a sign with which the verb will combine, reflecting an entity parameter in the situation type expressed by the verb. What the discussion in Sections 3.1 and 3.2 aims to establish, then, is that the partitioning of a situational content into signs follows certain non-arbitrary lines: on the one hand, it may reflect lexical semantics on the other, it may reflect the distinction between conservative and radical combination inside a verbal construction. These are, in slightly different terms, answers to question (i) in Section 3.1.

Some further upshots of the discussion should be mentioned. First, contrary to what is assumed in most grammatical frameworks, semantic analysis requires *two* types of indexing, not just one (commonly called 'referential indexing'): conceptual indexing (reflecting role complex and ultimately sign identity), and referential indexing (indicating discourse referent). More precisely, conceptual co-indexation indicates membership in the same role complex; referential coindexation indicates instantiation of the same discourse referent.

Secondly, both co-relations just mentioned are distinct from the grammatical relation of binding, that is, the relation between an anaphor and its antecedent (binder). The latter relation obtains between morpho-syntactic elements (with the interpretation 'my semantic value is that of my binder'), not between roles or referents, and it is asymmetric—the binder binds the anaphor, not vice versa—whereas conceptual coindexation and referential coindexation are both symmetrical. To the extent that binding is to be represented through indexing, this is thus a third type of indexing.

Although the modelling of sign combination, in connection with the contrast conservative–radical combination, may take different shapes according to underlying assumptions, all proposals now made can in principle be accommodated in most or all grammatical frameworks.

PART TWO

Constraints on the Conceptual-Structure-
to-Spatial-Structure Interface

4

Some Restrictions in Linguistic Expressions of Spatial Movement

URPO NIKANNE

This chapter discusses the link between spatial cognition and language. The investigation supports the idea of Jackendoff (1983) that linking between these two representations is not direct; it is intermediated by a level of representation referred to as conceptual structure. The constraints that govern the form of conceptual structure are also the reason for some structural differences between spatial structures and the linguistic structures expressing them. The theoretical assumptions are based on the approach of Conceptual Semantics (Jackendoff 1983, 1987a, 1990; Nikanne 1990). The main focus is on the constraints of conceptual-structure formation and their effects on the linking between linguistic and spatial representations.

4.1. Introduction

In this chapter, I will discuss the interaction between linguistic and spatial representations in the light of the traditional gestalt Figure/Ground distinction. I will only concentrate on events in which the Figure is moving along a path.

According to Jackendoff (1983, 1987a) and Jackendoff and Landau (1992), there is a single representation, *conceptual structure*, that functions—for one thing—as a lingua franca between spatial and linguistic representations (cf. Section 4.2). Following Jackendoff and Landau (1992: 99), spatial representation is 'a format or level of mental representation devoted to encoding the geometric properties of objects in the world and the relationships among them in space'.

The well-formedness of each level of mental representation is defined by a set of formal constraints that apply only at that particular level of representation. Given that conceptual structure is the intermediate representation between linguistic and spatial representations, the constraints of conceptual-structure formation (as formalized by Nikanne 1990) are crucial for our purposes.

This chapter has benefitted greatly by Emile van der Zee's valuable comments. I am also grateful to Ingebrit Scheltens for her comments on an earlier version. This chapter is an elaborated version of my paper presented at the conference of the International Society of Theoretical Psychology in Ottawa in 1995 and at the University of Utrecht in June 1996. I would also like to thank the audiences at those talks for their comments.

I will argue that even though the linguistic and spatial representations are linked together, both of them have their own characteristics due to the different constraints governing the form of these representations and also the intermediate representation, conceptual structure. To simplify things a great deal: a linguistic expression with a single (abstract) path may require several separate paths at the spatial level of representation (e.g. *Three men went to New York [from different cities and using different routes]*). We can understand this mismatch in linking if we understand the formation conditions of conceptual structure.

In Section 4.2, the assumptions of the modular organization of mind are explained. Section 4.3 discusses the relevant conceptual-structure constraints. Section 4.4 deals with the effects of these constraints on the linking between the spatial understanding and linguistic expressions of situations in which a Figure is moving along a path.

4.2. Organization of Mental Modules

According to Jackendoff (1987*a*, 1990, 1992, 1997), the human cognitive system is organized in modules, as illustrated schematically in Figure 4.1. In this figure, only some cognitive areas are present and only linguistic and visual 'faculties' are

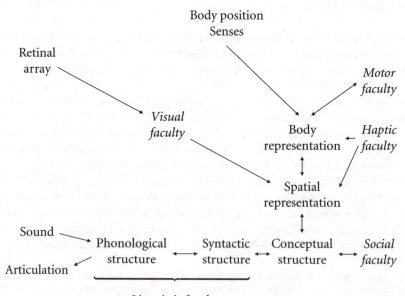

FIGURE 4.1. Representational modularity of mind

analysed in more detail (on the visual faculty, see Marr 1982). I have written the labels of so-called 'faculties' of the mind in italics and the labels of representational modules in roman type.

The modules are assumed to be very specialized, such that each one contains one level of representation. Basically, each module is autonomous and has its own primitive categories and principles of combination. Here the theory differs from for instance Fodor's (1983) theory of modularity. Technically, Fodorian kinds of 'large' faculties (for example, *'language faculty'* that includes everything linguistic) do not have a status in the present model. Because the system in (2) is based on representational modules, it doesn't actually matter whether, for instance, conceptual structure is part of the linguistic faculty or not: its status and function in the system remains the same. Thus, notions such as *'visual faculty'*, *'linguistic faculty'*, etc. are used only for convenience to refer to certain groups of representational modules.

The primitive categories of phonological structure include, among others, consonant, vowel, voiced, round, nasal, syllable. The primitives of syntactic structure are, for instance, noun, verb, adjective. Thus, for instance, a property like 'being pronounced with round lips' (phonological feature [round]) does not play any role in syntax but it is crucial in phonology.

Conceptual structure, spatial structure, and body representation are called *central formats* as they organize and integrate the information from several peripheral faculties and at the same time enable systematic linking between the peripheral faculties. In that sense, they can be called 'levels of understanding'.

Even though the representational modules are built of different primitive categories, they must be able to communicate with each other. In the model presented in (2), the communication (mapping relations) is handled by linking rules. A linking rule maps together fragments of structures of two or more modules. For instance, each word is a linking rule: a typical word, the English word *cat*, is presented in (1).

(1)	Phonology	/kæt/
	Syntax	Noun
	Conceptual structure	THING
	3D-model	
	Audial representation	(*meaoww . . .*)
	Etc.	. . .

Words are often considered to be a part of language. However, in the present account, words are not just linguistic items. Actually, the only linguistically relevant fragments of representation in (1) are the fragments of phonology, syntax, and conceptual structure. Phonological structure is needed for the identification and pronounciation of the word, syntactic structure gives the limits of the syntactic behaviour of the word *cat*, and the conceptual structure enables the concept CAT to function as a certain kind of argument of some predicate. The 3D shape associated with the word *cat* does not affect the linguistic behaviour of the word, and vice versa: such information that the word cat is a noun does not play any role in the way we picture cats visually. However, the non-linguistic fragments of representation are parts of the meaning of the word cat. Given that only syntactic and phonological structures are parts of the linguistic system, the meaning of a linguistic utterance consists of all its associations to non-linguistic levels of representation (including conceptual structure).[1] Thus, following Jackendoff (1997), I assume that a word is a linking device between linguistic and non-linguistic representations.

4.3. Conceptual-structure Constraints of 'Figure'

Conceptual structure has its own categories, such as those in (2). (Examples—or, actually, their linguistic expressions—are given in parentheses.)

(2)   Some conceptual categories
      SITUATION   (e.g. *The boy hit the ball; I am tired; I knew the answer; It is raining.*)
      PLACE   (e.g. *In the yard; At my place; There; Under the table.*)
      PATH   (e.g. *To the yard; From my place; Down; Through the wall.*)
      THING   (e.g. *Dog; She; The guy with the beer can; Table; Church.*)
      PROPERTY   (e.g. *Yellow; Funny; Tall; Square; Amazing; Out of his/her mind.*)
      AMOUNT   (e.g. *An inch; Five cubic feet; Pretty much.*)

As pointed out in (3), these categories can be divided into simple and complex categories such that the complex categories must be function-argument structures at event-structure level. The simple categories do not have to (Nikanne 1987).

(3)   Two types of conceptual category
      (*a*)   *Complex categories* (SITUATION, PLACE, PATH) must be governed by event structure functions
      (*b*)   *Simple categories* (THING, PROPERTY, AMOUNT, etc.) are not governed by event structure functions.

For instance, THING, PROPERTY, and AMOUNT are simple categories. They are typically in argument positions of complex categories. The complex categories such as SITUATION, PLACE, and PATH, are complexes of functions and

---

[1] In addition to structure-specific linking rules like (3), there are also more general, more schematic linking rules. These rules map very general, schematic, configurations of separate levels together (for details and examples, see Jackendoff 1990; Nikanne 1990).

their arguments. When these categories are expressed linguistically, they are typically based on a linguistic predicate word. In English, SITUATIONS are most normally built around verbs (e.g. *hit*, *be*, *know*, and *rain* in (2)) and PATHS and PLACES around prepositions (e.g. *in*, *at*, *under*, *to*, *from*, and *through* in (2)). We will concentrate on the complex categories.

Now we can go into the concepual structure representation of the category SITUATION, as it is crucial for our topic. The conceptual structure of SITUATION is assumed to be multi-tiered with at least two major tiers, or levels, given in (4).

(4) Two major tiers of the conceptual structure of SITUATION
Thematic tier: Deals with causation, movement along a PATH, and staying in a PLACE
Action tier: Deals with domination and active vs. passive role among the participants of the SITUATION

Those aspects of the situation that deal with causation, movement, and staying in a place are in one tier, called the 'thematic tier', and those aspects that deal with domination of the SITUATION are in another tier, which is called the 'action tier' (see Jackendoff 1987*b*, 1990; Nikanne 1995). In the SITUATION expressed by the sentence *John sent Bill to the supermarket*, the thematic tier contains the information that 'John caused that Bill went to the supermarket' and the action tier contains the information that 'John did something to Bill', that is, John dominated Bill in the situation. If there is only one participant in a situation, the action tier expresses whether the participant is active: 'John was jumping around' or passive 'John collapsed'. In this chapter we only discuss the thematic tier because it is the part of conceptual structure that is responsible for concepts of movements along a path. According to Nikanne (1995*a*) this tier is the backbone of the whole conceptual representation.

The backbone of the thematic tier, in turn, is the string of functions that select the arguments for the different roles required in a SITUATION. In (5) is an illustration of the linking of the thematic structure to some sentences. The functions (CAUSE, GO, TO, IN) in (5) are, however, in an unanalysed form, and we will analyse some of them in more detail shortly. The subscripts indicate linking. For instance, both semantic functions TO and IN are linked to the preposition *into*, CAUSE is linked to the verb *make*, etc.

(5) (*a*) John$_4$ made$_1$ Bill$_5$ go$_2$ into$_3$ the store$_6$
$\quad\quad$ JOHN$_4$$\quad$ BILL$_5$$\quad$ STORE$_6$$\quad\quad\quad$ arguments
$\quad\quad\quad$ ‖$\quad\quad\quad$ ‖$\quad\quad\quad$ ‖
$\quad\quad$ CAUSE$_1$=GO$_2$=TO$_3$=IN$_3$$\quad\quad$ string of functions = f-chain

$\quad$ (*b*) John$_3$ sent$_1$ Bill$_4$ into$_2$ the store$_5$
$\quad\quad$ JOHN$_3$$\quad\quad$ BILL$_4$$\quad\quad$ STORE$_5$
$\quad\quad\quad$ ‖$\quad\quad\quad$ ‖$\quad\quad\quad$ ‖
$\quad\quad$ CAUSE$_1$=GO$_1$=TO$_2$=IN$_2$

(c) John$_3$ made$_1$ Bill$_4$ enter$_2$ the store$_5$
    JOHN$_1$ BILL$_4$ STORE$_5$
     ‖   ‖   ‖
    CAUSE$_1$=GO$_2$=TO$_2$=IN$_2$

The thematic structure of all the sentences in (5) is the same. The functions that are connected with double horizontal lines belong to the so-called lexical f-chain—the chain whose functions encode a particular predicate (i.e. *send, make, enter, go, into*). The indexes indicate syntactic-structure-to-conceptual-structure linkings. The arguments and the string of functions—that is, the f-chain—are at separate levels.[2] The double lines in conceptual structure indicate selection and, thus, scope, which goes from left to right and from f-chain to the argument level.

The f-chain has a syntax of its own. The key observation in Nikanne (1990) is that thematic functions belong to three separate zones, illustrated in Table 4.1.[3]

The notation is taken from Jackendoff (1983, 1990), and is transparent. The meaning of the functions is very close to the corresponding English verbs and prepositions as their lexical conceptual structure contains basically the plain

TABLE 4.1. *The f-chain functions and the three zones*

	Causative zone (Zone 3)	Figure zone (Zone 2)	Ground/Location zone (Zone 1)
More-than-monadic functions:	CAUSE LET	GO BE STAY ORIENT EXTEND	
Monadic functions:	INCHOATIVE	MOVE CONFIG	TO, FROM, VIA, AWAY-FROM, TOWARD; AT, IN, ON, UNDER . . .
Semantic argument	Causer	Theme	Landmark (Goal, Source, Role of route; Location)

[2] Of course, in an f-chain of the form . . . F=G . . ., where F and G are functions, G . . . is an argument of F as well. In linguistics the arguments referred to here as 'arguments' are called 'thematic arguments' or 'theta arguments', to keep them apart from other selected items. However, in the linguistic literature, the terminology often varies when it comes to argument structure.

[3] The labels for semantic roles vary a lot in literature, according to the theoretical tradition within which they are used. The term Theme is a traditional term used in generative grammar, but meaning especially the participant whose location or motion we are talking about. This idea is taken from Gruber (1965) and Jackendoff (1972). The term Landmark is a standard term used in cognitive grammar (see e.g. Langacker 1986).

function. Still, it must be kept in mind that a verb is a linguistic entity, and the function is an abstract conceptual structure operator. In spatial concepts, the argument of GO moves along a PATH (e.g. *Howard ran/walked/went/. . . to the supermarket*), the argument of BE is in a place (*Howard is in the supermarket*), the argument of STAY stays in a place (*Howard stays/remains/. . . in the super-market*), the argument of ORIENT points to some direction (*The arrow points to the supermarket*), the argument of EXTEND has an extension along some PATH (*The road goes to the supermarket*). The argument of MOVE is doing or undergoing some activity but there is no change of location involved (e.g. *Mary is laughing*). The argument of CONFIG is in a position but the place of the argument is not required as a part of the concept (e.g. *The flagpole is standing*).

The main division among functions in the same zone is between monadic and non-monadic functions. Monadic functions can have only one complement, either another function (notated to its right) or an argument (notated above it). The non-monadic functions can have more than one complement, even more than two, as in (*6a, b*).

(6)　(*a*)　Mary drove from Boston to Ottawa via Montreal.

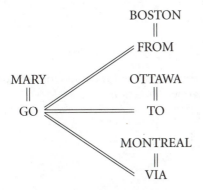

　(*b*)　Bill Clinton was standing in front of the audience, beside Hillary Clinton, under the American flag.

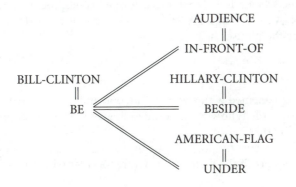

A schematic form of a function chain (f-chain) is illustrated in the structure in (7). A well-formed f-chain must follow the schema in (7).

(7) $F_3^* = F_2 = F_1^*$

('F' stands for any function; the numbers 1, 2, and 3 indicate the zone; the asterisk (*) indicates that there may be no, one, or more occurrences of the type of function in the f-chain.)

Note that the schema of a well-formed f-chain very much resembles the schematic representations of a well-formed phrase in syntax and a well-formed syllable in phonology. Linguistic representations tend to have a head, the most important part of the structure, such as a noun in a noun phrase (for instance *boy* in *The young boy who was laughing at me*) or the vowel in an English syllable. As well, in 3D model structure, the main axis of a geon (a primitive 3D shape in Biederman's 1987 theory) might be considered to be the geon's head. The head is a necessary part of the representation, and there may only be one instance of the head per (relevant part of) the representation.

The schema rules out conceptual anomalies like that in (8) because the functions are not in the correct order.

(8)   TOM   MIKE   HOUSE
         ‖   ‖   ‖
       *GO = CAUSE = IN

The schema in (7) also rules out structures like (9) because of two zone-2 functions and (10) because it has no zone-2 functions.

(9)   TOM   MIKE MARY HOUSE
           ‖   ‖   ‖   ‖
         *CAUSE = GO = STAY = IN

(10)   TOM   HOUSE
           ‖   ‖
         *CAUSE = IN

It follows from the schema in (7) that a well-formed conceptual structure must be a SITUATION. A PLACE or a PATH alone is not a well-formed concept. For instance, consider the phrases in (11):

(11)   (*a*)   in the yard
         (*b*)   to England

They must be complemented with a zone-2 function and its argument (Theme): Who/what is in the yard? Who/what is going to England? The expressions in (11) are not complete by themselves.

Note also that it is possible to use a plain causative verb (e.g. *let* or *force*) expressing a zone-3 part of the thematic structure together with a PP expressing a PATH. This is illustrated in (12) and (13). (Note that not all the elements of a conceptual structure need a correspondent in the linguistic expression.)

(12) John$_3$ let$_1$ Bill$_4$ in$_2$
       JOHN$_3$ BILL$_4$ DEICTIC
         ‖   ‖   ‖
         LET$_1$＝GO＝TO＝IN$_2$

(13) John$_3$ forced$_1$ Bill$_4$ into$_2$ the car$_5$
       JOHN$_3$ BILL$_4$ CAR$_5$
         ‖   ‖   ‖
       CAUSE$_1$＝GO＝TO$_2$＝IN$_2$

The sentences must be understood to mean something like 'John let Bill go in' and 'John forced Bill to go into the car'. However, sentences with only a causative verb without a zone-2 interpretation are ungrammatical. For instance, such utterances as *John forced or *Bill let are not complete sentences and they do not express a complete conceptual structure.

Arguments are selected by the f-chain. This selection is constrained by principles given in (14).

(14) Selection of arguments by the f-chain
       (*a*) All non-monadic functions must have an argument.
       (*b*) All functions of zone 2 must have an argument.
       (*c*) No function can have more than one argument.

Now we can compare the present conceptual semantics analysis to the traditional Gestalt psychology idea of Figure and Ground. The main idea is given in (15). Recall that Theme (the argument of an f2) is that participant of the SITUATION that moves long a PATH or stays in a PLACE:

(15) Spatial structure   **Figure**   /   **Ground**
       Corresponds to   :   :
                              Theme   Landmark

       Conceptual structure   . . . F2＝ . . . ＝F1

(The argument of the zone-2 function—i.e. Theme—in conceptual structure corresponds to a Figure in spatial **Figure/Ground** distinction and the argument of a zone-1 function (i.e. Landmark) corresponds to the **Ground**.)

It should be emphasized that (15) is only about linking between conceptual and spatial representations. I am not, for instance, assuming any constraints to limit the number of **Figures** in spatial representation.

It follows from principles (9) and (14) that a SITUATION in conceptual structure always has one Theme but never more than one. According to our theory, the reason for the obligatoriness of the Theme is the obligatoriness of the function whose argument it is. It is interesting that there are also situations in which there is a Theme but no argument that corresponds to **Ground,** for example *John is laughing, Mary is dancing,* etc. This means that a counterpart of **Ground** is not a necessary part of a concept but the counterpart of **Figure** is. These SITU-ATIONS, that only have a Theme but not a counterpart for **Ground,** are headed by a monadic zone-2 function. The present theory covers these cases as well.

Note that the restriction of one Theme is a restriction that constraints the potential arguments in zone 2 of the thematic structure (see Table 4.1). Interest-ingly, we can apply coordination and quantification to the Theme and it still functions formally as one argument. For instance, *John and Mary* corresponds to one Theme in the Event expressed by the sentence *John and Mary went home* and *three boys* corresponds to a single Theme in the Event expressed by the sentence *Three boys drove to Chicago.*[4]

4.4. Dealing with Paths

In this section I illustrate how the different constraints of different levels of representation affect the linking of these representations to each other. The focus is on conceptual structure, and the spatial and linguistic levels of representation are only very superficially described.

4.4.1. *Spatial Path*

The scheme of a spatial **path** is illustrated in (16) (spatial categories are written in bold). A **Path** starts from a **Source,** goes through a **Route,** and ends in a **Goal. Path** can be bounded or unbounded in its ends, which is indicated by the dotted line at the ends of the arrow that illustrates the schematic **path.**

(16) The schema of spatial **path**

> ⋯⋯ ⟶ ⋯⋯ >

Source   Route   Goal

In (16) the spatial **path** is described as an element having a starting point (= **Source**), a (set of) middle point(s) (= **Route**), and an end point which are all more or less specified. I assume that these points are specified in the case of movement, because, according to the standard idea (see e.g. the discussion in Marr 1982: 159 ff.), the whole idea of movement is a consequence of the interpre-tation that one and the same **Figure** is first observed at one place and later at

---

[4] I would like to emphasize here that the conceptual-structure formation principles discussed in this chapter do not only apply to concepts dealing with space. They are also followed in other semantic areas, such as possession (*John gave Bill money*), characterization (*John made Bill nervous*), temporal concepts (*John postponed the meeting to Wednesday*), etc. in which the movement of spatial field corresponds to other types of change and the starting, middle, and ending points of PATHS are not spatial but TIMES, PROPERTIES, etc. (see Jackendoff 1983, 1990; Nikanne 1990).

another place. The points of these observations are assumed to be on the **path** and the earlier observation is at or towards the **Source**-end of the **path** and the later one at or towards the **Goal**-end of the **path**. However, I am well aware that (16) is based mostly on common sense, which can be a rather unreliable source.[5]

As we are discussing only movement in this chapter, (16) is sufficient for our purposes. **Path** may be involved in situations with no movement, e.g. pointing toward something or extending somewhere, it is not so clear that all the features **Source**, **Route**, and **Goal** are specified in the spatial representation of the **path**. That I must, however, leave for future research.

4.4.2. *Conceptual PATH*

According to Nikanne (1990), the conceptual-structure functions in the f-chain can be analysed as hierarchically organized sets of features: [Directional], [bounded], [distributed], etc. I will only discuss some of them in this chapter, but it will be clear that a great deal of linking **paths** to PATHS is based on this feature system.

From the point of view of our topic, it is important to observe that some non-monadic zone-2 functions select PATH functions (TO, FROM, VIA, TO-WARD, or AWAY-FROM), and that the rest select PLACE functions (AT, UN-DER, ON, IN, etc.). I will assume that the relevant principle is something like the one in (16), which actually follows from a more general principle, called the Directionality Filter.

(17)   The Directionality Filter (for a more generalized formulation, see Nikanne 1990)
Zone-2 functions GO, EXT, and ORIENT have the feature [Directional]. A function carrying the feature [Directional] must be followed by a PATH-function in the f-chain, and a function not carrying the feature [Directional] cannot be followed by a PATH-function in the f-chain.

This filter rules out f-chains like the ones in (18):

(18)   *GO=AT
       *BE=TO
       *ORIENT=IN

I will now analyse the conceptual structure feature [Directional] in more detail. If a function of zone 1 carries the feature [Directional], it is a Path-function, and

---

[5] As far as I know, not much has been written on **path**-representation. Elisenkolb *et al.* (1998) introduce a theory of path-representation based on movement of a Figure—even if the Figure itself is not a part of their **path**-representation. The main goal of their theory is a description of the shape of **path** in a representational framework. For the argumentation in this chapter, the shape of the **path** is not relevant. I am concentrating on the constraints on the Figure and such restrictions on the path-representation that are not dependent on the shape of the path. However, there is no contradiction between their theory and mine.

if not, it is a PLACE-function. The feature [Directional] has three subfeatures, at least one of which must be present. As illustrated in (19), the subfeatures are [Goal], [Source], and [Route], which correspond to the 'end of the PATH', 'the beginning of the PATH', and the 'middle of the PATH', respectively.

(19)   Directional

       Source   Route   Goal

The feature [Goal] is in common with the PATH-functions TO and TOWARD; the feature [Source] is carried by the functions FROM and AWAY-FROM; and the feature [Route] is carried by the function VIA. If we add the feature [bounded] to the analysis, we can reduce the PATH functions into the feature hierarchies given in (20). (The abbreviation F'1 indicates a monadic function of zone 1; the prime (') indicates monadicity.)

(20) TO =

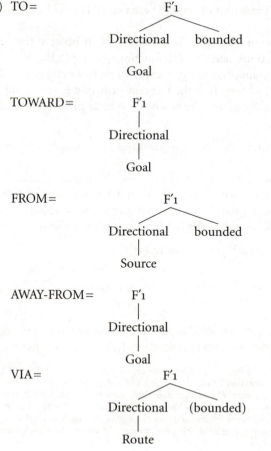

$F'1$

Directional   bounded

Goal

TOWARD = $F'1$

Directional

Goal

FROM = $F'1$

Directional   bounded

Source

AWAY-FROM = $F'1$

Directional

Goal

VIA = $F'1$

Directional   (bounded)

Route

The feature Directional is not only a part of PATH functions but also of some zone-2 functions. Zone-2 functions too may carry the feature [Directional]. Another feature that is needed for zone-2 functions is the feature [Time]. The SITUATIONS that carry the feature [Time] are EVENTS and those that do not, STATES. The zone-2 functions can be presented as feature hierarchies. They can differ either as to their features (e.g. GO and BE) or as to the monadicity of their functions (e.g. BE and CONFIG). Some of the zone-2 functions are analysed in (21) ('F2' indicates a non-monadic function of zone 2 and 'F'2', a monadic one; see Nikanne 1990 for more details).

(21) GO= F_2

                   Time   Directional

      BE= F_2

      ORIENT= F_2
                        |
                    Directional

      CONFIG= F'_2

      MOVE= F'_2
                        |
                      Time

The well-formedness of PATH as a part of a SITUATION is restricted by the principles in (22). The fact that zone 1 must be licensed by zone 2 follows from the principles in (22*b*) and (*c*):

(22) Restrictions of PATH formation
      (*a*) A zone-1 function cannot have more than one subfeature of the feature [Directional] (i.e. [Goal], [Route], or [Source]).
      (*b*) A zone-1 function must share its subfeature of the feature [Directional] with the function of zone 2.
      (*c*) The zone-2 function can share its subfeature of the feature [Directional] with no more than one function of zone 1.

For instance, the analysis of the sentence *John went from Helsinki to Stockholm via Tallinn* is as given in (23).

(23) John$_5$ went$_1$ from$_2$ Helsinki$_6$ to$_3$ Stockholm$_7$ via$_4$ Tallinn$_8$

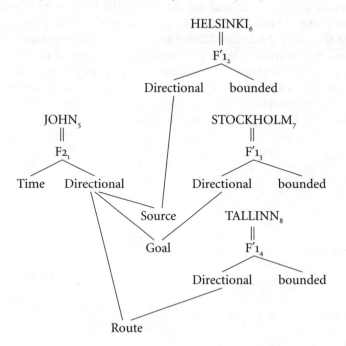

4.4.3. *Linguistic Expressions of Paths*

In linguistic representation, there is no such syntactic constituent that would correspond to the conceptual PATH (or spatial **path**) (see Nikanne 1990). This can be illustrated by the Finnish examples in (24).[6]

(24) (*a*) John matkusti Helsingistä   Vilnan   kautta Tukholmaan.
           John travelled Helsinki-ELA Vilnius-GEN via   Stockholm-ILL
           'John travelled from Helsinki to Stockholm via Vilnius.'
      (*b*) John matkusti Vilnan kautta Helsingistä Tukholmaan.
      (*c*) John matkusti Tukholmaan Helsingistä Vilnan kautta.
      (*d*) John matkusti Helsingistä Tukholmaan Vilnan kautta.
      (*e*) Helsingistä John matkusti Vilnan kautta Tukholmaan.
      (*f*) Tukholmaan John matkusti Helsingistä Vilnan kautta.
      (*g*) Vilnan kautta John matkusti Helsingistä Tukholmaan.

Word order is not fixed and one can change the order of the PPs freely (24*a–d*) and break the cluster of PPs without difficulty (24*e–g*).

---

[6] The grammaticality judgement of the Finnish data in this chapter is based on my intuition as a native speaker.

In English, PATHs are expressed by using prepositional phrases which correspond to PATH-functions, or by a cluster of f-chain functions governed with a PATH function. (A function governs those functions of the same f-chain that are in its scope.) For instance, the English preposition *to* is linked to the function TO (cf. the more detailed description in (20)), and the preposition *into* is linked to the function cluster TO=IN. Linking of an English sentence to a conceptual structure is, thus, licensed by the lexical forms (in linguistics terms, 'lexical entries') of these prepositions. As mentioned in Section 4.1 (recall the discussion of example (1)), each word is a linking rule in itself. The lexical form of *to*, for instance, is as follows:

(25) Phonology: to

  Syntax: Preposition

                           F'1
                            |
  Conceptual structure: Directional
                            |
                          Goal

(For more details on syntactico-conceptual linking, see Jackendoff 1990; Nikanne 1990, 1995*a*, 1997*a*, 1997*b*.)

The form of the feature hiearchy of Directionality given in (19) and the principles in (22) restrict the form of a possible PATH such that the PATH can consist of one, two, or three PATH functions, each of which has a different subfeature of the feature [Directional]. Thus, sentences like those in (26) do not make sense:

(26) *John went from Helsinki via Tallinn to Stockholm to Gothenburg.
  *John went from Helsinki from Oslo to Stockholm via Tallinn.
  *John went from Helsinki via Tallinn via Vilnius to Stockholm.

It is of course possible to use coordination of arguments and say, for instance, *John went from Helsinki via Tallinn and Vilnius to Stockholm*. But a coordinated argument behaves as a single argument.

Also note that the syntactic structure of the linguistic faculty does not rule out the structures like those in (26). It is grammatical to have several *to*-phrases or *from*-phrases one after another as long as we are talking about places that are parts of each other. At least in Finnish, it is grammatical—although a little odd—to say, for instance (27):

(27) (*a*) Menin Helsingistä   Ruotsiin   Tukholmaan.
           I-went Helsinki-from Sweden-to Stockholm-to
           'I went from Helsinki to Sweden to Stockholm.'

(*b*) Lähdin Helsingistä   Suomesta   kohti Ruotsia.
I-left   Helsinki-from Finland-from toward Sweden
'I left from Helsinki from Finland toward Sweden.'

4.4.4. *Comparing Spatial, Conceptual, and Linguistic Representations of Paths*

At least in movement contexts, PATHs differ from paths in that a well-formed PATH requires that one of the features [Source], [Route], and [Goal] must be present. They do not all have to be specified. In addition, as the Theme in conceptual structure is defined as the category in the argument position of a zone-2 function, it is possible to apply quantification or coordination to it and still it functions as a single argument. In spatial structure, on the other hand, the **Figure** is always one single object or a group of objects traveling at the same time at the same speed in the same direction (Emile van der Zee, p.c.). This makes the conceptual structure use of PATH different from its spatial counterpart. For instance, we can have an EVENT like *All the boys left the house* in which only the Source is specified. In this case, even if the boys would all go to different Goals using different routes and leaving at different times, they are on the same abstract conceptual structure PATH and can function as the same **Figure**. In the same way, it is possible to specify just the Route, as in *All the passengers must go through passport control*, or the Goal as in *We have all come to Ottawa*, or the Goal and the Route as in *Emile and I came to Ottawa via London*, etc.

The schema in (28) shows the main differences (discussed in this chapter) in the constraints of conceptual structure and spatial structure when it comes to events in which a Figure is moving along a path ('Figure' covers both spatial **Figures** and conceptual Themes; 'Path' covers both spatial **path** and conceptual PATH).

(28)

	CONCEPTUAL STRUCTURE	SPATIAL STRUCTURE
Quantification or coordination of separate 'Figures' possible	Yes	No
All 'Path' features must be specified	No	Yes

Language allows structures with several path prepositions (*to, toward, from, via*, etc.) but in order for the sentence to sound grammatical, the interpretation of the sentence cannot violate conceptual structure well-formedness constraints. This is because each sentence must have an interpretation in conceptual structure; see Nikanne (1997*b*). The spatial representation constraints cannot directly affect the linguistic structures expressing spatial meanings. The linguistic expression of spatial SITUATIONS is filtered by conceptual structure.

4.5. Concluding Discussion

I have discussed the Gestalt Figure and its movement along a PATH in the light of a representational analysis of conceptual semantics. We have found that the conceptualization of this kind of a SITUATION is based on abstract and highly restricted principles. I hope that I have shown that a representational analysis of conceptual structure can give a new perspective to some aspects of the human mind. Restrictions like the schema in (7) and of PATH formation are not logical necessities, but simply empirical observations of those small restrictions that limit our concepts.

5

Object Use and Object Location: The Effect of Function on Spatial Relations

LAURA A. CARLSON

Spatial relations indicate the location of one object by specifying its position relative to a second object. Most theories of spatial relations assume that the identities of the objects and their relationship are irrelevant to this process. This chapter suggests that an important characteristic of the objects—their function—plays a critical role in constraining the use of spatial relations. Research is reviewed that demonstrates an influence of function on the preferences for using reference frames to define spatial relations and on the designation of a region as the most acceptable use of the spatial relation. Such functional influence has implications for the interface between conceptual and spatial representations. One possibility is that functional properties represented within conceptual structure may generate a reference frame whose output is combined with the perceptually based reference frames that are represented in spatial representation, with such combination occurring within a spatial mental model.

5.1. Introduction

Everyday tasks often require spatially locating one object with respect to another, such as placing one's fingers on top of the keyboard, placing a coffee mug under a coffee pot, and positioning a remote control in front of the television. In English, we can describe the spatial relationship between these objects using locative prepositions such as *above*, *below*, and *in front of* (for example *my fingers are above the keyboard*; *the mug is below the coffee pot*; *the remote control is in front of the television set*). Spatial terms specify the location of one object (the located object) by referring to the known location of a second object (the reference object). In the utterances above, *keyboard*, *coffee pot* and *television set* are all reference objects. To find the located objects, one would start at the reference object, move in the direction specified by the spatial relation (for example *above*,

This work is supported by NSF grant SBR 97–27638. I thank Eric Covey for helpful comments and assistance.

below, in front of), and search the surrounding space for the located object (*fingers, mug, remote control*) (Logan and Sadler 1996; Carlson-Radvansky and Logan 1997). It has been implicitly assumed that the identities of the objects and their relationship are not relevant to this process, in that the same algorithm applies whether the objects are the letters X and O (Logan and Sadler 1996) or line drawings of objects such as trees, buildings, fish, and animals (Carlson-Radvansky and Irwin 1994; Hayward and Tarr 1995; Carlson-Radvansky and Logan 1997). Indeed, many theories of spatial relational use invoke a process of schematization, in which particular details of the objects are disregarded or abstracted over (Talmy 1983; Herskovits 1986; Landau and Jackendoff 1993). The difficulty with this approach is that it ignores the fact that the purpose of putting objects into such spatial arrangements is to fulfill some function, such as typing, pouring a cup of coffee, and changing the channels. Because these objects interact in order to serve a particular function, they are functionally related. Other objects may enter into the same spatial relationship, but if they do not interact to fulfill a designated function, they are functionally unrelated, such as a pencil above the keyboard, a sealed can under the coffee pot, and a block in front of the television.

Most previous work has examined spatial relational use with objects that are not functionally related. The goals of the current chapter are twofold: (1) to demonstrate that the identity of the located and reference objects and their interactive functional relationship do influence the characterization of their spatial relationship, and (2) to discuss the implications of such influences on the interface between conceptual structure and spatial representations.

5.1.1. *Schematization*

Theoretical accounts of spatial relational use have largely ignored the identity of the objects and their functions, and have posited geometric or topological approaches (Clark 1973; Bennett 1975; Fillmore 1975; Talmy 1983; Landau and Jackendoff 1993). For instance, some spatial relations can be classified according to the number of dimensions required by the reference object to satisfy the relation. For example, the relation *at* requires a reference object with at least one dimension; the relation *on* requires one with at least two dimensions; and the relation *in* requires a reference object with three dimensions (Clark 1973). Within such a view, the identity of the object is irrelevant insofar as the object is reduced to a set of dimensions. Alternatively, *in* has been defined in terms of the topology of the reference object, reducing the reference object to a set of contours that includes the located object in the region denoted by the reference object (Miller and Johnson-Laird 1976).

Such definitions are consistent with a process of schematization (Talmy 1983; Herskovits 1986; Landau and Jackendoff 1993). According to Talmy, schematization involves selecting some aspects of the objects as representative and disregarding other aspects. This is achieved through the processes of idealization (finding critical features of the object that match the schema invoked by the relation) and abstraction (selectively ignoring other features that are irrelevant to the schema). For example, for the spatial relation *along*, a linear schema is applied to both the reference and located objects. Thus, in the sentence *The snake is along the road*, both the snake and the road are conceived of as linear. Moreover, *along* requires that these shapes be parallel. If the linear shape corresponding to the snake is perpendicular to the linear shape corresponding to the road, then the schemas required by *along* are not fulfilled—rather, the snake is said to be *across* the road. Furthermore, this linear schema can apply to a cluster of objects rather than to a single object. For example, a row of trees can be said to be along the road (Landau and Jackendoff 1993), given that the row is schematized as a linear shape, with the shapes and features of the individual trees ignored.

Notwithstanding the case with *along*, in English there are very few spatial relations that require that the reference and located object exhibit specific properties or characteristics; most relations allow wide variations in shape and size (Talmy 1983; Landau and Jackendoff 1993; Jackendoff 1996a). This has thus led to the idea that characteristics of the objects are irrelevant to the spatial relational term used to describe their configuration. That is, if a term such as *above* does not require a reference or located object to exhibit any specific feature, then in principle it is possible to use *above* to relate any two objects. This idea leads to the supposition that the identity of the objects and their function do not play a role in constraining the meaning of spatial relational terms. The current chapter questions this supposition.

Recently, Herskovits (1998) has elaborated on the idea of schematization, to allow for the application of different degrees of abstraction, invoked by various features of the objects and situation. For example, for projective prepositions such as *above* or *in front of*, the degree of schematization depends on the distance of the objects to the viewer. According to Herskovits, when the distance between the reference and located objects is large, then the objects are schematized as points; however, when the distance between the figure and ground is small, their shape and precise relative placement influence how the spatial relationship is described. In addition, how the objects are schematized is dependent upon a number of other factors, including context and the geometric and functional properties of the objects. Thus, Herskovits allows for characteristics of objects to play an important role in how their configuration is described, although the mechanisms by which these features constrain spatial relational use is not disclosed. The purpose of this chapter is to provide evidence for the idea that functional properties of the objects do directly influence the way in which the objects are represented, as indicated by the manner in which the spatial relationship between the objects is described.

5.1.2. *Why Function May Be Important*

Objects like coffee pots, pencils, and television sets are artifacts created to fulfill some function. Indeed, Miller and Johnson-Laird (1976) suggest that function is more critical than shape in the categorization of most human artifacts, such that objects that afford sitting can be categorized as CHAIRS, even though most may have four legs, some may have no legs (beanbag chairs, for instance), and some may hang from the ceiling. As such, the function of these objects should be integrally tied to their representations. Empirical evidence consistent with this idea has come from the object-naming and object-recognition literature (see for instance Rosch *et al.* 1976; Merriman, Scott, and Marazita 1993; Landau, Smith, and Jones 1998). For example, Landau, Smith, and Jones (1998) looked at the development of the bias to categorize on the basis of function instead of shape. In their task, they showed 3-year-olds, 5-year-olds, and college students novel objects constructed of a particular substance (sponge or cork) that were in a particular shape (two attached circles or a u-shape). There were two groups of participants. In the function group, participants were shown the objects (the standards), and their function was demonstrated. For example, the experimenters showed the participants how the sponge object could be used to soak up water, and how the cork object could be used to hold pins. In the non-function group, participants were simply shown the standard objects. Participants were then shown test items that either were made of the same substance or had the same shape as the standards (see Figure 5.1 for a sample standard and test items). For example, for the sponge set, they were shown sponge objects in different shapes, or non-porous objects in the shape of the standard. For each test item, subjects were asked whether or not they would call it by the name of the standard for that set. For the non-function group, children and adults generalized objects on the basis of shape, calling objects of the same shape by the same name. In contrast, for the function group, adults generalized on the basis of function. The 5-year-olds were influenced by the functional instructions but showed a somewhat different pattern, and the 3-year-olds were not affected by the instructional manipulation. These findings were replicated in an additional experiment using objects whose functions children have mastered. These data suggest that the bias

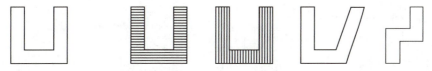

Standard   Test items

FIGURE 5.1. Standard and test items from Landau, Smith, and Jones (1998)

to categorize on the basis of function instead of shape is one that is acquired over time, presumably as a function of experience with the objects.

Recently, Lin and Murphy (1997) examined whether background information about the function of an object would influence performance on tasks requiring speeded access to the object's perceptual representation. Such a finding would suggest that function was an intimate part of the object's representation, such that access to the representation includes access to functional information about the object. To investigate this question, they used speeded categorization and part detection tasks. More specifically, they showed participants pictures of multi-part novel objects and read them descriptions of the function of the objects. Importantly, each object had two possible functions, with different parts critical for performing each of the functions. For example, Figure 5.2 shows an object referred to as a 'jid'. For half of the subjects, the jid was described as an incense burner, with part 1 designated as the place to hold the burning incense. Part 2 was mentioned in the description as a convenient place to store incense that was not being used. As such, for this description, part 1 was the functional part and part 2 was the non-functional part. For the other half of the subjects, the jid was described as a log smoother, with part 2 designated as the place where the logs were pushed through to become smooth. Part 1 was mentioned as a convenient place to hold the jid. For this description, part 2 was the functional part and part 1 was the non-functional part. Note that both parts were explicitly mentioned in all descriptions.

For the speeded classification task, participants first learned the object categories and then were shown test items and asked to decide whether they were members of the relevant object category as quickly as possible. There were three test items for a given description: (*a*) an object that contained the critical functional part but not the non-functional part; (*b*) an object that contained the non-functional part but not the critical functional part; and (*c*) an object that contained neither the critical functional part nor the non-functional part. For example, in Figure 5.2, the first test object contains part 1 but not part 2. For the jid described as the incense burner, this object contains the functional part; however, for the jid described as a log smoother, this object contains the non-functional part. The second test object contains part 2 but not part 1, and thus

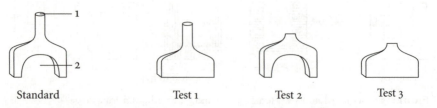

Standard   Test 1   Test 2   Test 3

FIGURE 5.2. Standard and test items from Lin and Murphy (1997)

depicts the functional part for the log smoother but the non-functional part for the incense burner. Finally, the third test object has neither part 1 nor part 2.

The hypothesis was that participants would base their speeded categorization decisions on whether or not the object contained the critical functional part necessary for fulfilling the object's function. If so, then participants who were given the incense-burner description should classify test object 1 as a jid because it has the critical functional part, but should not classify test objects 2 and 3 as jids because they do not have functional parts. In contrast, participants who were given the log-smoother description should classify test object 2 as a jid because it has the critical part, but should not classify test objects 1 and 3 as jids because they do not have functional parts.

As predicted, Lin and Murphy found that both the speed of the categorization and the categorization decision were directly influenced by background knowledge about the object. Categorization decisions were not perfect; however, the presence of functional parts had an influence on both types of decisions (yes, the object was a member of the category and, no, it was not a member). More specifically, when objects were deemed to be members of the category, objects with functional parts were classified more quickly than objects with non-functional parts. Thus, functional parts were accessed faster than non-functional parts. When objects were deemed not to be members of the category, objects with non-functional parts were more quickly rejected as members than objects with functional parts. Thus, the presence of functional parts made it more difficult to reject the object from the category. Finally, in a part detection task, participants were better able to verify that a functional part of the object was present than a non-functional part when the object was displayed under limited viewing conditions. This suggests that the functional part was more salient in the object representation than the non-functional part.

These demonstrations—that function is integrally tied up in an object's representation—suggest that function may influence other interactions with the object, including its spatial relationships with other objects. Some initial indications in support of this idea come from theoretical (Vandeloise 1991, 1994) and empirical work (Coventry 1992, 1998; Coventry, Carmichael, and Garrod 1994; Coventry and Prat-Sala 1998). For example, for the preposition *in* in English (or *dans* in French), Vandeloise favours a functional definition that emphasizes the containment function that the reference object fulfils for the located object, rather than geometric or topological definitions. Coventry (1992) offers evidence against a geometric definition by showing that a given spatial configuration that violates a geometric definition of IN can nevertheless be described with the relation *in* when a context is provided that motivates the functional containment of the located object by the reference object. For example, Figure 5.3 shows a pear hanging from a string above a bowl. When participants were given task instructions to place the pear within the circumference of a bowl, they were significantly more willing to use the relation *in* to describe the configuration than participants who were not given the game context. On the basis of these and other data, Coventry (see also Coventry, Carmichael, and Garrod 1994) argues for a functional definition of IN that includes the notion of containment.

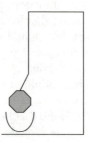

FIGURE 5.3. Pear-in-bowl example
from Coventry (1998)

More generally, Ullmer-Ehrich (1982) has shown that the functional relationship among the objects influences the manner in which they are described. In her study, participants verbally described the layouts of their apartments. She found that clusters of functionally related objects (such as a desk, chair, and lamp) were described using a grouping technique that linked the objects together, but non-functionally related objects were described using a sequencing technique that just listed one object after another.

Thus, the nature of the relationship between the objects and their identity seems to influence the applicability of the spatial relations used to describe the objects' configuration. Function affects spatial relational use. However, the direct evidence in favour of this idea is scant, especially for projective relations such as *above*. To remedy this, across a number of different projects I have examined the influence of function within a computational model of spatial relational use.

5.1.3. *Using Spatial Relations*

Spatial relations indicate the position of a located object relative to the reference object by specifying a direction, such as *above* or *in front of*. Direction is defined with respect to a reference frame, a set of three-coordinate orthogonal axes whose intersection point is the origin (Miller and Johnson-Laird 1976). Reference frames have a number of parameters, including a scale that defines units of distance, an orientation that is assigned to each axis that specifies whether it corresponds to the above/below, front/back, or left/right dimension, and a direction that defines the endpoint of each axis (which endpoint is 'above' on the vertical above/below axis, for instance). These parameters are not fixed (see for example Morrow and Clark 1988; Logan and Sadler 1996). For example, the axes of a reference frame may be rotated in space about the origin, in accordance with various sources of information. This results in three distinct classes of reference frames (Fillmore 1975; Miller and Johnson-Laird 1976; Hinton and Parsons 1988; Farah *et al.* 1990; Friederici and Levelt 1990; Levinson 1996). Adopting Levinson's (1996) taxonomy, the relative reference-frame (also known as viewer-centered or deictic) relies on the orientation of the viewer in the scene to define the orientation of the axes. The intrinsic reference-frame (also known as object-centered) relies on the predefined intrinsic sides of the reference object (top, bottom, for instance) to define the orientation of the axes. Finally, the absolute reference-frame (also known as environment-centered or extrinsic) relies on salient properties of the environment to orient the axes, such as gravity for the vertical axis or the sides of a room for the horizontal axes.

Sometimes the axes of the three reference frames are aligned and assign the same direction to a spatial relation. For example, consider the scenario depicted in Figure 5.4. Suppose that the person in the picture says *There is a fly above the trashcan*. In Panel (*a*), there is only one possible location for the fly (position 1), because all the vertical axes of all the reference frames are oriented in the same way, thus assigning the same direction to ABOVE. However, because people and objects in the world can move and rotate about in space, sometimes the axes of the three reference frames are misaligned and assign competing directions to the same spatial relation. For example, in Panel (*b*), there are three possible locations for the fly because the vertical axes of the reference frames are oriented in different ways, thus assigning competing directions to the term ABOVE. For example, according to the absolute reference-frame based on gravity, a fly at position 2 is above the trashcan. However, according to the intrinsic reference-

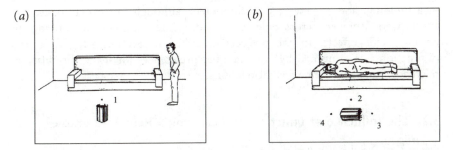

FIGURE 5.4. Definitions of *above* when reference frames are aligned (Panel (*a*)) and misaligned (Panel (*b*)) (adapted from Carlson-Radvansky and Irwin 1993). Position 1: *above* with respect to relative, absolute, and intrinsic reference-frames; position 2: *above* with respect to the absolute reference-frame; position 3: *above* with respect to the intrinsic reference-frame; position 4: *above* with respect to the relative reference-frame

frame based on the overturned trashcan, position 3 is above the trashcan. According to the relative reference-frame based on the person who is now reclining on a couch, position 4 is above the trashcan.

Given multiple definitions of ABOVE, which one do people choose? Carlson-Radvansky and Irwin (1993) used a number of tasks to show that people prefer to use the absolute reference-frame to define ABOVE, with a smaller but nonetheless significant preference for using the intrinsic reference-frame. There was no evidence that the relative reference was used. However, Friederici and Levelt (1990) showed that in the absence of gravity (an absolute reference-frame), and in the absence of an intrinsic reference-frame (the reference object was a ball), the relative reference-frame was used. In a further examination of this issue, Carlson-Radvansky and Logan (1997) found different sets of preferences for using reference frames to define ABOVE. More specifically, some participants preferred to use the intrinsic reference-frame, some preferred to use the coincident relative/absolute reference-frames, and some preferred to use both reference frames, defining ABOVE with respect to the intrinsic reference-frame on some trials and with respect to the relative/absolute reference-frames on other trials.

The existence of different preferences suggests that certain characteristics may influence the reference frame that is selected. Such factors include the need for coordination between speaker and listener (Garrod and Anderson 1987; Schober 1993); the relative communicative ease of the speaker and listener (Clark and Wilkes-Gibbs 1986); the size of the environment being described (Taylor and Tversky 1996); aspects of the individual objects in the scene, such as movement (Fillmore 1975; Levelt 1982); and the manner in which the objects are presented. In most of the previous work involving reference frames it was not possible to assess the impact of function because the objects were not functionally related: the located object was always either a fly (Carlson-Radvansky and Irwin 1993, 1994) or a small box (Carlson-Radvansky and Logan 1997). In Hayward and Tarr (1995) the objects were somewhat related (a raft and a bird or a fish; two offices in a building; and a circle and a computer), although not functionally, and effects were averaged across objects precluding the possibility of looking for object-specific effects. In the projects described in Section 5.2, the impact of function was examined by documenting preferences for using the different reference-frames to define spatial relations.

5.2. The Influence of Function on Choosing a Reference Frame

5.2.1. *Across Different Spatial Relations*

It has been suggested that deictic terms defined by the relative reference-frame emphasize the relation between the viewer and are thus more perceptual, while intrinsic terms defined by the intrinsic reference-frame focus attention on the objects and are thus more functional (Miller and Johnson-Laird 1976; Ullmer-

Ehrich 1982). If so, then the presence of a functional relation between the located and reference objects should result in a preference to describe the objects' spatial layout using intrinsic terms; in the absence of such a functional relationship, there should be a preference for using the relative or absolute reference-frame. It should be noted that in all of the projects to be described, participants were upright. Thus, the vertical axes of the relative and absolute reference-frames were aligned, rendering it difficult to determine which reference frame was in use. Therefore, the contrast in preferences for reference frames is between the intrinsic reference-frame and the coincident relative/absolute reference-frames.

Carlson-Radvansky and Radvansky (1996) tested the idea that a functional relationship would elicit a preference for the intrinsic reference-frame. To do this, they showed participants pictures for which the intrinsic reference-frame described the spatial configuration between the objects using a particular spatial term, whereas the relative/absolute reference-frames described the same configuration using a different spatial term. For example, consider the picture of the mail carrier and the mailbox shown in Panel (a) in Figure 5.5. There are two possible descriptions of the spatial relationship between these objects. According to the relative or absolute reference-frames one would say *The mail carrier is to the left of the mailbox*; however, according to the intrinsic reference-frame one would say *The mail carrier is in front of the mailbox.* The picture in Panel (a) shows a mail carrier and a mailbox in their typical functionally interactive arrangement. These are the functionally related/interactive pictures. It was predicted that participants would prefer to use the intrinsic relation IN FRONT OF to describe this spatial arrangement rather than the relative/absolute relation TO THE LEFT OF, even though both are acceptable descriptions of the picture.

In contrast, consider the picture in Panel (b). This also shows a mail carrier and a mailbox but they are no longer depicted in their functionally interactive manner; the mail carrier is facing away from the mailbox, a position hardly conducive to delivering the mail. These are the functionally related/non-interactive

FIGURE 5.5. Functional and non-functional conditions from Carlson-Radvansky and Radvansky (1996). Panel (a) is functionally related/interactive; (b) is functionally related/non-interactive; (c) is unrelated

pictures. For this situation, it was predicted that the relative/absolute relation TO THE LEFT OF would be more preferred than the intrinsic relation IN FRONT OF, even though, again, both relations are acceptable descriptions of the picture. Note that the objects are the same in both Panels (*a*) and (*b*). Therefore, any difference in preferences for using the reference frames to define the spatial relation should be due to a change in the depicted interaction between the objects and not in the identity of the objects themselves. Such a finding would suggest that the interaction between the located and reference objects is a component to any functional influence that is found.

Finally, consider the picture in Panel (*c*), which shows a mail carrier and a birdhouse. The objects are placed in the same relative orientation as in Panel (*a*) for the functionally interacting mail carrier and mailbox. However, the mailbox has been replaced with a unrelated reference object, a birdhouse. Mail carriers and birdhouses do not typically interact in the depicted manner. These are the unrelated pictures. It was predicted that the relative/absolute relation TO THE LEFT OF would be preferred to describe this situation rather than the intrinsic IN FRONT OF. Note that this condition offers an alternative definition of non-functional that emphasizes the identity of the objects rather than their interaction. Thus, any difference in preferences for using reference frames to define spatial relations that are found across Panels (*a*) and (*b*) should be due to a change in the identity of the objects and not to the depicted interaction. Such a finding would suggest that the identity of the objects is an important component to any functional influence that is found.

Participants were given sentence–picture pairs, and asked to rate the acceptability of the sentence as a description of the picture on a 5-point scale, with 1 labelled *not at all acceptable*; 3 labelled *moderately acceptable*, and 5 labelled *perfectly acceptable*. In one experiment, participants were shown the functionally related/interactive and functionally related/non-interactive pictures; in the other experiment, different participants were shown the functionally related/interactive and unrelated pictures. For the unrelated pictures, the reference object was replaced with an unrelated object that was similar in size and shape (e.g., replacing the mailbox with the birdhouse).

The results supported a functional influence on reference-frame selection. For the functionally related/interactive pictures, intrinsic terms were considered more acceptable than relative/absolute terms; however, for the other types of pictures (functionally related/non-interactive and unrelated), relative/absolute terms were considered more acceptable than intrinsic terms. This pattern was also replicated in companion production experiments in which participants were given a sentence frame such as *the mailman is _____ the mailbox* and asked to supply the appropriate spatial relation. The results showed that for the functional pictures, participants more often supplied the intrinsic term than the relative/absolute term; however, for non-functional pictures, the relative/absolute term was supplied more often than the intrinsic term.

These data demonstrate that the nature of the objects and their relationship strongly influences the characterization that people apply to the spatial configuration of the objects, as reflected in their choice of a spatial relation. Moreover, this influence appears to have two components. First, the depicted interaction between the objects is important, given that the functional effect was obtained when the same objects were in their typical interactive configuration, relative to conditions in which the same objects were shown in a non-interactive configuration. Second, functional effects were found when the objects were functionally related, relative to conditions in which the same interaction was depicted between unrelated objects.

5.2.2. *Within the Spatial Relation ABOVE*

In the study described in the previous section, Carlson-Radvansky and Radvansky (1996) examined reference-frame selection by showing a given picture and documenting the preferences for the different ways of describing it (that is, using the intrinsic or relative/absolute reference-frames). Thus, the display was constant and the spatial relational terms varied. An alternative approach is to take a single spatial relation, and document the preferences for pictures that depict different interpretations. Thus, the term is held constant and the spatial relationship among the objects in the picture varies. This approach is consistent with earlier work by Carlson-Radvansky and Irwin (1993, 1994) that examined preferences for interpreting the spatial relation ABOVE. The specific question addressed in this next project was whether there would be a preference to use the intrinsic reference-frame to define ABOVE when the reference and located objects were functionally related. ABOVE is an interesting relation to study because it is not thought to require certain features of a reference object and located object, unlike ALONG or ACROSS (Talmy 1983; Landau and Jackendoff 1993). Moreover, Coventry and Prat-Sala (1998) have suggested that ABOVE may be less influenced by functional constraints than other spatial relations such as OVER. Thus, it may be reasonable to expect not much of an influence of a functional relationship between the located and reference objects on the selection of a reference frame to define ABOVE.

Carlson-Radvansky and Tang (in press) examined this issue by using functionally related and functionally unrelated reference and located objects while manipulating the placement of the located object, and the orientation of the reference object. As in Carlson-Radvansky and Radvansky (1996) there were three types of pictures (shown in Figure 5.6: functionally related/interactive pictures with related reference and located objects placed in a typical interactive configuration (a hot dog and a bottle of mustard); functionally related/non-interactive pictures with related reference and located objects placed in a non-interactive configuration (an upside down mustard bottle and a hot dog); and unrelated pictures with unrelated reference and located objects placed in the

(*a*) Functionally related/   (*b*) Functionally related/   (*c*) Unrelated
interactive   non-interactive

FIGURE 5.6. Functional and non-functional conditions from Carlson-Radvansky and Tang (in press)

same relative orientation as in the functional pictures (a bottle of ant killer and a hot dog).

To test for preferences for using the intrinsic or relative/absolute reference-frames, five types of configurations of reference and located objects were used; these are illustrated in Figure 5.7. For two configurations, the reference object was upright in a canonical orientation; thus, the intrinsic reference-frame was perfectly aligned with the absolute and relative reference-frames, yielding only one definition of ABOVE. The located object could either be placed above the reference object or not above the reference object. Ratings of sentences containing the term ABOVE for these pictures should be very high and very low, respectively; as such, these are control conditions. For the other three configurations, the reference and located objects were rotated ninety degrees into a non-canonical orientation, thereby dissociating the intrinsic reference-frame from the coincident relative and absolute reference-frames. Thus, for these configurations there were two possible definitions of ABOVE: intrinsic and relative/absolute. Accordingly, the located object could be placed above the reference frame according to the relative/absolute reference-frames, above according to the intrinsic reference-frame, or not above the reference object according to any reference frame.

Participants were shown a number of pictures in each configuration. As in Carlson-Radvansky and Radvansky (1996), some participants saw the functionally related/interactive and functionally related/non-interactive pictures; other participants saw the functionally related/interactive and the unrelated pictures. Each picture was paired with a sentence of the form *The LOCATED OBJECT is above the REFERENCE OBJECT*, with the names of the located and reference objects from the picture appearing in the sentence. The task was to rate the acceptability

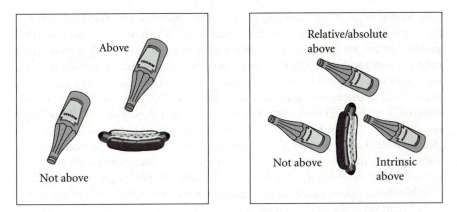

FIGURE 5.7. Five possible placements of the located object (bottle of mustard) around a canonical or noncanonical reference object (hot dog)

of the sentence as a description of the picture on a scale ranging from 1 to 7, with 1 labelled *not acceptable*, 4 labelled *moderately acceptable*, and 7 labelled *perfectly acceptable*.

For the canonical pictures, not surprisingly, 'above' placements received high ratings and 'not above' placements received low ratings. More importantly, for the non-canonical pictures, the critical finding was a greater preference for placements of the located object with respect to the intrinsic reference-frame for the functionally related/interactive picture than for either the functionally related/non-interactive pictures or unrelated pictures. In contrast, there was no difference in preference for the relative/absolute reference-frames across picture types. Thus, the functional interactive relationship increased preference for the intrinsic reference-frame. This replicates the effect found in Carlson-Radvansky and Radvansky (1996), discussed earlier, and lends support to the idea that there are two sources of functional influence: the identity of the located and reference objects and their functional interaction.

5.3. The Influence of Function on Imposing a Reference Frame

Given that function influences reference-frame selection, the next project addressed whether function also affects another feature of reference frames: the manner in which reference frames are imposed on reference objects. Most theories of spatial relational use assume that reference frames are imposed on reference objects (Levelt 1984; Garnham 1989; Carlson-Radvansky and Irwin 1994; Logan and Sadler 1996; Carlson-Radvansky and Logan 1997). However, the factors that influence how the reference frame is placed on the object have not been identified, although recently van der Zee (1996) has suggested the shape of the reference object influences the manner in which intrinsic and relative/ absolute terms are mapped onto space surrounding the object. The most common assumption is that the reference frame is centered on the reference object (for example Carlson-Radvansky and Irwin 1994; Carlson-Radvansky and Logan 1997). Such a placement coincides with the object's center-of-mass, a feature believed to be integral to the acceptable uses of the spatial relations (Regier 1996; see Regier and Carlson-Radvansky 1999 for a test of this idea). However, it is also possible that the function of an object dictates the manner in which a reference frame is imposed on it. As discussed above, the functional parts of an object are particularly salient (for instance Lin and Murphy 1997). Therefore, it is possible that a reference frame is imposed on the functional parts of the object rather than on its center-of-mass.

Carlson-Radvansky, Covey, and Lattanzi (1999) recently investigated this issue by using reference objects whose functional parts occurred to one side. This allowed us to present a front view of the object with the functional part aligned with the center-of-mass of the object, or a side view with the functional part misaligned with the center-of-mass. For example, consider Panels (*a*) and (*b*) in Figure 5.8. Panel (*a*) depicts a front view of a toothbrush; from this view, lines running through the functional part (the bristles) and the center-of-mass of the toothbrush coincide. Panel (*b*) depicts a side view of the toothbrush; from this view, one line runs through the center-of-mass of the toothbrush and a different line runs through the object's functional part. The task involved placing a

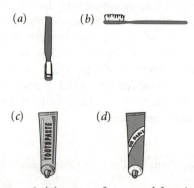

FIGURE 5.8. (*a*) center-of-mass and function of object (bristles) are aligned in this front view of the toothbrush; (*b*) center-of-mass and function of object (bristles) are misaligned in this side view of a toothbrush; (*c*) functionally related located object (toothpaste tube); (*d*) functionally unrelated located object (tube of oil paint). (From Carlson-Radvansky *et al.* 1999)

located object so that it was above or below the reference object. When the center-of-mass and the functional parts of the object were aligned (Panel (*a*)), only one placement of the located object was possible. When the functional part of the object was offset from the center-of-mass of the object (Panel (*b*)), there were two possible placements. If the functional part of the object is salient and plays a strong role in how spatial relations are defined, then placements should be made in alignment with the functional part and not the center-of-mass. It is assumed that such placements are taken to indicate the axis of the reference frame, given evidence that the most prototypical use of a spatial relation corresponds to positions that fall along the axis of a reference frame (Hayward and Tarr 1995; Logan and Sadler 1996; Carlson-Radvansky and Logan 1997). As such, the placements serve as an initial measure of how reference frames are imposed on reference objects.

In addition, because the two projects described earlier implicated the identity of the objects as a component of the functional influence, we also manipulated whether the located and reference objects were functionally related. For example, the toothbrush could be paired with a tube of toothpaste (functionally related, shown in Panel (*c*) of Figure 5.8) or a tube of oil paint functionally unrelated, shown in Panel (*d*). Note that the related and unrelated located objects were matched as closely as possible in shape and size. The idea was that a functional relation may strengthen the salience of the functional part and make it even more likely that spatial terms are defined with respect to the functional part of the object as opposed to its center-of-mass.

In the experiment, we presented pairs of pictures of reference and located objects to participants, and asked them to place the picture of the located object above or below the picture of the reference object. The dependent measure was the deviation in millimeters of the center of the located object from the center-of-mass line.

The results were examined for the aligned and misaligned pictures separately. For the aligned conditions, placements were virtually on top of the coincident center-of-mass and functional lines, with only very small deviations on either side of the center-of-mass line. However, for the misaligned conditions, there were significant deviations that were biased toward the functional line. Moreover, the deviations in the misaligned conditions differed, with a greater bias toward the functional part for the functionally related pictures than for the functionally unrelated pictures. To get a sense of the size of these deviations, we translated the deviations into percentages of the distance between the center-of-mass line and the functional line. Placements of the located object toward the functional line were more biased for functionally related located objects than for unrelated located objects; however, the bias was not complete (deviations were not 100 per cent). Assuming that the placement reflects the best use of the spatial relation, and that the best uses of the relation tend to occur along the axis of a reference frame (Hayward and Tarr 1995; Logan and Sadler 1996), these data

FIGURE 5.9. Piggy bank as the reference object and coin as the located object. The three possible slot placement are shown on the pig; each participant saw only one placement. Three critical placements of the located object are shown; on a given trial, only one coin appeared (adapted from Carlson-Radvansky *et al.* 1999)

suggest that imposing an axis of a reference frame on the reference object was influenced by functional characteristics of the object. This is an important finding, and has implications for the interface between spatial representation and conceptual structure, as discussed in Section 5.4.

Carlson-Radvansky *et al.* (1999) further examined how function may influence how a reference frame is imposed on a reference object by employing a stronger test and using a different task. Specifically, they asked whether the region that corresponds to the most acceptable use of the spatial relation would shift as the functional part of the object shifts. For example, Figure 5.9 shows a piggy bank serving as a reference object. The slot in its back into which coins are placed is functionally very important. The hypothesis was that placements of a coin above the piggy bank should shift in accordance with shifts in the location of the functionally important part (the slot). For example, if the slot moves from the tail end of the pig (slot 1) to the middle of the pig (slot 2) to the front of the pig (slot 3), acceptability ratings for a coin placed over the slot should similarily shift, with the most acceptable placement moving from the tail to the middle to the front.

To test this, Carlson-Radvansky *et al.* (1999) showed people sentence/picture pairs. The pictures contained the piggy bank as the reference object, with the slot located either at the tail, in the middle, or in the front of the pig. A given participant saw only one placement of the slot. The picture also contained a coin that served as a located object. Across trials, the coin could be placed in various locations around the pig. The critical locations were placements above the three possible slot locations. The sentence was *The coin is above the pig*, and participants were asked to rated the sentence as a description of the picture using a scale from 0 (not at all acceptable) to 7 (perfectly acceptable).

The results were as expected. For participants with the slot at the tail, the placements over the tail were rated more highly than the placements over the middle or the front of the pig. For participants with the slot in the middle, placements over the middle were rated more highly than those over either the tail or the head. Finally, for participants with the slot at the head, placements over the head were rated more highly than those over either the tail or the middle. These results demonstrate a systematic shift in the most acceptable use of the spatial relation ABOVE that is in accordance with the systematic shift of the functional part.

In the remainder of the chapter I will discuss how these functional influences may operate on the spatial relations.

5.4. How Function Influences Reference Frames

Across the set of projects described in the chapter, function has influenced how a reference frame is selected and how a reference frame is imposed on a reference object. These influences have some implications for how spatial and linguistic information is represented. According to Jackendoff (1996a; see also Jackendoff 1983, 1987a; Jackendoff and Landau 1991; Landau and Jackendoff 1993), spatial information is represented within a spatial representation module, and conceptual information is represented within a conceptual structure module. The important issue that serves as the basis for this book is identifying the nature of the information that is contained within each of these modules, and identifying the information that is shared in the interface between them. This is relevant to the current chapter because Jackendoff (1996a) suggests that functional information resides in conceptual structure, whereas spatial reference-frames and axes reside in the spatial representation system. Given this, how does function influence reference frames?

5.4.1. *Functional Influences on Imposing a Reference Frame*

Let us start first with the functional influences on how a reference frame is imposed on a reference object. One possibility is that function dictates where to put the reference frame. This is clearly wrong on both theoretical and empirical grounds. Theoretically, such an idea is inconsistent with Jackendoff's (1996a) suggestion that spatial reference-frames and axes reside in the spatial representation module, and are set via perceptual processes, *à la* Marr (1982) and Biederman (1987). Empirically, the data from the placement study discussed in Section 5.3.1 show that the placements were biased away from the center-of-mass of the object in the direction of the functional part. However, importantly, this bias was not complete. Placements were not directly aligned with the functional part.

A more promising possibility is that perceptual information and functional information jointly determine where a reference frame will be imposed on a reference object. One way in which this could be accomplished is with the function of an object generating its own reference frame that gets imposed upon the functional part. According to Jackendoff (1996*a*) the function of the object is detailed in its lexical entry in conceptual structure, and this entry can contain some shape information consistent with the spatial representation. So, it is possible that the functional information specifies not only what the object does, but also the part that is critical for performing the function. Thus, there would be two active reference frames, one based on function, and one based on perceptual aspects of the stimuli, including geometric characteristics such as center-of-mass. The output of the perceptual reference-frame and the output of the functional reference-frame would then be additively combined in accordance with a set of weights attached to both frames. Many theorists believe that spatial relations are calculated within a spatial mental model of the scene (for example, Mani and Johnson-Laird 1982; Tversky 1991; Coventry, Carmichael, and Garrod 1994). Therefore, it is possible that within this mental model, the output of the spatial representation system with its perceptually derived information is combined with information from conceptual structure. Presumably, then, this mental model resides in the interface between conceptual structure and the spatial representation system. The combination of reference frames produces the optimal location for imposing a reference frame. Because this optimal location reflects the best example of the spatial relation, a new reference frame would be imposed with its origin at this location; as a consequence, the best examples of the relation would fall along its axes.

Let us examine a number of assumptions underlying this idea. First, the assumption that multiple reference-frames are active is not new. Carlson-Radvansky and Irwin (1993, 1994) demonstrated that multiple reference-frames are initially active and define directions to the spatial relation 'above'. Similarly, Behrmann and Tipper (1999) show that attended locations can be coded within competing reference-frames. Moreover, such activation seems to be automatic (Carlson-Radvansky and Logan 1997).

Second, a definition of the spatial relation must emerge from some combination of the multiple reference-frames. Studies in mental rotation have shown that when people have their heads tilted 90 degrees from upright, they mentally rotated a figure to a location that is in between upright vertical and retinally-based vertical (for example Attneave and Reid 1968; Corballis *et al.* 1978; McMullen and Jolicoeur 1990). Similarly, Carlson-Radvansky and Logan (1997) showed that participants additively combine the outputs of active intrinsic and relative/absolute reference-frames with selective weights attached to each frame.

It should be noted that sometimes instead of combining the active reference-frames, one reference frame is selected over another. For example, Carlson-

Radvansky and Irwin (1993) showed that 93 per cent of the time participants choose a single reference-frame to define 'above'. Carlson-Radvansky and Jiang (1998) showed that this type of selection involves inhibition of the non-selected reference-frames. Within the framework of assigning weights to the active reference-frames, this would just mean that the selected reference-frame receives a maximum weight (e.g., 1.0), whereas the non-selected reference-frames receive a minimum weight (e.g., 0). An important question for future research is understanding how various weights are assigned to these different sources of information. As a start, Coventry and Prat-Sala (1998) demonstrate differential influences of functional and geometric contraints on the use of the relations 'over/under' and 'above/below', implicating differential weights attached to these two sources of information. Note that this idea is also consistent with the results of Carlson-Radvansky and Tang (in press) discussed in Section 5.2.2 that suggest that function influences the selection of the intrinsic reference-frame. Within this view, the role of function is to increase the weight attached to the intrinsic reference-frame, so that it becomes the one that is preferred. Presumably, this selection would also take place within the spatial mental model where the perceptually derived reference-frames and axes are combined with the functional information to enable selection.

A third assumption is that there is a function-based reference-frame that resides in conceptual structure and not in the spatial representation system. If this is the case, then this reference frame should not be dependent upon form. However, to the extent that form and function cannot be separated (Miller and Johnson-Laird 1976), it is possible that this functional reference-frame is derived through perceptual information. For example, figures can be decomposed into hierarchical representations, with axes imposed on parts in a similar manner as axes are imposed on the whole object (Marr 1982; Biederman 1987). Therefore, it is possible that the functional parts in the study described in Section 5.3.1 could have a set of perceptual axes running through them, and that these subsidiary perceptual axes are being combined with the perceptual axes that run through the main part of the objects. If this were the case, then the active reference-frames and their combination could be contained strictly within the spatial representation module.

To assess this possibility, the reference objects used in Carlson-Radvansky, Covey, and Lattanzi (1998) were classified with respect to whether a perceptual vertical axis ran through the functional part. This group of objects (that is, the toothbrush, N=13) was contrasted with a group of objects for which the functional part was contained within the main part of the axis, and thus could not receive its own set of axes (that is, the piggybank, N=7). For both groups, the deviations were positive, and in the direction of the functional part. More importantly, the magnitude of the deviations did not differ. Therefore, it is not the case that the functional reference-frame derives strictly from perceptual characteristics, because this second group of objects (piggy bank, for example) lacks the perceptual characteristics that would support the generation of another set of axes. Instead, it would be more parsimonious to assume that information about the function of the object that is already contained within conceptual structure (Jackendoff 1996a) is augmented with information about the part that supports that function.

A final assumption is that there is a function-based reference-frame. This idea is consistent with the fact that there are many different types of reference frame that can be applied to objects, dependent upon the task that involves the object. For example, the haptic perceptual system relies on different sources of information for grasping, determining orientation, and determining length than those implicated for linguistic or visual interaction with the object (for a review, see Turvey and Carello 1995). Levinson (1996) presents an analysis of the different classifications of reference frames that are implicated across different disciplines of cognitive science, including linguistics, psycholinguistics, developmental and behavioural psychology, brain sciences, visual perception and philosophy. An important issue will be evaluating the similarities and differences across these reference frames, and determining whether the same reference frames underlie performance across these disciplines (see also Hayward and Tarr 1995; Herskovits, in press).

5.4.2. *Functional Influences on Selecting a Reference Frame*

The projects described in Section 5.2 demonstrated functional effects on the selection of a reference frame. The basic finding was a preference for using the intrinsic reference-frame when the reference and located objects were functionally related and depicted in an interactive relationship. As such, functional influences can be added to the list of factors that seem to mediate reference-frame selection. An important open question in this regard, however, is what exactly is meant by 'function'. A diverse set of objects and consequent functions is represented across the projects described in this chapter. These functions include the reference objects that serve as containers (e.g., pencil sharpener, piggy bank), reference objects that transfer force (hammer, dolly), and reference objects that direct a flow of liquid (gas pump, tea kettle, for instance). An important issue will be to evaluate whether these various functions influence the use of spatial relations differently, and if so, why (for a theoretical treatment of function, see Pustejovsky 1995; for some initial empirical work see Coventry and Prat-Sala 1998). More generally, undercutting these various functions is an implied motion and eventual contact between the located and reference objects (for example, coin and piggy bank). It will also be important to assess whether this more general characteristic is responsible for the functional influences that were observed rather than the more specific individual functions. Finally, each object may be said to have many functional parts. Note that in the research discussed above, there was never any mention of the specific functional part that we selected.

Nevertheless, performance was significantly influenced by these particular parts. This suggests that the parts and their functions may be represented hierarchically. As such, determining at what level 'function' should be defined (for example, with respect to the whole object or with respect to the purpose of specific parts) is also important for understanding the nature of the functional influence (for some initial ideas, see Tversky and Hemenway 1984; Tversky 1989).

5.5. Concluding Discussion

The evidence reported in this chapter supports the view that the identity of reference and located objects and their functional interaction influences how projective spatial relational terms are used. Systematic functional effects were obtained by looking at preferences for selecting reference frames for defining spatial relations, both when examined across a set of spatial relations (Carlson-Radvansky and Radvansky 1996), and when examined for the relation ABOVE (Carlson-Radvansky and Tang, in press). Functional effects were also found to influence how a reference frame was imposed on a reference object (Carlson-Radvansky *et al.* 1999). Thus, the claim that objects are schematized to geometric or topological constructs and that their identities and functions are largely ignored in the context of spatial relations is not sufficient.

More generally, the functional effects are a specific example of a class of effects attributable to background knowledge or context. The finding of such influences within spatial relational tasks implicates an interaction between spatial representations and conceptual representations. One suggestion is that the function of an object is represented in conceptual structure (Jackendoff 1996*a*), and generates a functional reference-frame. The output from this reference frame is combined with the perceptually derived reference-frames emerging from the spatial representation module within a spatial mental model.

6

Retrieving Spatial Relations From Observation and Memory

DAVID J. BRYANT, BARBARA TVERSKY,
and MARGARET LANCA

According to the classical view of imagery, images have analogue properties and are like internalized perceptions. Mental representations of some spatial situations, such as the one investigated here, do not conform to that view. In the present research, people studied spatial scenes consisting of an array of objects either around themselves or around a doll. To direction probes, they reported the objects lying in different directions from the body either from observation or from memory. The patterns of retrieval times from observation and memory differed, and were not analogue in memory, indicating that mental representations of these scenes are more like mental models than like images. Three models that account for the behaviour in the different tasks are presented. In contrast to images, mental models reflect conceptions of space rather than perceptions of it. Mental models are more schematic or categorical than images and incorporate knowledge about the world that is not purely perceptual.

6.1. Retrieving Spatial Relations from Observation and Memory

Knowledge about our spatial surroundings is acquired from many different modalities, from sight, from sound, from touch. Knowledge about space may also be acquired from language. Retrieval time and memory accuracy data indicate that vivid spatial descriptions can induce mental representations that reflect relative directions (see for example Mani and Johnson-Laird 1982; Perrig and Kintsch 1985; Franklin and Tversky 1990; Bryant, Tversky, and Franklin 1992; Taylor and Tversky 1992) and relative distance (e.g. Glenberg, Meyer, and Lindem 1987; Denis and Cocude 1989, 1992; Morrow, Bower, and Greenspan 1989; Wagener-Wender and Wender 1990; but see also Gray *et al.* 1993). Mental representations induced by language not only represent the spatial arrangement of characters, objects, and landmarks, but also allow changes in perspective (Franklin, Tversky, and Coon 1992) and updating relative positions as new information becomes available (for example Glenberg *et al.* 1987; Morrow *et al.* 1989; Franklin and Tversky 1990; Bryant *et al.* 1992).

The fact that complex spatial properties are spontaneously and coherently represented and updated in mental representations constructed from discourse suggests that these representations resemble those constructed from experience. In the present experiments, we directly compare mental representations of space that are constructed from descriptions with those that are constructed from actual experience. Several approaches—specifically imagery, spatial frameworks, and intrinsic computation—predict different patterns of results. We will describe each in turn.

6.1.1. *Imagery*

The similarities between spatial properties of mental representations formed from language and spatial properties of the world have led many to conclude that these mental representations are like mental images. The classic accounts of imagery have stressed the similarity of images to perceptions, and of transforming images to transforming perceptions (see among others Shepard and Podgorny 1978; Finke 1980; Kosslyn 1980; Finke and Shepard 1986; Paivio 1986; Farah 1988). In support of this position, several studies have demonstrated that examining an image is like examining a percept of an object. For example, searching an image of an animal for a larger part takes less time than searching an image for a smaller part (Kosslyn 1976). In visual search, too, due to visual acuity, larger things are located faster than smaller ones. Other experiments have demonstrated that transforming an image is like perceiving a transformation. For example, the time it takes to mentally rotate an image is proportional to the angle of rotation (Shepard and Cooper 1982). Similarly, mentally scanning a long distance takes longer than mentally scanning a short distance (Kosslyn, Ball, and Reiser 1978). Finally, images, like percepts, have a specific spatial perspective (Pinker 1980).

Together, these findings have been used to support the view that imagery is like internalized perception (Shepard and Podgorny 1978; Kosslyn 1980). Images and transformations of images appear to be analogue, as they are assumed to be in perception. They are bound to a specific perspective, like perception. Recent neuro-imaging data indicate that imagery can activate the same brain structures as perception (Kosslyn *et al.* 1993). This account of imagery has intuitive appeal as well. It provides an account for the origin of mental images and a mechanism for the transformation of them, through internalizing perception. It also provides a rationale for their existence, to support visual and spatial thinking and memory in the absence of perception. A strong prediction from this position is analogue performance. A weaker prediction is identical performance in perception and imagery.

With rare exceptions, imagery experiments have not included perception conditions, so what happens in perception can only be surmised (but see Denis and Cocude 1992; Denis and Zimmer 1992; Denis, Goncalves, and Memmi 1995). Moreover, because using imagery is an optional and often burdensome strategy, participants in imagery experiments have frequently been instructed, and sometimes trained, in the use of mental images. Often, the subjective experience of having a mental image is equated with the processing that is revealed in reaction time tasks.

6.1.2. *Mental Models*

Appealing as the imagery-as-internalized-perception view is, there is growing evidence for mental representations of objects and space that do not have the properties ascribed to images. The inspirations for the classical view of imagery have been among those who have noted this (e.g. Finke and Shepard 1986; Kosslyn 1987). An alternative kind of mental representation has been proposed for such situations, namely, spatial mental models. The term 'mental model' has been used in different ways, sometimes causing confusion. By some, the term has been used to characterize people's mental representations of dynamic (in contrast to) static systems, such as a doorbell, a calculator, or a steam plant (Miller 1979; Gentner and Stevens 1983; Halasz and Moran 1983; Kieras and Bovair 1984). Others have used the term to characterize a component of deductive reasoning, in contrast to formal logic (Johnson-Laird 1983; Johnson-Laird and Byrne 1991). Finally, the term 'mental model' has been used to characterize the mental representations readers construct of situations described by discourse, in contrast to a mental representation of the language of discourse (e.g. Bransford, Barclay, and Franks 1972; Clark and Haviland 1974; van Dijk and Kintsch 1983; Glenberg *et al.* 1987; Tversky 1991). Despite these differences, for all, the term mental model is meant in two of its senses, in the sense of capturing some, but not all, aspects of the world and in the sense of being a system of postulates and inferences. A mental model consists of elements and the relations between them. Elements are typically objects in the world, or things that can be conceptualized as objects. Various properties may be ascribed to the objects, though for many purposes, their existence in space and perhaps time is all that is imputed. Relations between objects may be spatial, temporal, causal, etc.

Mental models of spatial relations among objects are the case considered here. Spatial mental models are more abstract, more schematic, than images (Johnson-Laird 1983; Taylor and Tversky 1992). The spatial relations within or between objects need not be analogue. Objects may be represented incompletely, even one-dimensionally, as markers. An image, then, can be viewed as a special case of a mental model, where the spatial relations are analogue and there is a single perspective. Although mental models represent states of the world, they are not necessarily equivalent to perceptions of the world.

6.1.3. *Spatial Framework Model*

Spatial mental models have received support from a paradigm examining the spatial situation that people are usually in—standing, sitting, or reclining in a setting surrounded by objects (Franklin and Tversky 1990; Bryant *et al.* 1992). In the prototypic internal situation (Franklin and Tversky 1990), participants read narratives describing themselves in a scene, such as a hotel lobby or workshed, with objects—such as a hammer, basket, or saw—located to their fronts, backs, left, and right sides, above their heads, and below their feet. After studying a narrative, participants turned to a computer that presented further text orienting participants to face one of the objects, and then probing them with probe terms; *front, right, head,* etc. Participants responded with the object located in that direction. After all directions were probed, participants were reoriented and probed again. Participants made few errors, so the data of interest were response times to the six directions.

Franklin and Tversky (1990) considered three possible models to account for the pattern of reaction times. The data rejected an equiavailability model, according to which all directions should be equally fast, as would be expected in scanning a picture or looking at a scene. The data also rejected a mental transformation model, derived from theories of imagery. According to a mental transformation model, participants should imagine themselves in the scene, and then imagine themselves turning to mentally inspect the probed directions. If that model held, times to respond to probes to the *front* would be fastest, followed by probes 90 degrees from *front*, namely, *left, right, head,* and *feet*. Probes to *back*, 180 degrees from *front*, would be slowest. This pattern was not obtained. Instead, the data supported the spatial framework model.

According to the spatial framework model, participants construct a mental spatial framework consisting of extensions of the three body axes, head–feet, front–back, and left–right, and associate objects to the framework. The accessibility of an axis depends on characteristics of the body and the world, and the posture of the observer in the narrative (this model is partially based on work by Clark 1973; Fillmore 1971; Miller and Johnson-Laird 1976; Levelt 1984; and Shepard and Hurwitz 1984). Table 6.1 shows the predictions of response times for the spatial framework model.

For an upright observer, the head–feet axis is most accessible because of properties of the world and properties of the body. For the canonically oriented upright person, the head–feet axis is correlated with the environmental axis of gravity, which is the only salient, fixed asymmetric axis of the world. As observers navigate the world, vertical relations among objects remain largely constant with respect to the viewer whereas relations in the horizontal plane change. The head–feet axis is also physically asymmetric, so that physically distinct body sides correspond to head and feet. Both the biological asymmetry and the correlation with gravity impart a special status to the head–feet axis, making it a salient indicator of location. This leads to easy and rapid access of objects beyond the head and feet. The front–back axis is next most salient. Its asymmetry separates the world that can be seen and manipulated from the world that cannot be easily perceived or manipulated. The left–right axis is least accessible as it has no

TABLE 6.1. *Predicted response times (RT) for the spatial framework and intrinsic computation models ('<' indicates 'significantly faster than')*

Prediction	Posture Upright	Reclining
Spatial framework model		
P1	RT(Head–Feet) < RT(Front–Back)	RT(Front–Back) < RT(Head–Feet)
P2	RT(Head–Feet) < RT(Left–Right)	RT(Head–Feet) < RT(Left–Right)
P3	RT(Front–Back) < RT(Left–Right)	RT(Front–Back) < RT(Left–Right)
Intrinsic computation model		
P1	RT(Head–Feet) < RT(Front–Back)	RT(Head–Feet) < RT(Front–Back)
P2	RT(Head–Feet) < RT(Left–Right)	RT(Head–Feet) < RT(Left–Right)
P3	RT(Front–Back) < RT(Left–Right)	RT(Front–Back) < RT(Left–Right)

salient asymmetries. Thus, for an upright observer, the spatial framework model predicts that participants will be fastest to identify objects to the *head* and *feet*, followed by *front* and *back*, followed by *left* and *right*. Franklin and Tversky (1990) obtained this pattern of data in four experiments, and parts of the pattern had been obtained by others (for instance Farrell 1979; Hintzman, O'Dell, and Arndt 1981; Sholl and Egeth 1981; Maki and Braine 1985; Sholl 1987). In addition, because perceptual and behavioural asymmetries so strongly favour *front* over *back*, the spatial framework model predicts faster response times to *front* than *back* when the observer is surrounded by objects.

When the observer in the scene reclines, the situation changes. In this case, no axis of the body is correlated with gravity, so the relative salience of axes depends solely on the importance of their asymmetries. The perceptual and behavioural asymmetries of the front–back axis are stronger than those of the head–feet axis, so front–back should be faster than head–feet for the reclining case. The left–right axis has the weakest asymmetries, so it should be slowest. This pattern was obtained in two experiments by Franklin and Tversky (1990).[1]

The pattern of retrieval times is not a simple consequence of the verbal labels used. For one thing, the head–feet axis is fastest in the upright condition but the front–back axis is fastest in the reclining condition. Moreover, in several more complex situations with two characters, where participants were required to answer from both points of view, no differences in response times to the three axes were found (Franklin *et al.* 1992; but see also Maki and Marek 1997). Thus, the patterns of response times to retrieve objects located at different axes can be

---

[1] The reclining situation eliminates two alternative explanations for the primacy of head–feet in the upright situation. That primacy cannot be due to verticality or to the fact that objects at *head* and *feet* were constant. In the reclining case, response times to vertically arranged objects were not fastest. Also, in the reclining case, objects to *head* and *feet* were constant, but response times to the front–back axis were faster than those to the head–feet axis. Both upright and reclining patterns were replicated using objects to probe for directions rather than vice versa (Bryant and Tversky 1992).

attributed to conceptual factors. These differences were accounted for by variants in the mental models induced by the situations, specifically in perspective in the situation and in interpretations of the axes (see Bryant *et al.* 1992; Franklin *et al.* 1992; Bryant and Wright 1999).

6.1.4. *Intrinsic Computation Model*

The spatial framework model provides an account of the accessibility in memory of objects located beyond the intrinsic sides of a body. The model holds when participants take the point of view of the character in the scene. It also holds when the scene contains a central object surrounded by other objects rather than a central person, as long as participants adopt the object's point of view. However, a different model, the Intrinsic Computation Model, may be appropriate when viewing a body or an object from an outside viewpoint. In that case, in order to identify the objects at specified directions from a body or object, participants may first determine the intrinsic sides of the body or object using general perceptual mechanisms, and then identify the objects located beyond each intrinsic side. Some intrinsic sides are more readily determined than others (see Table 6.1 for predictions of the intrinsic-computation model). Several lines of research suggest that people first identify the top, and by contrast, the bottom of an object, followed by the *front* and *back*, and lastly, *left* and *right* (Rock 1973; Braine, Plastow, and Greene 1977; Jolicoeur 1985; Corballis and Cullen 1986; Maki 1986; Jolicoeur *et al.* 1993). *Left* and *right* can be determined only after the top (*head*), bottom (*feet*), *front*, and *back* are known. Consequently, determining *top* and *bottom* should be faster than *front* and *back*, which in turn should be faster than *left* and *right*. Identifying the objects located beyond the intrinsic sides should be the same irrespective of side.

According to this model, the relative accessibility of the intrinsic sides does not depend on the posture of the body or the orientation of the object. Orientations other than upright may (and often do) yield longer reaction times, but the increases should be the same for all sides. Logan (1995) adapted the situation of Franklin and Tversky (1990) and Bryant *et al.* (1992) to a diagram task. Participants saw diagrams of heads at varying orientations and identified what was located at specified directions from the heads. Logan found what we have termed the intrinsic computation pattern of data, namely, head–feet faster than front–back faster than left–right for all head orientations. Whether the retrieval times correspond to the spatial framework pattern or to the intrinsic-computation pattern may be a consequence of the perspective taken on the scene.

The spatial framework and intrinsic computation analyses can easily be distinguished by their predictions for a character that is not upright. According to the spatial framework model, participants mentally take the perspective of the character in the scene. When the character is reclining, the head–feet axis is out of its canonical alignment with gravity and participants are faster for front–behind than head–feet relations. According to the intrinsic computation model, the participant identifies the sides of the character, beginning with the axis of the intrinsic top. As a consequence, participants should be faster to head–feet than front–back at all orientations of the person.

6.1.5. *Present Experiments*

The first question we posed is whether mental representations established from narrative are functionally equivalent to those established from observation. To address it, we compared patterns of retrieval times of participants for memory of scenes learned by observation to the patterns of retrieval times for memory of scenes learned from descriptions. The second question we posed was whether mental representations for these scenes are like internalized perceptions. To address it, we compared patterns of retrieval times for answering from memory to patterns of retrieval times for answering from observation. In the first experiment, the participant was internal to the scene, that is, surrounded by objects. In the second experiment, the participant was external to the scene, observing a doll surrounded by objects. Thus, we were able to determine the patterns of reaction times for actually observing scenes from two perspectives, one external, and one internal.

6.2. Experiment 1: Responding from Memory or Observation: Surrounding Spatial Array

In this experiment, participants learned a spatial array of objects that surrounded them by perceptual observation. Participants stood or reclined on a bench in an empty room. Large pictures of objects were hung on the walls, ceiling, and floor at the six directions from the participant's body. The objects were thematically related (e.g., kitchen objects), and were changed for each scene. Participants responded to direction probes either from memory, or while looking at the scene.

There are two issues of interest. The first is whether response times in the present memory condition will show the same pattern observed in previous research, where memory was established by narrative. The second is whether response times in the present memory condition will show the same pattern as the present perception condition. If the pattern of response times from memory of a perceived scene is the same as the pattern of response times from memory of a described scene, then the claim that spatial mental representations constructed from descriptions are in some way equivalent to those constructed from experience is supported. This inference relies on comparison of data across experiments, which does not allow for ready statistical analysis. The general spatial framework pattern, however, has been independently replicated in memory for narratives in a number of studies, each with several experiments (Franklin and

Tversky 1990; Bryant *et al.* 1992; Franklin *et al.* 1992). Although some variability exists among these studies, the critical differences between axes have appeared reliably in nearly a dozen experiments and seem to reflect a stable pattern for comparison.

For the case of perception, if participants look at the direction probed to find the object, then response times should conform to a physical transformation model. Specifically, times to *front* should be fastest, times to *back* should be slowest, and times to the other four directions, all 90 degrees from *front*, should be in between because the time to physically turn to a direction will determine response time. If memory is like internalized perception, as classical views of imagery maintain, the pattern of responding from perception should be like that of responding from memory.

In a pilot study for this experiment, we found that participants in the perception condition quickly learned the arrays and then stopped looking at them. Instead of using the perceptually available array to ascertain which object was at a probed direction, they relied on memory. Thus, in the perception condition of this experiment, we frequently changed the objects so that the array was difficult to learn.

6.2.1. *Method*

6.2.1.1. *Participants*

Sixteen Stanford University undergraduates (eight male and eight female) participated in the memory condition. Twelve Northeastern University undergraduates (eight males and four females) participated in the perception condition. All participants received credit in an introductory psychology class.

6.2.1.2. *Materials and Equipment*

A set of 42 black and white drawings of common objects was employed to represent seven scenes (one a practice scene) in both the memory and perception conditions. The objects and scenes are listed in Table 6.2. Each picture was roughly 15 × 22 cm and mounted on black poster board.

TABLE 6.2. *Scenes and objects used in Experiment 1*

Scene	Objects
Kitchen	Cake, calendar, hotdog, kettle, pear, tomato
Parent's bedroom	Boots, glasses, hat, pants, purse, shirt
Child's bedroom	Bed, chair, globe, microscope, radio, raincoat
Living room	Book, candle, flowers, lamp, telephone, television
Backyard	Broom, flashlight, hose, lawnmower, pitchfork, rake
Laundry room	Clock, iron, sewing machine, table, towel, vacuum
Workshed	Axe, crowbar, hammer, pliers, screwdriver, wrench

Direction probes were presented by a stereo tape recorder. One channel of the audiotape contained a sequence of direction probes for each scene. The probes were spoken by the experimenter and recorded on the tape. The second channel contained a series of tones that were coordinated with the auditory probes and controlled an electronic timing device. When a probe was presented, a tone on the second channel of the tape sent a signal to start an electronic timer. The timer in the memory condition measured response times accurately to 10 msec, whereas the timer in the perception condition measured response times accurately to 1 msec. Participants used a hand-held response button to stop the timer in the memory condition. In the perception condition, the timer was connected to a voice key. Participants spoke their response into a microphone connected to the voice key, which sent a signal to stop the timer.

The experimental situation is diagrammed in Figure 6.1. The experimental room for the memory condition was not perfectly square, measuring 9′5″ × 11′7″, with a ceiling 8′2″ high. The experimental room for the perception condition measured 12′ × 12′ with a ceiling 8′1″ high. In both conditions, a bench was placed such that one end was at the centre of the room (i.e. at the midpoint horizontal and vertical distances of each wall), so that when a participant was standing on the bench he or she would be in the centre, and when the participant reclined his or her head would be at the centre. Pictures of objects were hung on hooks placed at the centre of each wall and the ceiling. The object below the participant was simply placed face up on the floor immediately before the bench. Although distances between objects and the participant were not all equal, the relatively small deviations do not affect predictions of either the spatial framework model or the physical rotation models.

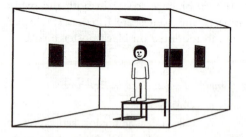

FIGURE 6.1. Sketch of the experimental situation of Experiment 1. The dark rectangles surrounding the person represent the object pictures placed on the walls, ceiling, and floor. The drawing is not to scale

6.2.1.3. *Procedure*

6.2.1.3.1. *Memory condition*   For each scene, the participant stood on the bench, facing one of four directions. The experimenter then placed pictures of six objects on the walls, ceiling, and floor of the experimental room, so that the objects were above, below, to the front, back, left, and right of the participant. Participants were told the theme of the scene and the name of each object and instructed to study the scene so they could answer questions concerning the whereabouts of objects in the scene. They were allowed to view the scenes as long as they wished and to turn to inspect all directions. When participants indicated that they were ready, the objects were removed, and the questioning sequence began.

For the questioning procedure, participants stepped off the bench and sat at a table in one corner of the room, facing directly into the corner so their orientation never matched any orientation they were to imagine. Once seated, participants were instructed to think of themselves standing on the bench in the centre of the room. At the beginning of each block, the experimenter told the participant to imagine that he or she had turned to face a new object, either standing or reclining. Then the audiotape was started and six direction probes were presented, each six seconds apart. At each probe, participants were to simultaneously: (*a*) say the name of the object located at that direction, and (*b*) press the response button. Participants were instructed to respond as quickly as possible while maintaining accuracy. The experimenter recorded the participant's response time and accuracy. The relative looseness in coupling participants' spoken and button responses could add variability to response times. The results of this experiment, however, have been independently replicated in similar designs which have collected responses by voicekey or other procedures that collect responses in one step (Experiment 2; Bryant and Tversky 1999).

There were eight blocks of trials, four in the upright posture and four in the reclining. The order of postures was counterbalanced across scenes. For the upright posture, participants imagined themselves turning to face each of the four objects on the walls, rotating either clockwise or counterclockwise with each new block of probes. For the reclining posture, they imagined themselves turning around their head–feet axis, facing two objects on the walls and the objects on the ceiling and floor.

Participants began the questioning procedure in either the upright or reclining postures. Posture was alternated between scenes and the order of posture was counterbalanced across participants. The participant turned clockwise in half the scenes and counterclockwise in the other half. Direction probes within a given block were assigned to one of six counterbalanced orders, which assured that each probe appeared in each serial position an equal number of times across all scenes. The objects in a scene were placed in one of six counterbalanced sets of locations. Locations were fully counterbalanced across the first 12 participants, and four sets of locations were randomly selected for the last four participants. The first object faced during questioning was randomly selected and was never the object faced during initial learning.

6.2.1.3.2. *Perception condition*   Participants were not allowed to study the scenes prior to the probing procedure. The experimenter placed each object in its location, naming it for the participant, then immediately started the audio-tape containing the direction probes. The objects in the scene were left visible for the questioning procedure and the participant physically stood while responding to direction probes. The participant was told to face a particular object, answer six direction probes, turn to face another object, and so on. The participant turned to face each of the four objects on the walls, rotating clockwise or counterclockwise. Participants did not recline in this condition; participants responded to just four blocks of probes from the upright posture. Participants in the pilot study were found to have had limited movement while reclining, making physical rotation difficult. As in the memory condition, participants turned clockwise in half the scenes and counterclockwise in the other half. The order of probes and the placement of objects were counterbalanced as in the memory condition as well.

The procedure for responding to direction probes was the same as in the memory condition, except that participants spoke their responses into a microphone. Participants were not instructed to visually inspect probed directions, nor were they told not to do so. After finishing all eight blocks of probes in a scene, the experimental room was set up as the next scene, and the procedure repeated. The pilot experiment revealed that participants physically turn to respond to some probes but not others. This behaviour was coded to allow comparison of response times for these two different strategies. For each probe, the experimenter coded whether the participant turned to look at least once in the probed direction (scanning strategy) or not (memory strategy).

6.2.1.4. *Design*

The independent variables were direction (*front, back, head, feet, left,* or *right*), posture (upright or reclining), and response condition (memory or perception). Direction and posture were varied within participant and response condition varied between participants. The dependent variable was the time participants took to press the response button when probed.

6.2.2. *Results*

6.2.2.1. *Data Treatment*

In the memory condition, 3.1 per cent of participants' responses were lost either because the participant made an inappropriate response (e.g., giving an answer without pressing the response button or pressing the button before saying the answer) or because the timing device malfunctioned. The remaining data were adjusted according to the following criteria. Participants made errors in response to 1.9 per cent of the probes. Outliers, defined as response times greater than a participant's direction cell mean plus two standard deviations, accounted for 4.6 per cent of the data. Errors and outliers were discarded from analysis. Response times were collapsed across blocks within each scene to form participant means.

In the perception condition, 5.9 per cent of participants' responses were lost due to inappropriate responses or timing device malfunction. Participants made errors on an additional 0.6 per cent of probes. Outliers accounted for 4.2 per cent of responses. Errors and outliers were discarded from analysis.

6.2.2.2. Memory Condition

Mean direction by posture response times are presented in Table 6.3.

Effect of direction and posture. Participants responded faster overall when imagining themselves upright than reclining and the pattern of response times conformed to the spatial framework model for both postures. A two-factor analysis of variance (ANOVA) with repeated measures revealed significant effects of posture [$F(1,15)=5.31$, $MSe=0.39$, $p<.05$], direction [$F(5,75)=18.50$, $MSe=0.48$, $p<.05$], and their interaction [$F(5,75)=2.84$, $MSe=0.06$, $p<.05$]. Differences between subsets of levels of direction in this and subsequent experiments were tested by contrasts. For the upright posture, participants were faster to head–feet than front–back [$F(1,15)=8.97$, $MSe=0.16$, $p<.01$], which was faster than left–right [$F(1,15)=46.43$, $MSe=0.85$, $p<.01$]. For the reclining posture, participants were slightly faster to front–back than head–feet, but this difference was not significant [$F(1,15)=2.30$, $MSe=0.04$, n.s.], although responses to front–back were faster than those to head–feet for a significant majority of participants (see below). Participants were reliably faster to head–feet than left–right [$F(1,15)=36.34$, $MSe=0.66$, $p<.01$].

Constant and vertical dimensions. In the upright and reclining postures, the objects located to the head and feet did not change with reorientations, whereas objects located did change with reorientations. One might hypothesize that the advantage of the head–feet axis might be due to this constant association. If so, however, that advantage should occur for both upright and reclining postures.

TABLE 6.3. *Mean response times (in seconds) in the Memory Condition (Experiment 1)*

Orientation	Direction					
	Head	Feet	Front	Back	Left	Right
Upright	1.14	1.14	1.18	1.29	1.48	1.46
Mean	1.14		1.24		1.47	
Reclining	1.32	1.35	1.26	1.31	1.52	1.46
Mean	1.34		1.28		1.49	

In the reclining posture, however, participants were faster to respond to front–back than head–feet. Thus, constancy of objects in and of itself did not make objects at the head and feet more accessible. In the reclining posture, all directions except head and feet were sometimes associated with the gravitational axis, depending on which side participants imagined themselves reclining. To examine the effect of this, a mean response time for the vertical axis was calculated by averaging response times for left–right when participants reclined on their side with response times to front–back when they reclined on their front or back—that is, the axes were aligned with the vertical gravitational axis. The mean response time for objects located on the vertical axis (1.40 s) was slower than response times to front–back (1.28 s) and head–feet (1.34 s). Being associated with gravity did not in itself convey fast access to *front, back, left,* or *right.*

Individual effects. Data of individual participants were generally consistent with the predictions of the spatial framework. To assess whether individual participants tended to display the predicted pattern, participants' response times were treated as the product of a random binomial process. There were six possible orders of response times to the three axes so that the spatial framework pattern had a 1/6th probability of occurring by chance. The binomial probability indicated is the probability that the given number of participants exhibited the predicted pattern by chance. Fifteen of 16 participants produced the general spatial framework pattern of response times for the upright posture (head–feet < front–back < left–right) (binomial probability < .001). The remaining participant did not exhibit the pattern predicted by the physical transformation model. Ten of the 16 participants were faster to *front* than *back* (binomial probability < .05). None of the remaining participants exhibited the pattern by the physical transformation model. Their response times displayed no consistent or readily interpretable pattern. For the reclining posture, 10 of 16 participants produced the predicted pattern (front–back < head–feet < left–right) (binomial probability < .01). There was no effect of participant gender [$F(1,14)=0.12$, $MSe=0.05$, n.s], and this factor did not interact with any other.

6.2.2.3. Perception condition

Participants' data were divided into two conditions on the basis of the experimenter's observation of participant behaviour on each trial. Response times for trials in which the participant gave no indication of physically turning to inspect the probed direction were assigned to the memory-strategy condition. Response times for trials in which the participant physically turned to the probed direction (even if they did not fully turn) were assigned to the scanning strategy condition. All response times to *front* were assigned to the scanning-strategy condition because participants could always see that object.

Participants used the scanning strategy on 71.1 per cent of trials and the memory strategy on 28.9 per cent of trials. They tended to use the memory strategy more for later blocks of probes. Otherwise, loss of data to the memory strategy was not differential across any counterbalancing factors. A repeated measures ANOVA revealed no significant effect of direction in the memory strategy data [$F(5,55)=0.37$, $MSe=0.01$, n.s.]. This is probably due to the fact that participants used the memory strategy on so few trials (average of 38.9 per participant) and provided too few data points for a reliable spatial framework effect.

Table 6.4 displays mean response times when participants employed the scanning strategy. Because participants scanned in 71.1 per cent of trials, these means are based on an average of 96.34 responses per participant.

TABLE 6.4. *Mean response times (in seconds) for participants who used the Scanning Strategy in the Perception Condition (Experiment 1)*

	Direction					
	Front	Head	Feet	Left	Right	Back
	0°	90°	90°	90°	90°	180°
Scanning strategy	0.89	1.21	1.15	1.28	1.24	1.70

Effect of direction. A repeated measures ANOVA revealed a significant effect of direction [$F(5,55)=30.12$, $MSe=0.82$, $p < .01$]. Response times conformed entirely to predictions of the physical transformation model.

Individual patterns: All twelve participants displayed the general pattern predicted by the physical transformation model (*front < head–feet–left–right < back*) (binomial probability $< .001$). Participant gender did not affect response times [$F(1,10)=1.79$, $MSe=0.09$, n.s.], nor did this factor interact with direction [$F(5,50)=2.10$, $MSe=0.05$, n.s.].

6.2.3. *Discussion*

Participants learned an array of objects beyond their heads, feet, fronts, backs, and sides by observing a real scene. They were later tested either from memory or while the scene remained visible. In the memory condition, response times exhibited the same pattern as that for scenes acquired from narratives, namely the spatial framework pattern. When upright, participants were fastest to head–feet, followed by front–back, followed by left–right. When reclining, participants were fastest to front–back, followed by head–feet, followed by left–right. In the perception condition, participants were induced to look at the array in order to respond to direction probes. The pattern of response times for trials in which participants physically scanned the probed direction did not conform to the spatial framework pattern. Instead, as expected, the pattern conformed to the physical transformation model. Participants were fastest to identify objects to the *front*, followed by directions offset by 90 degrees (*head, feet, left,* and *right*), followed by the direction offset by 180 degrees (*back*). Response times depended on how far the participant had to turn to the specified direction. Thus, the patterns of responses from perception and memory differ, indicating that spatial mental models are not like internalized perceptions.

The results do not imply that perception operates without reference to a mental model, only that it operates with reference to a different mental model than that used in memory of these scenes. Thus, perception of the scenes was organized on the basis of different physical and spatial factors, or with a different emphasis on the salience of factors. The physical dynamics of turning were obviously crucial for the perception condition but not salient in memory, where participants could inspect locations without mentally simulating physical transformations.

6.3. Experiment 2: Responding from Memory or Observation: External Spatial Array

The first experiment showed that when participants learn a surrounding array of objects by observation and identify objects in the directions around their bodies from memory, the pattern of response times is the same as when participants learn the array from narrative. The current experiment demonstrates the same phenomenon in a different situation. The array of objects is entirely in front of the participant, surrounding a doll, and the participants respond either from memory or from observation of the scene. This situation corresponds to the third-person narratives employed by Bryant *et al.* (1992). Participants view the model from an external viewpoint, but the direction probes require participants to locate objects with respect to the doll's intrinsic body sides. This experiment explores whether people employ spatial frameworks or intrinsic computation for external arrays.

Based on the results of Experiment 1, we expected that participants who had learned the scene from observation and responded from memory would respond like participants in the studies of Bryant *et al.* (1992) who learned scenes from narratives and responded from memory. Specifically, we expected that they would construct mental spatial frameworks from the doll's point of view to keep track of the directions of objects relative to the doll and to update them as the doll is turned in the scene.

Participants in the perception condition responded to direction probes from the doll's perspective while observing the model scene. The doll was physically rotated and reclined in the model. Participants could perform this task in one of two ways. They could adopt the perspective of the doll, as they did in the third-person narratives. If so, the spatial framework pattern of data would be expected. However, this would entail mentally adopting a perspective that conflicts with the participant's own perspective on the scene. For the case of reading narratives or responding from memory, there is no such conflict. Alternatively, participants could keep their own perspective by determining the intrinsic sides of the doll and then searching for the object lying beyond the probed intrinsic side. This is the intrinsic computation model described earlier. It makes the same predictions as the spatial framework model for the upright case, but predicts faster responses to head–feet than front–back for the reclining case, unlike the spatial framework model.

6.3.1. *Method*

6.3.1.1. *Participants*

Forty-eight Northeastern University students participated in the experiment for credit in an introductory psychology class or pay. Eleven men and 13 women served in the memory condition and 12 men and 12 women in the perception condition.

6.3.1.2. *Materials and Equipment*

A physical model portrayed the scenes. In the centre of each scene was a 'Homer Simpson' doll (28 cm tall). The doll stood on a platform 14 cm high, and could be rotated to face four directions or reclined and rotated to face in four directions. Drawings of objects were hung from narrow wooden shafts to the front, back, head, feet, left, and right of the doll, such that they faced the participant at all times. A set of 42 object drawings was used to represent objects in seven scenes (one a practice trial). The objects and scenes (shown in Table 6.5) were meant to represent common situations. The same apparatus from Experiment 2 was used to present probes, and the voicekey used to collect participants' response times.

TABLE 6.5. *Scenes and objects used in Experiment 2*

Scene	Objects
Kitchen	Bread, fork, pie, plate, pot, spoon
Bedroom	Cap, dress, pants, purse, shirt, sock
Living room	Chair, clock, lamp, painting, table, vase
Backyard	Bird, cat, drum, flower, kite, (toy) truck
Zoo	Bear, camel, elephant, lion, monkey, tiger
Workshed	Axe, desk, ruler, saw, scissors, soap
Rec. room	Bell, (toy) boat, dice, glass, shoes, (toy) top

6.3.1.3. *Procedure*

Two variants of the general procedure were employed. In both the memory and perception conditions, participants responded to either eight blocks of probes for a scene or to just one block per scene. Pilot studies indicated that participants might be able to predict or precompute object locations prior to receiving probes if the participants respond to the same objects in the same positions over several blocks of trials. Thus, we included one condition with eight blocks of probes per scene to encourage participants to treat scenes as stable and realistic, but a second condition with a single block per scene to prevent precomputation of responses. This factor, however, turned out not to affect participants' performance and is not reported in the analyses of data.

6.3.1.3.1. *Memory condition*   Multiple-Blocks-per-Scene Condition. For each scene, the experimenter placed six objects around the Homer figure. The participant sat about two feet from the model, which rested on a table. Participants were allowed to study the scene for as long as they wished. They were instructed to study the model until they were confident that they could answer questions concerning the whereabouts of the objects in the scenes. When participants indicated that they were ready, they were told to turn their seat so that they faced away from the model and could not see it.

Participants responded to eight blocks of probes per scene from memory. Rotations of the doll were described verbally to participants. For four blocks, the doll was said to be upright and for the other four it was reclining. The order of upright and reclining postures was counterbalanced across scenes and participants. Four blocks of trials were completed within a posture before the doll was changed to a new posture. A block began when the experimenter told the participant that the doll had turned to face a new object. For each block, six direction probes (*front, back, head, feet, left,* and *right*) were presented by audiotape, separated by six seconds of silence. Participants were instructed that the directions were to be interpreted with respect to the doll's body-sides and current direction it was facing. They were also instructed to say aloud, upon hearing a probe, the name of the object that was located at the probed direction, as quickly as possible, without sacrificing accuracy. The experimenter recorded the participant's response time and accuracy. Participants completed six scenes in this fashion, after an initial practice scene.

The objects in a scene appeared in one of six counterbalanced sets of locations around the doll so that each object occupied each location an equal number of times across participants. The first object faced by the doll during questioning was randomly selected and was never the object faced during initial learning. In half of the scenes, the doll was rotated clockwise about its head–feet axis, and in the other half counterclockwise, for both postures. The direction of rotation was counterbalanced across scenes and participants.

Single-Block-per-Scene Condition. The procedure was generally the same as the multiple-block condition except that an entirely new scene was set up after each block of six direction probes. Participants completed 48 separate scenes, responding to six direction probes. The objects in each scene were randomly selected from the total set of 42 objects and randomly located in the model. The direction the Homer doll faced was randomly determined for each scene, with the provisions that it was upright and reclining in half the scenes and that it faced each of the four directions of rotation within a posture six times during the entire procedure.

6.3.1.3.2. *Perception condition*   Multiple-Blocks-per-Scene Condition. For each scene, the experimenter placed six objects around the Homer figure. As in the memory condition, the participant sat about two feet from the model. The model with Homer and objects was visible to the participant during the entire procedure. Participants were instructed to look at Homer between probes and were seated at a slight angle relative to the model so that they could see all the objects surrounding the doll. Participants were not given time to study the scene prior to the probing procedure.

The probing procedure was similar to that of the memory condition except that rotations of the doll were performed physically in the model and participants responded while viewing the scene. Participants responded to eight blocks of probes for each scene, counterbalanced for upright and reclining postures as in the memory condition. A block began when the experimenter rotated the doll to face a new object. Then six probes were presented by audiotape and participants named the object currently at the probed location with respect to the doll's body sides. Within a block, participants received the six direction probes one after the other, separated by four seconds (participants generally needed less time to respond from perception than from memory). The experimenter recorded the participant's response time and accuracy.

Single-Block-per-Scene-Condition.The procedure was the same as the single block per trial memory condition except that participants responded to probes while viewing the scenes.

6.3.1.4. *Design*

The independent variables were response condition (perception or memory), blocks per scene (multiple or single), posture (upright and reclining), and direction (*front, back, head, feet, left,* and *right*). Response condition and blocks per scene were varied between participants, and posture and direction were varied within participant. The dependent variable was the time it took participants to say the name of the object located at a probed direction. Direction probes within a block were assigned one of six counterbalanced orders that assured that each probe appeared in each serial position an equal number of times.

6.3.2. *Results*

In the memory/multiple-blocks-per-scene condition, 6.8 per cent of participants' responses were lost, either because the participant made an inappropriate response or because of a timing device malfunction, 7.7 per cent were errors, and 3.0 per cent were outliers. In the memory/single-block-per-scene condition, nine participants failed to complete a total of 79 scenes (474 probes or 13.7 per cent of possible responses of all participants), 1.8 per cent of responses were lost, 4.4 per cent were errors, and 3.5 per cent were outliers. In the perception/multiple-block-per-scene condition, 0.7 per cent of responses were lost, 1.4 per cent were errors, and 2.8 per cent were outliers. In the perception/single-block-per-scene condition, 1.7 per cent of responses were lost, 1.4 per cent were errors, and 2.4 per cent were outliers. All errors and outliers were discarded from analysis. The remaining response times were collapsed to form participant direction by posture means for the four conditions.

An ANOVA with response condition and blocks per scene as between participants' variables and direction and posture revealed no significant main effect of blocks per scene [$F(1,44)=0.18$, $MSe=0.350$, n.s.], nor did this factor interact with any other. Thus, it made no difference whether participants responded to only one or to eight blocks of trials for a scene. A significant main effect of test condition was observed [$F(2,44)=59.96$, $MSe=118.51$, $p < .01$], and this factor interacted with both posture [$F(2,44)=8.69$, $MSe=2.21$, $p < .01$] and direction [$F(10,220)=11.12$, $MSe=0.89$, $p < .01$]. In light of these results, data were analysed separately for the memory and perception response conditions but combined across levels of blocks per scene within each response condition. Table 6.6 presents mean direction by posture response times for the memory and perception conditions.

TABLE 6.6. *Mean response times (in seconds) for memory and perception of a model scene (Experiment 2)*

Orientation	Direction					
	Head	Feet	Front	Back	Left	Right
Memory Condition						
Upright	1.80	1.84	2.02	2.27	2.67	2.73
Mean		1.82		2.15		2.70
Reclining	2.58	2.60	2.28	2.31	3.13	3.24
Mean		2.59		2.29		3.18
Perception Condition						
Upright	1.01	1.00	1.07	1.08	1.25	1.28
Mean		1.00		1.08		1.26
Reclining	1.12	1.12	1.20	1.21	1.36	1.39
Mean		1.12		1.20		1.38

6.3.2.1. *Memory condition*

Effect of posture and direction. Participants' pattern of response times conformed to predictions of the spatial framework model for both postures, and participants responded faster when the doll was upright than reclining. A two-factor ANOVA with repeated measures revealed significant effects of posture

[$F(1,23)=33.54$, $MSe=15.74$, $p < .01$], direction [$F(5,115)=52.22$, $MSe=6.96$, $p <$ .01], and their interaction [$F(5,115)=14.39$, $MSe=0.99$, $p < .01$]. When the doll was upright, head–feet was faster than front–back [$F(1,23)=36.63$, $MSe=2.53$, $p <$ .01], which was faster than left–right [$F(1,23)=107.47$, $MSe=7.42$, $p < .01$]. When the doll reclined, however, front–back was faster than head–feet [$F(1,23)=31.03$, $MSe=2.14$, $p < .01$], which was faster than left–right [$F(1,23)=121.82$, $MSe=8.41$, $p < .01$].

Constant and vertical dimensions. As in Experiment 1, participants were faster to front–back than head–feet in the reclining posture, even though the objects to head and feet were constant across rotations. In the reclining posture, the mean vertical response time, calculated as in Experiment 1, (2.74 s) was slower than that of front–back (2.29 s) and head–feet (2.59 s). Being associated with gravity did not itself convey fast access to *front, back, left,* and *right.*

Individual effects. The data of individual participants were generally consistent with the spatial framework model. In the upright posture, 22 of 24 participants produced the general spatial framework pattern (head–feet < front–back < left–right) (binomial probability < .001). Neither of the remaining participants exhibited the intrinsic computation pattern. Twenty of 24 participants were faster to *front* than *back* (binomial probability < .02). In the reclining posture, 20 of 24 participants displayed the general spatial framework pattern (front–back < head–feet < left–right) (binomial probability < .001). Only one of the remaining participants exhibited the intrinsic computation pattern; the rest showed no consistent pattern. Only 14 of 24 participants were faster to *front* than *back* (binomial probability > .05). There was no effect of participant gender on response times [$F(1,22)=0.34$, $MSe=1.128$, n.s.], and this factor did not interact with any other.

6.3.2.2. *Perception Response Condition*

Effect of posture and direction. Participants responded faster when the doll was upright than reclining, and the pattern of response times predicted by the internal spatial framework model was not observed for the reclining posture. Instead, participants were faster to head–feet than front–back in both postures. A two-factor ANOVA with repeated measures revealed significant effects of posture [$F(1,23)=52.19$, $MSe=0.986$, $p < .01$] and direction [$F(5,115)=37.74$, $MSe=0.689$, $p < .01$], but their interaction was not significant [$F(5,115)=0.13$, $MSe=0.0004$, n.s.]. When the doll was upright, head–feet was faster than front–back [$F(1,23)=38.86$, $MSe=0.14$, $p < .01$], which was faster than left–right [$F(1,23)=225.39$, $MSe=0.84$, $p < .01$]. Similarly, when the doll reclined, head–feet was faster than front–back [$F(1,23)=42.76$, $MSe=0.16$, $p < .01$], which was faster than left–right [$F(1,23)=198.57$, $MSe=0.74$, $p < .01$]. This pattern is consistent with the intrinsic computation hypothesis.

Constant and vertical dimensions. Unlike the memory condition, participants were fastest to head–feet in both postures. Consequently, we cannot rule out the possibility that the advantage of head–feet relative to other directions was due to the fact that the objects located to the head and feet were constant across rotations of the doll. Bryant and Tversky (1999), however, have observed that participants responding in a perception condition to a physical model or a diagram of a scene are fastest to head–feet in all orientations of a doll when the objects are not constant along the head–feet axis across rotations. Logan (1995) has also found head–feet to be faster than front–back for all orientations in a dot localization task. Thus, it seems unlikely that the advantage of head–feet in this particular experiment is due to the constancy of objects. In the reclining posture, all directions except head and feet were sometimes associated with the gravitational axis, depending on which side the doll was reclining. The mean vertical response time (1.30 s), however, was slower than that of front–back (1.20 s) and head–feet (1.12 s). Thus, neither the front–back nor left–right axes gained any advantage by being temporarily aligned with gravity.

Individual effects. In the upright posture, 20 of 24 participants produced the overall observed pattern (head–feet < front–back < left–right), which is consistent with both the spatial framework and intrinsic computation models (binomial probability <.001). The remaining participants exhibited no consistent pattern. However, only 14 of 24 participants were faster to *front* than *back* (binomial probability > .05), which is inconsistent with spatial framework model but consistent with the intrinsic computation model. In the reclining posture, 18 of 24 participants displayed the overall pattern (binomial probability < .001), which is consistent with the intrinsic computation model. Only 4 of 24 participants displayed the pattern predicted by the spatial framework model (front–back < head–feet < left–right) (binomial probability > .05) and the rest exhibited no consistent pattern. There was no effect of participant gender on response times [$F(1,22)=0.023$, $MSe=0.014$, n.s.], and this factor did not interact with any other.

6.3.3. *Discussion*

In this experiment, participants learned an array of objects located to all sides of a doll from observation, and responded to direction probes from memory or from observation. When participants responded from memory, their response times conformed to predictions of the spatial framework for both upright and reclining postures. This pattern has been obtained in experiments where participants learned arrays from narratives rather than observation (Franklin and Tversky 1990; Bryant *et al.* 1992). The results suggest that, as for narratives, when participants observe a model of a doll in a scene, they mentally adopt the doll's perspective and construct a mental spatial framework centered on the doll. These data add to the evidence that for these types of spatial arrays, mental representations of spatial relations established from experience are functionally identical to those induced by description.

When participants viewed the same arrays but responded to direction probes while viewing the scene, their responses conformed to the intrinsic computation pattern. The pattern for the reclining posture was the same as for the upright posture, consistent with the intrinsic computation model but not the spatial framework model. These results indicate that participants do not employ spatial frameworks for responding during perception of a person in a scene.

6.4. Concluding Discussion

6.4.1. *Summary*

In two experiments, participants learned a spatial array of objects from observing a scene. In the first two experiments, participants were embedded in an array of objects to all six sides of their bodies. In the second experiment, participants viewed an array consisting of a doll with objects to its head, feet, front, back, left, and right, and responded from the doll's internal perspective. For both situations, participants' knowledge of the spatial arrays was tested either from observation or from memory. In all cases, participants were given probe terms and asked to name the objects in those directions. The data of interest were the patterns of response times to those directions.

Two major findings emerged from these experiments. First, in both situations, when participants responded from memory, the pattern of response times was identical to the spatial framework pattern found in previous work where participants learned the scenes from descriptions rather than from direct experience (Franklin and Tversky 1990; Bryant *et al.* 1992). This implies that the spatial mental representations constructed from perceptual observation are functionally similar to those constructed from descriptions. Second, the patterns of response times obtained while participants observed the scene was considerably different from the patterns obtained when participants responded from memory. This was true when participants scanned scenes surrounding themselves (Experiment 1) and when they viewed a model scene (Experiment 2). For arrays of objects surrounding the participant, retrieval times corresponded to the physical transformation model, with longer retrieval times for longer distances from *front*. For perception of model scenes, retrieval times corresponded to the intrinsic computation model according to which participants determine the intrinsic sides of an object in an order from top and bottom to front and back to left and right. Thus, spatial mental representations are not like images or internalized perceptions.

6.4.2. *Spatial Representations*

We contrasted the physical transformation, spatial framework, and intrinsic computation models of spatial representation. Each posits a particular perspective, which is needed to establish a frame of reference. The frame of reference defines the spatial directions used to locate objects. The models differ with respect to frame of reference and/or means of accessing directions.

The physical transformation model posits an internal perspective. People use their own body axes as a frame of reference and mentally project the body frame into a scene. Directions are accessed by imagining a rotation from one's front to a probed direction, which is an analogue process. The spatial framework model also assumes an internal perspective; one's own body axes serve as a reference frame that can be projected into a scene. This model, however, posits categorical access to directions. Physical and perceptual asymmetries affect the salience of the body axes and determine how quickly one can access information from the mental model. The intrinsic computation model posits an external perspective. The frame of reference is the set of body axes of another person or a set of intrinsically defined object axes outside the self. Participants maintain their outside perspective and compute directions within the object-centered frame of the other person. Directions are accessed as they are in spatial frameworks but different physical and perceptual factors determine the salience of directions, leading to different patterns of responding.

6.4.3. *Using Memory Instead of Looking*

Although participants in a pilot and the first experiment could inspect the scene around them to answer the direction probes, they rarely did so after learning the scene. This implies that while perceiving the scene, participants constructed mental spatial representations of the scene. Once the mental representations were constructed, information about the directions of objects in the scene was apparently more accessible from memory of the scene than from looking at the scene. Hence, it cannot be assumed that information is derived from perception simply because a scene is perceptually available to a viewer. Memory is part and parcel of perception, especially for maintaining awareness of elements of a scene that are not in direct line of sight. Information that is in the world may be more easily accessed by searching memory than by searching the world.

6.4.4. *Mental Models and Images*

The memory representations participants used in order to provide the objects at the probed directions are more like mental models than like images. Images are usually conceived of as internalized perceptions. Like perceptions, they have a point of view, and like perceptions, they have analogue properties. However, performance in this task entailed taking many different perspectives. Moreover, performance in this task was not analogue; in particular, times to retrieve objects displaced 180 degrees was less than times to retrieve objects to right and left, displaced only 90 degrees. Furthermore, when reorientation times are measured, 180 degrees reorientations are even shorter than 90 degrees reorientations (Tversky, Kim, and Cohen, in press). In contrast, studies of pointing to locations in arrays have shown what looks like analogue processing (for example Rieser 1989).

The present situation may have encouraged more categorical representations by using only categorical spatial relations and aligning the array with the observer's body. It is certainly possible that language and memory can capture and convey more refined spatial information than projections of the six body surfaces. The language people spontaneously use to describe spatial locations around the body is category plus hedge, for example, *slightly to the right*, where *front* is presupposed. Memory errors are biased consistently with the descriptions (Franklin, Henkel, and Zangas 1995). A model that incorporates both categorical and graded effects has been developed by Huttenlocher, Hedges, and Duncan (1991).

For two different situations, performance from memory was not like performance from perception so that the mental representations are not like internalized perceptions. Mental models are more schematic than images, capturing some elements and relations in a situation, but not all. They are not restricted to a specific point of view, and they may contain categorical rather than analogue properties. Though the mental model account given here differs from an imaginal account, it also differs from a propositional account. For one thing, a propositional account cannot naturally incorporate the differences in accessibility of body axes or the interaction of that with body posture.

The theory of imagery as internalized perception is both elegant and simple. It accounts for the origins of images and provides insight into their nature. Although it explains behaviour in many contexts, it does not provide an account of all spatial thinking. Mental representations of the situation under investigation, the situation that people find themselves in most of their lives, are not like images. Rather than deriving from our momentary perceptions of the spatial world, mental representations of this situation derive from our conceptions of the spatial world. Our conceptions of the spatial world are based on our extended interactions with the world (cf. Clark 1973; Shepard 1984). In those interactions, we are three-dimensional creatures, with a front–back axis that is asymmetric and orients both our perception and our behaviour, a head–feet axis that is asymmetric and canonically upright, and a left–right axis that is more or less symmetric. The world we interact in is three-dimensional with a single asymmetric axis determined by gravity. These properties of the world and ourselves constrain our perception and our behaviour and form the foundation for our conceptions of the world and the mental representations we create of it.

PART THREE

Constraints on the Lexical Interface

7

Why We Can Talk About Bulging Barrels and Spinning Spirals: Curvature Representation in the Lexical Interface

EMILE VAN DER ZEE

This chapter considers Dutch nouns, verbs, adjectives, and adverbs that refer to path curvature, object curvature, and surface curvature (e.g. *a kink, to zigzag, bent,* and *circling*). It is shown (1) that part of the meaning of such words is described by spatial features encoding axis and contour curvature, (2) that certain features encoding axis curvature behave like focal values, (3) that there is a systematic link between conceptual and spatial representations in the lexical structure of Dutch curvature words, and (4) that semi-productive rules explain how Dutch curvature verbs, adjectives, and adverbs can be derived from Dutch nouns. The formal tools that are used to describe the lexical structure of curvature words derive from Conceptual Semantics (for example Jackendoff 1983) and Recognition by Components theory (for example Biederman 1987). The conclusions, however, are phrased in a theory-neutral way, and are accessible to other frameworks in lexical semantics and visual perception.

7.1. Introduction

Every language contains words or expressions that refer to path curvature, object curvature, and surface curvature. For example, in English it is possible to say that *Andy zigzagged down the hill,* that *Penny's dress has pleats in it,* and that *Muttley's tail is curved.* These examples show that such different words as verbs, nouns, and adjectives may refer to particular curvature distinctions. In this

This chapter has profited extensively from discussions with Urpo Nikanne, Kerstin Meints, Ray Jackendoff, John Slack, Rik Eshuis, Lars Kulik, Joost Zwarts, those present at the Symposium on Verbs and Situations in Bielefeld in October 1997, and the people at the Department of Linguistics in Joensuu in Finland. I take full credit for all remaining mistakes. A less elaborate version of this chapter (not including sections 7.5 and 7.11, for example, and discussing fewer verbs) will appear as van der Zee (forthcoming). The terminology in the present chapter is also slightly different from the latter chapter, in that it more closely follows the mathematical notions of local and global curvature.

chapter I will consider Dutch nouns, verbs, adjectives, and adverbs that refer to curvature distinctions. Some of the questions that I will address are: Can we describe the meaning of Dutch curvature words in terms of conceptual features or do we also need spatial features? Is there any systematic relation between, e.g., the noun *bocht* 'bend', the verb *buigen* 'to bend', and the adjective or adverb *gebogen* 'bent'? Can Dutch curvature words refer to any possible curvature distinction, or do they preferably refer to schematized curvature distinctions, just like words that refer to spatial relations refer to schematized objects (Talmy 1983; Landau and Jackendoff 1993)? And, is it possible by looking at the meaning of curvature words to say something about the properties of the spatial to conceptual interface; a cognitive interface whose existence explains how it is possible for us to talk about what we see (Jackendoff 1987*b*, 1996*a*; Peterson *et al.* 1996)?

Few studies have so far addressed the role of curvature distinctions in language. Eschenbach *et al.* (1998) have looked at the German count nouns *Ecke* 'corner' and *Spitze* 'apex'. They show that these words refer, respectively, to unbounded and bounded vertices in an object's contour. The idea that *corner* refers to an unbounded vertex and *apex* to a bounded vertex explains, for example, the impossibility of saying ?*The table has a long corner* and the possibility of saying *The tower has a long apex*. Lessmoellmann (1999, forthcoming) considers the German adjective *rund* 'round'. Her results point out that *rund* can only be used if the object referred to, or its main part, has a cross-section with a circular contour, or if that object (part) can be schematized to a circular axis. Van der Zee (1996) and van der Zee and Eshuis (1997, 2000) describe a systematic influence of object-axis curvature on the use of Dutch directional nouns like *voorkant* 'front' and prepositions like *links van* 'to the left of'. For example, Dutch speakers refer to an axis that is orthogonal to a curved plane of symmetry in an object part as the front–back axis. And van der Zee (1999*a*) observes that Dutch verbs that refer to object and surface deformation, like *buigen* 'to bend' and *vouwen* 'to fold' refer to schematized curvature distinctions. All of these studies, however, limit themselves to particular word classes or particular spatial properties. Another aim of this chapter is, therefore, to formulate a general theory of lexical curvature representation.

Let us start by having a more detailed look at the mental architecture that allows us to represent curvature distinctions for language.

7.2. Representational Modularity

In Conceptual Semantics the human mind is assumed to represent knowledge of different kinds of information in a highly structured way (Jackendoff 1987*a*, 1997; Nikanne forthcoming; van der Zee 1996). Figure 7.1 describes our linguistic knowledge, our spatial knowledge, our knowledge of categorical information, and the way these kinds of knowledge are linked to each other. Linguistic know-

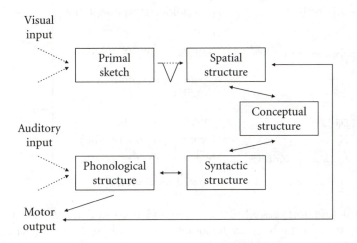

FIGURE 7.1. The structure of part of our knowledge system in terms of several modules of information representation (boxes) and interface modules (double headed arrows)

ledge is described in terms of phonological structure and syntactic structure; respectively our knowledge of linguistic sound patterns and our knowledge of the structure of sentences.

Conceptual structure (CS) is assumed to encode our knowledge of the categorical status of auditory, visual, olfactory and haptic information in a neutral or a-modal format. Spatial structure (SR) is assumed to a-modally represent our knowledge of the 3D structure of objects, their part structure, spatial relations between objects, object parts, regions, paths, etc.[1]

The information in each module is represented in terms of its own autonomous grammar. Interface modules describe unique links between two autonomous grammars. These modules explain how information distinctions at a particular representational module are linked to—or correspond to—distinctions at another representational module. The spatial to conceptual interface—called the SR/CS interface here—is of special interest in this chapter.

In Conceptual Semantics word representations are considered to be fixed sets of correspondences between different kinds of information. Elaborating on Jackendoff (1987*b*) we could represent words that refer to spatial entities, such as *giraffe* and *zebra*, in the following way:

[1] This is an idealization. It is clear from neurophysiological research that perceived facial features, objects, object locations and the direction in which we may find objects are represented in different brain structures (see for example Ungerleider and Mishkin 1982, Bruce and Young 1985, and O'Keefe 1990). And, as pointed out by Kappers, Koenderink, and Oudenaarden (1997), it may even be the case that surface curvature is represented in different ways for the visual and the haptic systems.

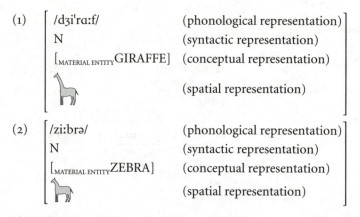

(1)
$$\begin{bmatrix} /\text{d}\text{ʒi'rɑːf}/ & \text{(phonological representation)} \\ \text{N} & \text{(syntactic representation)} \\ [_{\text{MATERIAL ENTITY}}\text{GIRAFFE}] & \text{(conceptual representation)} \\ & \text{(spatial representation)} \end{bmatrix}$$

(2)
$$\begin{bmatrix} /\text{ziːbrə}/ & \text{(phonological representation)} \\ \text{N} & \text{(syntactic representation)} \\ [_{\text{MATERIAL ENTITY}}\text{ZEBRA}] & \text{(conceptual representation)} \\ & \text{(spatial representation)} \end{bmatrix}$$

The structure in (1) describes the correspondence—in the long term memory of an English speaker—between the sound structure /dʒi'rɑːf/, the syntactic category noun, the concept GIRAFFE and the spatial representation ⌐.

This correspondence explains how it is possible for English speakers to know where to put the sound /dʒi'rɑːf/ in an English sentence, what category that sound refers to, and what the spatial structure of a GIRAFFE is like. (The 3D structure of a GIRAFFE is schematized here in terms of line segments. In our brain, shapes are most probably represented as generalized cones, in a viewer-independent fashion, in order to make recognition possible from almost any angle (Marr 1982; Biederman 1987; Biederman and Gerhardstein 1993, 1995).)

The CS representations in (1) and (2) encode both our semantic knowledge of the words *giraffe* and *zebra* (e.g. that these words refer to animate objects) as well as our encyclopedic knowledge of these words (how giraffes and zebras sound, what they eat, etc.).

Giraffes have relatively long necks, but zebras do not. As Jackendoff (1987*b*) observes, the grammar of SR seems more suitable for encoding such relative size distinctions than that of CS. This is why neck-length is encoded here in terms of SR structures. In other words, the meaning difference between the words *giraffe* and *zebra* is not only accounted for by their difference in conceptual structure, but also by their difference in spatial structure.

The idea that 3D representations may be part of the meaning of a word accounts for our ability to imagine ourselves a giraffe, upon hearing the sound /dʒi'rɑːf/, and also accounts for our ability to categorize more and less prototypical giraffes as members of the category GIRAFFE (where increasingly less prototypical giraffes have, e.g., increasingly shorter necks).

The examples that have been given so far are nouns that refer to object representations. Similar ideas, however, hold for verbs, adjectives, and adverbs that refer to curvature distinctions. For example, if we see or imagine a rope being rolled up, we know that the involved curvature change may be described with the verb *to roll up*, and the property of the rope or movement with *rolled up*, but not, respectively, with the words *to fold* and *folded up*. In other words, the fact that verbs, adjectives and adverbs can refer to particular curvature distinctions is used to communicate those observed or imagined curvature distinctions to other people.

The next two sections describe the way in which curvature distinctions may be represented at SR and CS for the purpose of language. Sections 7.5 through 7.10 use this machinery to describe the lexical conceptual structure (LCS) and lexical spatial structure (LSS) of Dutch nouns, verbs, adjectives, and adverbs that refer to curvature distinctions. Section 7.11 summarizes the main findings of this chapter.

7.3. How to Encode Curvature Distinctions for Language?

Let us start by looking at some words that encode object curvature. Part of the meaning of the word *pen* is that it is a straight object, and part of the meaning of the word *boomerang* is that it is a curved object. This becomes clear when we picture the spatial structures these words refer to. The pen or boomerang we imagine is clearly constrained in shape. By default we imagine a straight pen and a curved boomerang.

Curvature differences between pens and boomerangs can be represented in terms of the curvature of the main axis of these objects; the axis that generates such shapes if a contour is swept along it (usually the longest and/or symmetry axis of the shape). In order to describe the curvature properties of main axes, Biederman (1987) distinguishes between curved and non-curved main axes. For our purposes the feature opposition [+curved main axis] versus [−curved main axis] describes those properties.

It is not possible to see or imagine curvature distinctions of a point. So, apparently there are objects whose spatial structure cannot be described in terms of some curvature distinction, and objects (like pens and boomerangs) for which this is possible. This distinction can be captured—respectively—by the feature opposition [o-curved main axis] versus [±curved main axis]. These feature distinctions are summarized in a feature hierarchy in (3).

(3)   Main-axis curvature of object

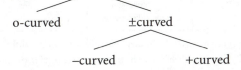

We are also able to perceive and describe differences in path curvature. For example, *John went (straight) down the hill* versus *John zigzagged down the hill*. Path curvature can be described as the sum of a translational and a rotational component. The translational component represents Figure displacement along a path, the orientation of which does not change in relation to any of the axes of an external reference frame (e.g. the North–South axis and East–West axis). **TRANS** here encodes the translational component; **NTRANS** its absence. The rotational component represents Figure displacement along a path that does change in orientation with respect to one of the axes of an external reference frame. **PATHR** describes this rotational component; **NPATHR** its absence. Differences in the relative strength of the translational and rotational component, or their absence, are responsible for differences in path curvature (e.g. a straight path, a smoothly curved path, a zigzag-like path, and a circular path). The translational and rotational component together describe extrinsic path-curvature. Figure 7.2 depicts possible extrinsic path-curvatures that result from the presence or absence of the translational and rotational component.

Examples like *Penny rolde zigzaggend over het gras* 'Penny rolled over the lawn zigzagging' show that Figure rotation must be specified independently of path rotation. Figure rotation is defined here as the rotation of at least one Figure

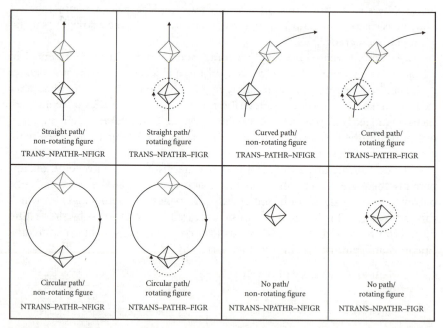

FIGURE 7.2. A helicopter perspective on possible Figure movements along differently curved paths. TRANS (translational movement), NTRANS (non-translational movement), PATHR (orientation change of the path axis with respect to an external axis) and NPATHR (no such change) account for differences in extrinsic path-curvature. FIGR (rotation of a Figure part around an axis represented on that Figure) and NFIGR (no such rotation) account for differences in intrinsic path-curvature

part (axis or contour) around an(other) axis represented on that Figure, where rotation direction is described in an external reference frame. **FIGR** encodes Figure rotation; **NFIGR** the absence of such rotation. Both of these components describe intrinsic path-curvature.

There is independent evidence for a distinction between some of the above path curvature components in relation to language. Kita and Özyürek (1999) asked Turkish speakers to recount a cartoon story about a cat rolling down a hill. They hypothesized that, because Turkish speakers use different verbs for describing Trajectory and Manner, these two elements would also be found separately in the gestures of these speakers when they recount the story. Kita and Özyürek indeed found separate components for translational movement and intrinsic movement. Furthermore, it also appears that Turkish does not contain any verbs in which the translational and rotational components are combined to express extrinsic (curved) movement (Özyürek p.c.), whereas English and Dutch verbs combine such components (as in *to zigzag*, for example).

The feature-combinations describing extrinsic and intrinsic path-curvature lead to some interesting empirical questions. E.g., would it be possible to describe a non-rotating Figure going along a curved path as in *John turned left*? At present I do not know of any empirical work that addresses such questions.

In (4) it is shown that path-axis and object-axis curvature features are part of the same feature hierarchy.

(4)   Main-axis curvature

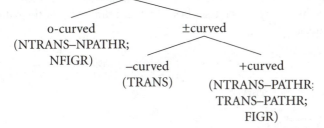

[o-curved] describes a situation in which the Figure is motionless, either because it does not go around some external axis, or around its own axis (both extrinsic and intrinsic path-curvature are o). [−curved] describes a straight (extrinsic) path axis, and [+curved] any kind of curved path, an extrinsic path being full circle, half circle, or zigzag-like, an intrinsic path, etc. Let us see whether the feature combinations that make up the +curved node can be given their own place in a more refined version of this feature hierarchy.

For the purpose of language it is not sufficient to only distinguish between [o-curved] and [±curved], or [−curved] and [+curved] axes. We are, for example, also able to perceive and describe the difference between a bend and a kink, or between a circular path and a zigzag-like path. The features [+smooth curvature] versus [−smooth curvature] capture such spatial distinctions.

[+smooth curvature] is defined in relation to some π-value, larger than 0π (e.g. the verb *buigen* 'to bend' refers to some [+smooth] deformation). [–smooth curvature] is defined in terms of some angle value, larger than 0 degrees (e.g. the verb *knikken* 'to kink' refers to any kind of [–smooth] deformation). Figure 7.3 depicts some π-values and angle values.

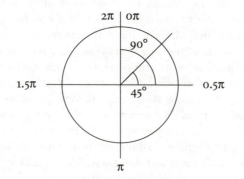

FIGURE 7.3. Some π-values and angle values

It seems necessary to further refine the features [+smooth] and [–smooth] in terms of some of the values in Figure 7.3. For example, the word *ring(-shaped)* refers to 2π-shaped objects, and *bow(-shaped)* to objects with a main axis around 0.5π. The feature hierarchy in (5) describes a further refinement of the path and object axis features.

(5)   Main-axis curvature

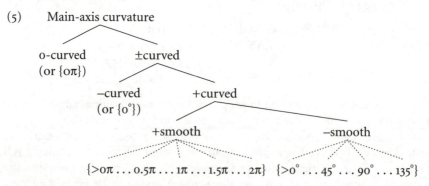

The feature hierarchy in (5) not only refines the [+smooth] and [–smooth] curvature features, but also makes it possible to distinguish between NTRANS–PATHR on one hand, and TRANS–PATHR on the other hand, by distinguishing between an extrinsic path-curvature of 2π, and all other [+smooth] and [–smooth] values. Furthermore, the [+smooth] subfeatures describe all intrinsic path lengths (FIGR), except 0-length (NFIGR).

Although the subfeatures under [+smooth] and [−smooth] contain all possible π-and angle-values larger than 0, (5) shows that certain values stand out as focal points (like pure red stands out as a focal point in color perception). Universally, there may be more focal values than indicated here. For example, Finnish has the verbs *koukata* (a path that becomes smooth, with path parts between .75π and 1π), and *aaltoilla* (an object that becomes smooth, with object parts being less than .25π) (van der Zee and Nikanne forthcoming). As we will see, however, the above set of focal values suffices for a description of the lexical structure of Dutch curvature words. More languages must be studied to determine whether there is a universal set of focal values from which different languages may make different selections.

An indication for at least a special role of the above [−smooth] subfeatures comes from vision research. Psychophysical evidence shows that the 45°, 90°, and 135° angles and the straight line have a special role in visual information processing, for example, in that participants tend to schematize angles in perception and in visual memory towards these angles (see Gray and Regan 1996; Regan, Gray, and Hamstra 1996; van der Zee 1999*b*, 1999*c*; van der Zee and Berni, forthcoming; but see Snippe and Koenderink 1994 for a different view). Let us now see whether we can use the features in (5) to represent surface curvature.

We are able to recognize differences in surface curvature, and use that information in naming-tasks. For instance, we use the word *egg(shaped)* in certain cases, and the word *cylinder(shaped)* in other cases, because the shapes referred to have different surface properties. In Biederman's (1987) Recognition-by-Components theory, the representation of surface curvature is a consequence of features representing axis properties and properties of the contour that is swept along an axis in order to generate an object part (or geon). Let us consider the contour features first. For present purposes I make a distinction between [+angular] versus [−angular] contours. Depending on whether the contour that is swept along an axis is [+angular] or [−angular,] for example, a beam-like or a tube-like geon is generated. Size variations in a geon's surface are represented by the features [constant] versus [expansion] and/or [contraction] (Biederman 1987). If a contour remains constant when it is swept along an axis, a tube-like structure of constant width is represented, but if this contour expands something like a cone results. In all those cases where the main axis of a geon is [−curved] the contour features directly represent surface curvature. For example, in order to represent the 3D shape of an egg (which has a [−curved] axis), a smooth contour is swept along an axis which first expands and subsequently contracts. But, in order to represent a horn—where the main axis is [+curved,] and the contour is [−angular] and expands (the default operation if both expansion or contraction apply)—the geon's surface curvature is both a consequence of contour and main axis properties.

We are now ready to address the issue of how changes in object curvature and surface curvature may be represented at SR for the purpose of language. Consider for example a sentence like *Andy bent the iron bar*, which refers to a main-axis curvature change. The bending of an iron bar can be represented at SR as a main-axis curvature change from [−smooth] to [+smooth,] or from [+smooth] to (another kind of) [+smooth.] The same features can also be used to represent surface-curvature changes, as referred to in, for example, *Andy bent the metal sheet.* A metal sheet can be bent at any possible spot. This means that the default main axis (the longest axis through the geometric mid-point and/or centroid) does not necessarily play a role in the representation of curvature change. We may assume, however, that in the case in which the default main axis does not play a role, a contextual main axis is represented in a metal sheet. The assumption is that the direction of bending induces a contextual main axis representation. Given this assumption it is possible to represent all surface-curvature changes that the verb *to bend* refers to in terms of a deformation of the default main axis or the contextual main axis. This assumption not only allows us to represent both object-curvature change and surface-curvature change in terms of features encoding axis curvature (a generalization required by verbs such as *to bend*), but also allows us to differentiate between the prototypical bending of a metal sheet and a less prototypical bending of that sheet. The prototypical bending of a metal sheet would involve bending along the default main axis, and an increasingly less prototypical bending would involve a bending of a contextual axis at increasingly different orientations and distances away from that default axis.

Another set of surface-curvature changes can be represented in terms of axis extension. Consider the sentence *I see a bulging sail.* Somebody who sees a bulging sail witnesses a convex or concave part growing into a surface, where this convex or concave part has different sizes at different time slices (that is, if we leave out a possible translational movement of such parts here). It is possible to describe the growing of a convex or concave part into a surface in terms of an axis that is growing into a geon's contour, thereby forming the basis for another geon (see Leyton 1988). The growing of a convex or concave geon in a surface is represented here, respectively, by the operators [+extension] and [−extension]. If both a convex and a concave geon may grow into a surface, the resulting surface-curvature change is encoded as [±extension]. In other words, the features [+extension] versus [−extension] versus [±extension] encode protrusions and/or indentations growing into a surface.

The features discussed so far describe all possible curvature distinctions for the purpose of language. Let us consider a formalism that ties these features together by looking at some examples.

(6)

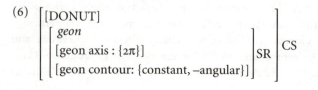

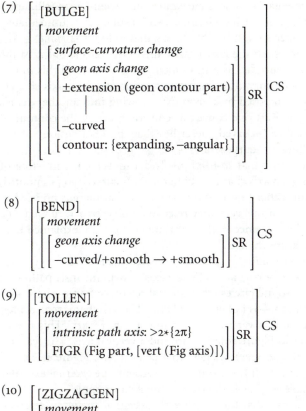

(7)
$$
\left[
\begin{array}{l}
\text{[BULGE]} \\
\left[
\begin{array}{l}
\textit{movement} \\
\left[
\begin{array}{l}
\textit{surface-curvature change} \\
\left[
\begin{array}{l}
\textit{geon axis change} \\
\left[
\begin{array}{l}
\pm\text{extension (geon contour part)} \\
\quad | \\
-\text{curved}
\end{array}
\right] \\
[\,\text{contour: \{expanding, }-\text{angular\}}\,]
\end{array}
\right]
\end{array}
\right] \text{SR}
\end{array}
\right] \text{CS}
$$

(8)
$$
\left[
\begin{array}{l}
\text{[BEND]} \\
\left[
\begin{array}{l}
\textit{movement} \\
\left[
\begin{array}{l}
\textit{geon axis change} \\
-\text{curved/}+\text{smooth} \rightarrow +\text{smooth}
\end{array}
\right] \text{SR}
\end{array}
\right] \text{CS}
\end{array}
\right]
$$

(9)
$$
\left[
\begin{array}{l}
\text{[TOLLEN]} \\
\left[
\begin{array}{l}
\textit{movement} \\
\left[
\begin{array}{l}
\textit{intrinsic path axis: } >2*\{2\pi\} \\
\text{FIGR (Fig part, [vert (Fig axis)])}
\end{array}
\right] \text{SR}
\end{array}
\right] \text{CS}
\end{array}
\right]
$$

(10)
$$
\left[
\begin{array}{l}
\text{[ZIGZAGGEN]} \\
\left[
\begin{array}{l}
\textit{movement} \\
\left[
\begin{array}{l}
\textit{global path axis: } \pm\textit{curvature} \\
\text{TRANS-PATHR/NPATHR (path part, external axis)}
\end{array}
\right] \\
\left[
\begin{array}{l}
\textit{local path axis: } >2*\{\ldots 45^\circ \ldots 90^\circ \ldots\} \\
\text{TRANS-PATHR (path part, external axis)}
\end{array}
\right]
\end{array}
\right] \text{SR}
\end{array}
\right] \text{CS}
$$

All examples point out that the lexical structure of a word may consist of a lexical conceptual structure (LCS), and a lexical spatial structure (LSS). It is assumed that the CS and SR structures within the outer brackets correspond to each other. In the course of this chapter I will refine the CS structures, and work out the correspondence in a more formal way. Let us consider each of the examples in more detail.

Example (6) describes the LSS of the noun *donut*. It represents the shape of a donut in terms of separate sets of axis features and contour features. The axis feature has the value 2π, and the contour feature the values constant and [$-$angular]. It is assumed that an operator (not represented explicitly) maps these two feature sets into the higher level SR category geon (represented in italics). (Given this representation of axis curvature, and given Lessmoellmann's (1999, forthcoming) criteria for using German *rund* 'round', it is immediately clear that a German speaker should be able to say that a donut is *rund*.

The structure in (7) represents the lexical structure of the verb *to bulge*. At the highest SR level *to bulge* is encoded as a movement. At a lower level this movement is encoded as a surface-curvature change, consisting of a geon axis change. The geon axis change is composed of a geon axis growing into another geon's contour, thus generating at least one convex or concave geon on the contour of that other geon. The feature [−curved] describes that the [±extension] of the geon axis takes place along a [−curved] axis.

The example in (8) encodes that *to bend* involves a movement consisting of a geon axis change. This geon axis change is either from [−curved] to [+smooth], or from +smooth to some other [+smooth] value. Note that there is no need to separately specify the fact that this verb may refer to an object-curvature change or a surface-curvature change, since both curvature changes are explained here in terms of an axis-curvature change.

The LSS of the Dutch verb *tollen* 'to spin' in (9) represents FIGR as a two-place function, which maps a Figure part and a Figure axis into an intrinsic path-axis, consisting of more than two full circles (the external reference frame—necessary to determine direction of spin—is not encoded here). The axis that is represented on the Figure is mapped into a vertical axis by the operator 'vert'. This means that *tollen* may only refer to Figure rotation around a vertical axis. The features [vertical] and [horizontal] are operators here that take either a Figure axis or an external axis as their argument. If these features are absent, the external axis may be oriented in any possible way, as is the case in the next example.

The structure in (10) shows that the Dutch verb *zigzaggen* 'to zigzag' refers to Figure movement along a global and a local path. This distinction between global- and local path-curvature is motivated by both linguistic and visual perception research. In Dutch, for example, it is possible to say *Jan zigzagde om het huis heen* 'John zigzagged all the way around the house'. Global-path curvature describes that John went all the way around the house (a circular path). Local-path curvature describes that at a lower level of spatial resolution there are zigzags in John's path. In (10) global-path curvature is not specified, although our example shows that its curvature may somehow be realized (see (29) for further discussion). Local-path curvature must be specified. The idea that paths are spatially represented at both a global and a local level is confirmed by Eisenkolb *et al.* (1998). These authors discuss a path discrimination task which shows that we visually discriminate paths on the basis of local properties, but not on the basis of global properties. Since prediction of future position is based on global properties Eisenkolb *et al.* interpret their findings within a two-layer model of visual path representation. Example (10) describes the local path-curvature of *zigzaggen* in terms of a range of curvature values between around 45 degrees and 90 degrees.

In summary, we can say that this section has shown that the LSS of curvature nouns, verbs, adjectives, and adverbs can in principle be described by features representing axis and contour properties. This idea can be stated in terms of the following hypothesis about the SR/CS interface:

(11)   General hypothesis about the SR/CS interface: the discussed features representing axis and contour curvature at SR are 'visible' at CS for the purpose of language

Hypothesis (11) is further refined in relation to Dutch words in the remainder of this chapter.

The next section considers the basic machinery that is necessary to represent the CS aspects of words.

7.4. The Formal Structure of CS Representations

7.4.1. *Sentential Conceptual Structure*

Let us start by considering the categorical status of perceived spatial configurations and sentences.

The basic conceptual categories at CS are (Jackendoff 1983, 1990; Nikanne 1990):

(12)   STATE   (Jon is there, The rod is bent, etc.)
        EVENT   (Jon left, Jon bent the rod, etc.)
        PLACE   (there, at the window, etc.)
        PATH   (from Utrecht, via Berlin, etc.)
        MATERIAL ENTITY   (nose, roof, stone, pig, etc.)

Each of these basic conceptual categories permits a different kind of *wh* question (Jackendoff 1983). It is therefore possible to find evidence for each basic category by posing a *wh* question. For example, *What happened . . . ?* can only be answered by giving an EVENT, *Where is/are . . . ?* by specifying a PLACE, etc.

Each of the concepts in (12) can be decomposed into more primitive conceptual items. A STATE, for instance, can be decomposed into a STATE function that maps a MATERIAL ENTITY and a PLACE into a STATE. Consider:

(13)   The table is at the window.

(14)   [TABLE] [WINDOW]
          ‖   ‖
         BE ═══════AT

In (14) the STATE function BE maps the MATERIAL ENTITY 'TABLE' and the PLACE 'AT THE WINDOW' into the STATE 'THE TABLE IS AT THE WINDOW'. The STATE function BE and the PLACE function AT are linked to each other by double horizontal lines at the so-called Functional Tier. The arguments that are linked to functions by double vertical lines belong to the Thematic Tier.

Nikanne (1990) argues that CS functions belong to different distributional classes, called Zones (see Table 7.1).

TABLE 7.1. *The distributional classes of CS functions and their arguments*

	Zone 3 (causative zone)	Zone 2 (figure zone)	Zone 1 (location zone)
	categories: EVENTS, STATES	categories: EVENTS, STATES	categories: PLACES, PATHS
Functions	2 arguments: CAUSE, LET	2 arguments: BE, GO, STAY, EXTEND, DIR, ORIENT	1 argument: Place functions: AT, IN, ON, . . . Path functions: FROM, TO, AWAY FROM, TOWARDS, VIA
	1 argument: INCHOATIVE	1 argument: MOVE, CONFIG	
Thematic role of Thematic Tier argument	Agent	Theme	Goal, Source
Spatial role of Thematic Tier argument	Agent	Figure	Reference object (PLACE or PATH are the 'Ground')

Rule (15) describes the possible ways in which CS functions are distributed at CS:

(15) $F_3{}^* = F_2 = F_1{}^*$

Rule (15) indicates that Zone-3 functions must—if present—always precede a Zone-2 function. A Zone-2 function must always precede a Zone-1 function. '*' indicates that no, one, or more than one function of this zone may be present. In other words, Zone-2 functions form the backbone of CS; a Zone-2 function must always be present in the categorical description of a sentence or a spatial configuration.

Table 7.1 and (15) together describe the properties of thematic structure; the level of CS at which spatial location and movement are encoded. This level formally encodes a description of the Theme (an argument of a Zone-2 function), the Source and Goal (arguments of Zone-1 functions) and the Agent (an argument of a Zone-3 function). Since verbs may encode movement, for example, we must expect to find parts of sentential conceptual structure in the LCS of such verbs.

Let us consider in more detail how the LCS of a word may be represented.

7.4.2. *The Lexical Conceptual Structure of Words that Refer to Objects or Object-parts*

As we have seen in (1) the concept GIRAFFE belongs to the category MATERIAL ENTITY. Jackendoff (1991) shows that CS encodes different kinds of material entities (objects, substances, etc.), and also that there are lexical functions that allow us to subdivide further those material entities (e.g. into PARTS or GROUPS). One such function, the PART function, is of interest for present purposes. The operation of this function can be illustrated by looking at the LCS of the Dutch word *tafelpoot* 'leg of a table':

(16)
$$\begin{bmatrix} \text{POOT} \\ \text{PART} \left(\begin{bmatrix} \text{TAFEL} \\ \text{\scriptsize MATERIAL ENTITY} \end{bmatrix} \right) \\ \text{\scriptsize MATERIAL ENTITY} \end{bmatrix}$$

The PART function extracts a PART (a POOT) from TAFEL, thereby specifying the concept TAFELPOOT. The lexical PART function makes it unnecessary to specify the information in the LCS of the word *tafelpoot* separately from the information in the LCS of the words *tafel* and *poot*.

Also of interest for present purposes is the function PLURAL. This lexical function makes it unnecessary to specify the LCS of a word like *tafelpoten* 'table legs' separately from the LCS of *tafelpoot* 'table leg':

(17)
$$\begin{bmatrix} \text{POTEN} \\ \text{PLURAL} \left(\begin{bmatrix} \text{POOT} \\ \text{PART} \left(\begin{bmatrix} \text{TAFEL} \\ \text{\scriptsize MATERIAL ENTITY} \end{bmatrix} \right) \\ \text{\scriptsize MATERIAL ENTITY} \end{bmatrix} \right) \\ \text{\scriptsize MATERIAL ENTITY} \end{bmatrix}$$

Van der Zee (1996) shows that PART functions can be further decomposed into more primitive features:

(18)
$$\begin{bmatrix} \text{KRAS} \\ -\text{PART} \left(\begin{bmatrix} \text{Y} \\ \text{\scriptsize MATERIAL ENTITY} \end{bmatrix} \right) \\ | \\ \text{1D} \\ \text{\scriptsize -MATERIAL ENTITY} \end{bmatrix}$$

The –PART function here encodes that a *kras* 'scratch' is a negative 1D part of Y. –MATERIAL ENTITY encodes reference to a non-material object part. The LCS's of words like *tunnel* 'tunnel' and *sjabloon* 'template' would contain 3D and 2D features indicating reference to, respectively, 3D and 2D non-material entities.

Material entities can be distinguished from non-material ones by filling in non-material entities for x and material entities for y in the phrase: *x was filled with y*. This fill test immediately shows that there are words that refer to both material entities and non-material entities. Consider:

(19) The bottle was filled with sand.

(20) The hole was filled with the bottle.

Conceptually, a bottle can be considered in terms of its negative or its positive space. Material entities like bottles are described as ±MATERIAL ENTITY. Entities to which the fill test cannot be applied (geometric objects, for instance) are represented as 0-MATERIAL ENTITY. So, the following ontology is assumed:

(21)   ENTITY

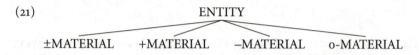

±MATERIAL   +MATERIAL   –MATERIAL   0-MATERIAL

We are now ready to apply both the SR and CS machinery to Dutch words that refer to curvature distinctions.

7.5. The Lexical Structure of Dutch Nouns that Refer to Curvature Distinctions

In the previous section I considered the LCS of the Dutch noun *tafelpoot* 'table leg'. Its LSS and LCS can be represented as follows (note that from here on I leave out the outer brackets that map together corresponding CS and SR structures):

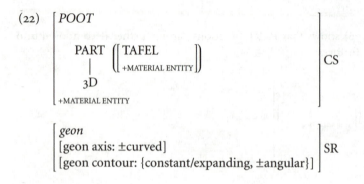

The structure in (22) describes that *tafelpoot* refers to a 3D object part, represented spatially by sweeping a contour of any size (constant or expanding) and any curvature (+ or −angular) along an axis of any curvature.

Structure (23) describes the lexical structure of the word *kras* 'scratch'.

(23)
$$\begin{bmatrix} KRAS \\ \\ -PART \begin{pmatrix} \begin{bmatrix} Y \\ \\ \text{\tiny +MATERIAL ENTITY} \end{bmatrix} \end{pmatrix} CS \\ | \\ \text{1D} \\ \\ \text{\tiny −MATERIAL ENTITY} \end{bmatrix}$$

$$\begin{bmatrix} -geon \\ \begin{bmatrix} -geon\ axis \\ \text{hor (axis extension (geon surface))} \\ | \\ \pm\text{curved} \end{bmatrix} SR \\ \\ [-\text{contour: \{constant/expanding, } \pm\text{angular\}}] \end{bmatrix}$$

At SR a scratch is represented as a negative geon, with a negative main axis of any possible curvature in and horizontally to the surface of another geon and with a negative contour of any curvature or size that is swept along this axis. In other words, SR represents the derivational history of a scratch, whereas CS represents its idealized shape.

The structures in (22) and (23) sum up most representational issues with respect to curvature nouns. (24) gives an overview of the SR and CS features that encode the meaning of some other curvature nouns. As we shall see below, the information in (24) will be important for representing Dutch curvature verbs, adjectives, and adverbs. This table represents either [expansion] or [constant], but not both. And, the dimensionality at CS is only indicated if main-axis curvature does not apply to both 1D and 2D objects by default.

(24) Dutch noun	English translation	SR curvature features of the main axis and the contour	CS features of the PART function (if applicable) and MATERIAL ENTITY
bocht	bend	$\{\ldots 0.5\pi \ldots \pi \ldots\}$; $\pm$angular	1D; +
breuk	breach	$\pm$curved; $\pm$angular	−
bult	bump	−curved; −angular, expansion	+
cirkel	circle	$\{2\pi\}$	1D; o

(24) *(cont.)* Dutch noun	English translation	SR curvature features	CS Features of the PART function
hoek	angle	{ . . . 90 ° . . .}; ±angular	o
knik	kink	{ . . . 45° . . .}; ±angular	+
kom	bowl	−curved; −angular, expansion	−
kreukel	crumple	−curved; ±angular	−
kromming	curve	+curved; ±angular	−
kronkel	twist	{ . . . π . . .}; ±angular	1D; +
krul	curl	{ . . . π . . . 2π}; ±angular	±
lus	loop	{2π}; ±angular, constant	1D; −
rol	roll	{2π}; ±angular, constant	±
plooi	pleat	+smooth; −angular	+
rimpel	wrinkle	+smooth; ±angular	+/−
rechte	straight line	−curved	1D; o
spiraal	spiral	{2π}	1D; o
vouw	fold	{ . . . 45° . . . 180°}; ±angular	2D; −
winding	winding	{2π}; ±angular, constant	1D; $\pm$
zigzag	zigzag	{ . . . 45° . . . 90° . . .}	1D; o

Let us now consider the lexical structure of Dutch verbs that refer to extrinsic path-curvature.

7.6. The Lexical Structure of Dutch Verbs that Refer to Extrinsic Path Curvature

Consider the following examples:

(25)   De auto zigzagde (om een pilaar heen/*in de kerk).
'The car zigzagged (around a pillar/*in the church).'

(26)   Jan slalomde (de heuvel af/*op de berg).
'John slalomed (down the hill/*on the mountain).'

(27)   De fietser cirkelde door de stad/op de parkeerplaats.
'The cyclist circled through the city/in the parking lot.'

(28)   Het boomblad spiraalde de tafel op/voor mijn neus.
'The leaf spiraled onto the table/in front of my nose.'

These examples show that *zigzaggen* 'to zigzag' and *slalommen* 'to slalom' may take an optional Path PP, but not an optional Place PP. *Cirkelen* 'to circle' and *spiralen* 'to spiral' must either take a Path PP or a Place PP. None of these verbs takes a bare object NP. Consider the lexical structure of *zigzaggen* in (29).

(29)

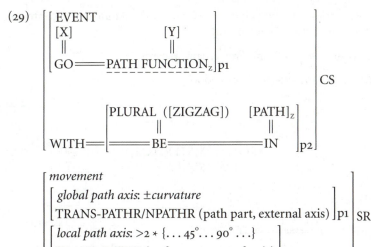

Let us consider how (29) describes the CS and SR structure of (25). At CS the Theme CAR would be fused with X. Intermittent underlining under PATH FUNCTION indicates that a curvature specification of global path-curvature is optional at CS. So only if *around a pillar* is present in syntax would the function AROUND be fused with PATH FUNCTION and PILLAR with Y. If no Path PP is present, PATH FUNCTION remains unspecified. The subscript z accounts for the idea that if a Path PP is absent, there are zigzags in an unspecified path, but that if a Path PP *is* present, there are zigzags in the path described by this PP. Specification of the curvature of the involved path at a local level is thus re-quired, whether the global structure of the path is known or not. The internal structure of ZIGZAG is not specified here. This is already done in the last sec-tion. Although the CS component introduced by WITH does not correspond to an adjunct in syntax, this component is in adjunct position here, thus expres-sing accompaniment of local path-curvature with global path-curvature (see Jackendoff 1990: 98 f. for details on WITH). *Zigzaggen* is therefore treated here as a verb with an 'obligatory adjunct' at CS, though not with an 'obligatory adjunct' at the level of syntax. At syntax the adjunct may be present, however, as shown in the paraphrase of (25): the car went along a path with zigzags in it. Details of the SR components have been explained before.

The impossibility of a Place PP adjunct in (25) may follow from having a non-specific path in the main CS structure (p1), together with a bound modifier in adjunct position (p2). If a Path PP is present, thus permitting fusion of a specific path function with PATH FUNCTION, a Place PP is possible (e.g. *De auto zigzagde om de pilaar in de kerk* 'The car zigzagged around the pillar in the church').

The representation of a PATH in the scope of a PLACE-function is new in

Conceptual Semantics. Its introduction is not only required by sentences like (25), but also by Path NPs as in (30).

(30) Brussels is on the way from Amsterdam to Paris.

The CS structure of (30) can be described as:

(31)

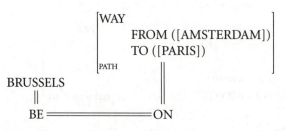

The lexical structure of *slalommen* 'to slalom' is similar to that of *zigzaggen*, except that in this case [+smooth] curvature parts—instead of zigzags—go into a path. [+smooth] curvature parts instead of slalom parts need to be assumed here, because the Dutch noun *slalom* refers to an EVENT. The path curvature referred to by *slingeren* 'to swing/wind' is [+smooth], and the external axis may be horizontal or vertical, but the exact curvature value depends on the functional properties of the Theme. If a path NP is used (such as *road*), or if the Theme is a vehicle, the resulting extrinsic path-curvature is like that of *slalommen*. However, if the Theme is an object that is attached to another object, like a pendulum, extrinsic path-curvature seems to be limited to 1.5π.

The lexical structure of the verb *cirkelen* 'to circle' is shown in (32).

(32)

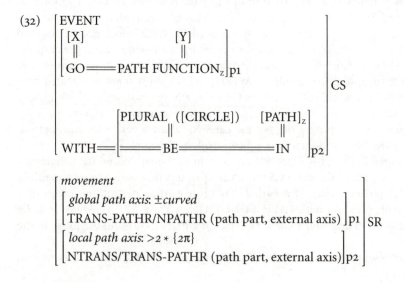

Example (32) shows that the lexical structure of *cirkelen* is similar to that of *zigzaggen*. One important difference, however, is that PATH FUNCTION is not marked as optional here. This means that a particular PATH FUNCTION must be present. If there is a Path PP in the sentence (as in the case *of door de stad* 'through the city' in (27)), the conceptual structure of this Path PP (here: VIA=IN) is fused with PATH FUNCTION. However, a Path NP (like *rondjes* 'circles') may do this job too, or even a Place PP, like *op de parkeerplaats* 'in the parking lot' in (27). In the latter case the conceptual structure of the object of the preposition is fused with Y, and a PATH FUNCTION is coerced (here: VIA=IN(SIDE)). (Type coercion into a path only seems possible if the Place PP does not bound the path, in the sense of being an end point to that path.)

The lexical structure of *spiralen* 'to spiral' is similar to that of *cirkelen*, except that some stretching operator must be represented at SR (thus encoding that *spiralen* refers to a sum of circular movements, stretched out along an axis). The lexical structures of *dwarrelen* 'to flutter' and *biggelen* 'to trickle along something' differ from that of *cirkelen* in that the external axis around which the Figure moves is horizontal. In the case of *zwenken* 'to swerve' the axis is vertical, and the global path parts are angular. There are no Dutch nouns that refer to path parts of *dwarrelen*, *biggelen*, or *zwenken*, so at CS circle parts or angle parts are encoded to go into a path.

Let us now consider some verbs that contain an intrinsic path-curvature specification at SR.

7.7. The Lexical Structure of Dutch Verbs that Refer to Intrinsic and/or Extrinsic Path Curvature

Consider the verb *rollen* 'to roll':

(33)   Jan rolde de bal door de kamer/*in de tuin.
        'John rolled the ball through the room/*in the garden.'

(34)   De bal rolt (door de kamer/*in de tuin).
        'The ball rolls (through the room/*in the garden).'

The lexical structure of *rollen* accounts for the observation that *rollen* demands a Path PP if an Agent is present, but cannot have a Place PP in either its causative interpretation in (33) or its non-causative interpretation in (34) (type coercion into a Path is blocked here, because such a coercion would result in 'the garden' to be the end point of the path):

(35)

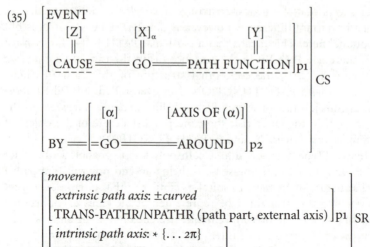

The optional marking of CAUSE indicates that if a verb-external argument is present an Agent (fused with Z) is described as causing the Theme to go along a particular extrinsic path. Depending on the Path PP the extrinsic path is either straight or curved (as indicated by SR component p1). Intrinsic path-curvature is described by SR component p2. The path axis features '* {. . . 2π}' encode that *rollen* refers to a rotation, the extent of which can be described by the product of any π-value, although preferably a product of 2π. (It must be noted that if the Figure is small in relation to its context, a product of 2π *is* expected—for instance, a small marble in a big room. However, if the Figure is big in comparison to its context, already a small π-value is enough to talk about a ball rolling through a room—for example, a huge ball in a small room.) The CS structure introduced with BY describes Theme rotation in terms of manner of motion in an adjunct position, even though an adjunct does not have to be present in syntax. Jackendoff (1990: 96 f.) introduces CS structures headed by BY only in case of optional Path PP's. His Spatial Resultative Adjunct rule allows him to represent the CS structure of such optional Path PP's in the main CS structure, and the CS structure of the main verb in adjunct position (see also Dorr 1993 and Dorr and Voss 1996). AROUND is a new Zone-1 function in Conceptual Semantics. I will discuss the properties of this function below.

Verbs with a similar lexical structure as *rollen* are: *buitelen* 'to tumble/to somersault', *duikelen* 'to turn somersaults', and *tuimelen* 'to tumble/to pivot'. All these verbs refer to rotation around a horizontal axis. They seem to differ from each other only in that they specify different moments of contact with the ground. *Buitelen* seems to refer to constant contact, *duikelen* to lack of contact, and *tuimelen* to intermittent contact.

Verbs that refer to rotation around a vertical axis are *tollen* 'to spin', *zwermen* 'to swarm', *wervelen* 'to whirl' and *kolken* 'to swirl'. The first verb refers to movement around a vertical axis, the second one to irregular movement of a distributed Theme around a vertical axis, the third one to regular movement around a vertical axis, and the last one to a revolving bounded quantity of water around a vertical axis.

A very interesting verb is the verb *draaien* 'to turn/to rotate'. Consider the following examples:

(36) Jan draaide de bal (het doel in/*rondjes/*op tafel).
    'John turned/rotated the ball (into the goal/*circles/*on the table).'

(37) De bal draaide (het doel in/rondjes/*op tafel).
    'The ball turned/rotated into the goal/circles/*on the table.'

Taking these examples into account, the lexical structure of the verb *draaien* can be described as follows:

(38)

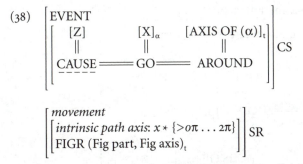

If an optional Path PP or Path NP is combined with the verb *draaien*, the sentential CS and SR structures are like those in (35). In such a case the main CS component describes the Theme going along the path described by the Path PP, and the CS structure describing the Theme rotating around itself is in adjunct position. Jackendoff (1990) describes this in terms of the Spatial Resultative Adjunct rule.

There are more verbs that can be analysed like *draaien*. *Kantelen* 'to topple' only differs from *draaien* in that it refers to main object axis rotation of approximately $1/2\pi$ around a horizontal object axis. *Wentelen* 'to turn/flip over' refers to secondary object axis rotation, that is a product of π, around a horizontal object axis. *Wippen* 'to seesaw' refers to the repetitive rotation of at least one endpoint of the main object axis around an object axis that is not marked for horizontal or vertical, in opposite directions, and of no more than 0.5π. *Zwaaien* 'to wave, to sway' only differs from *wippen* in that maximally one endpoint of the main axis rotates. *Schommelen* 'to swing' refers to an object rotating maximally 1.5π around a horizontal object axis. And *waggelen* 'to waggle' refers to the rotation of an animate object (part) around an object axis, not marked for horizontal or vertical, with an intrinsic path length of maximally 2π.

The interesting thing about the verb *draaien* is that its lexical structure is part of the lexical structure of the verbs *rollen* 'to roll', *buitelen* 'to tumble/to somersault', *duikelen* 'to turn somersaults', *tuimelen* 'to tumble/to pivot', *tollen* 'to spin', *zwermen* 'to swarm', *wervelen* 'to whirl', and *kolken* 'to swirl'. This accounts for Dutch native speakers' intuitions that a Theme *draait* 'turns/rotates', if any of these verbs is used. Such inferences, however, cannot be made in relation to any of the verbs in the previous paragraph. Apparently, the inference is only possible if AROUND is in adjunct position.

There are no Dutch verbs that refer to global path-curvature, local path-curvature, and intrinsic path-curvature at the same time. But such reference is possible in verb–adverb combinations:

(39) Jan rolde zigzaggend de heuvel af.
      'John rolled down the hill zigzagging.'

(40) Jan zigzagde rollend de heuvel af.
      'John zigzagged down the hill rolling.'

The CS and corresponding SR structure of (39) is:

(41)

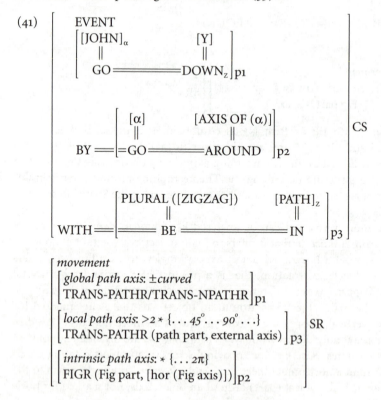

It follows from (41) that there are—in principle—no syntactic, semantic, or spatial representational objections to having verbs that refer to all three path components at the same time. It would be interesting to see whether such verbs exist in other languages.

The present analysis of Dutch verbs referring to path curvature and/or Figure rotation allows us to draw the following conclusions about the SR/CS interface:

(42) The representation of global path-axis curvature at SR corresponds to an encoding of path-axis curvature in the main CS structure

(43) The representation of local path-axis curvature at SR corresponds to an encoding of path-axis curvature in a modifying CS structure (introduced here by WITH)

(44) The representation of intrinsic path-axis curvature at SR corresponds to an encoding of path-axis curvature in a main CS structure (by using the function AROUND), except when also global path-curvature is described. In the latter case intrinsic path-axis curvature is described by a modifying CS structure (introduced with the function BY)

These structural rules allow us to formulate a semi-productive rule for Dutch verbs that refer to path-axis curvature:

(45) If N is a Dutch noun referring to some curved part, and V a Dutch verb referring to similarly curved parts in a path, than the curved parts encoded in the LCS of N must be part of the LCS of V, and V must be represented in agreement with (42) through (44)

At first glance there seems to be an important exception to (45). If intrinsic path-curvature is described in terms of the function AROUND (as with *to roll*), there are no CIRCLE parts in the LCS of the verb. This exception is only apparant, however, since AROUND encodes those circle parts in terms of the axis features that constitute this function (see van der Zee 1996: 36 and Nikanne 1999 for similar decompositions of F1 functions in terms of axis features)—see (46):

(46)

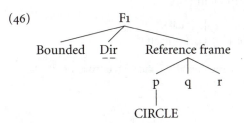

Example (46) describes AROUND as a Zone-1 function, which maps a Theme into a PATH or PLACE that is bounded by a reference object. This path or region is represented in relation to one of three possible axes (p) in a reference frame marked as being circle-shaped. Intermittent underlining under Dir indicates that the path or region may be directed, but need not be (if an EVENT function like GO is represented, Dir is present, but if a STATE function like BE is represented, it is absent. In the first case a PATH is projected, in the latter case a PLACE (Nikanne 1990)).

Lessmoellmann (forthcoming) observes that German does not contain prepositions (nor modified prepositional phrases) that allow German speakers to talk about paths going around some reference point. It is possible for German speakers, however, to say that a path has a circular shape by using a construction that has been analysed here in terms of a WITH adjunct at CS:

(47) Christopher geht in einen Kreis um seinen Schreibtisch herum.
      'Christopher is going "around" his desk with a circle in the path.'

Let us now come back to (45). The rule in (45) is called semi-productive, because it captures an important generalization across Dutch verbs referring to path curvature on the one hand, but it does not describe all possible lexical structures of Dutch path-curvature verbs on the other hand (for example, Dutch does not have a verb like 'triangling', referring to a going along a path with triangular shapes in it, although there is a Dutch noun for triangle. And, conversely, it is also the case that Dutch verbs like *slalommen* and *dwarrelen* do not have corresponding Dutch curvature nouns that refer to curved object or path parts).

The next section looks at verbs that refer to geon axis deformation.

7.8. Verbs that Refer to Geon Axis Deformation

Let us first consider Dutch verbs that refer to [+smooth] geon axis deformation. Consider:

(48) Jan krult het touw/het blad papier/*de tent.
      'John curls the rope/the page/*the tent.'

(49) De tuinslang/de pagina/*de tent krult (zich).
      'The garden hose/the page/*the tent curls (itself).'

On the basis of these distributional properties the lexical structure of *krullen* 'to curl' can be represented as in (50).

(50)

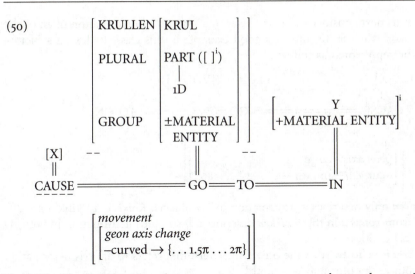

$$
\begin{bmatrix}
\text{movement} \\
\begin{bmatrix}
\text{geon axis change} \\
-\text{curved} \rightarrow \{\ldots 1.5\pi \ldots 2\pi\}
\end{bmatrix}
\end{bmatrix}
$$

The LCS of *krullen* describes that some Agent X causes a curl or curls to go into Y. The optional marking of PLURAL expresses that *krullen* does not specify whether one curl or more curls go into Y. The optional marking of CAUSE indicates that this function does not have to be present in a sentential conceptual structure. The 1D feature under the PART function encodes that the extracted PART (a curl) is an idealized 1D entity. Superscript 'i' ensures that the argument of GO represents a curved part of the Patient (Y). The LSS encodes *krullen* as a curvature change in the axis of a 1D or 2D entity from [–curved] to —preferably—a value between around 1.5 and 2π.

The lexical structure of *buigen* 'to bend', *krommen* 'to curve' and *oprollen* 'to roll up' is represented along the same lines. In the first two cases the LSS encodes an axis-curvature change to [+smooth,] and in the last case to a product of 2π.

A special case is the verb *kronkelen* 'to wriggle/to twist'. Let us only consider the LCS of this verb (from here on I do not represent the internal argument structure of the CS functions. These are given in Section 7.5):

(51)

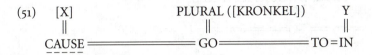

Kronkelen is special in that an intransitive use of the verb, combined with a volitional external argument of the verb, requires an identical Agent and Patient. That is, an Agent is read to cause *kronkels* 'wriggles' going into himself. If the external argument is non-volitional, as in *De tuinslang kronkelt* 'The garden hose is twisting', CAUSE along with its argument is not represented. Only 1D objects are able to *kronkelen*.

Let us next consider verbs that refer to a [–smooth] deformation of an object part axis. *Vouwen* 'to fold' is a good example in this class. Its lexical structure can be represented as follows:

(52)

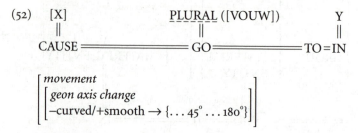

Vouwen only describes a deformation in 2D objects. *Knikken* 'to kink' only differs from *vouwen* in that *knikken* describes a [–smooth] deformation in both 1D and 2D entities.

Verbuigen 'to twist' is the only Dutch verb that refers to an axis deformation to both [+smooth] and [–smooth]:

(53)

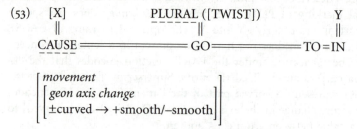

TWIST in the LCS of this verb indicates that Dutch does not contain a noun which refers to the meaning of this conceptual structure (*verbuiging* 'twist' is reserved for describing conjugation).

The verb *rechten* 'to straighten' does not encode that non-curved parts go into a Patient, but that curved parts go out of it. The lexical structure of this verb can be represented as in (54).

(54)

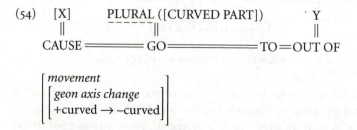

The LCS of *rechten* is very similar to that of certain deformation verbs that can be prefixed with the morpheme *-ont* (see van der Zee 1999*a* for a discussion). An example is *ontkrullen* 'to decurl':

(55)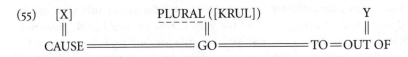

Let us now look at verbs that refer to axis extension.

7.9. Verbs that Refer to Geon Axis Extension

The lexical structure of the verb *bollen* 'to bulge' is representative for the verbs in this class. Consider first its distributional properties:

(56) De wind bolt de zeilen/Het zeil bolt.
 'The wind bulges the sails/The sail bulges.'

The lexical structure of this verb can be described as follows:

(57)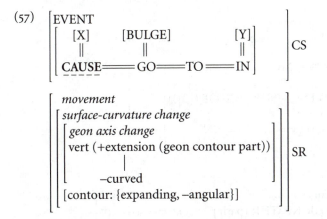

The LCS of this verb encodes that *bollen* refers to a BULGE going into a Patient. The LSS describes this in terms of a geon growing onto another geon's surface, along an axis vertical to that surface.

Other verbs that refer to geons growing into a surface can be represented along similar lines. *Uitstulpen* 'to get a convex part' refers to an Agent causing a bump to grow into himself. *Bobbelen* 'to become bumpy' does not allow an Agent, and encodes that more than one bump grows into a surface. *Indeuken* 'to dent inwards' and *instulpen* 'to get a concave part' refer to indentations growing into a surface, encoded by negative axes growing vertically into an object's surface. The verb *verkreukelen* 'to wrinkle/to crumple' optionally refers to an Agent, causing crumples to go into a surface, by negative axes growing into and horizontally to that surface. The lexical structure of the verb *bekrassen* 'to scratch into' is similar, except that it obligatorily refers to an Agent. The verb *breken* 'to break' may refer to 'cracks or breaches going into an object', or to 'a shattering of an object into many different parts'. The first meaning of this verb can be encoded along similar lines as that of the verb *bekrassen*. The LSS of *plooien* 'to pleat' refers to more than one positive axis growing horizontally to a surface, with [–angular] contours along these axes. *Rimpelen* 'to wrinkle' and *fronsen* 'to frown' are represented as *plooien*, except that *rimpelen* does not allow a volitional Agent, and *fronsen* 'to frown' must contain *voorhoofd* 'forehead' as an obligatory argument of the function IN at CS.

The lexical structure of *golven* 'to wave' is slightly different from that of *bollen*. Consider:

(58) *Jan/De wind golft het koren/Het koren golft.
      *Jan/The wind waves the corn/The corn is waving.

Example (58) shows that there is a restriction on the Agents that may cause something to *golven*. This can be explained in terms of restrictions on X in the following lexical structure:

(59)

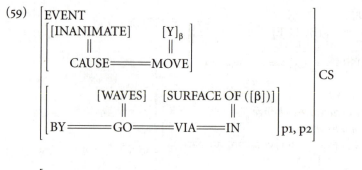

This lexical structure encodes that *golven* 'to wave' involves geons to protrude and indent along an axis that is vertical to a surface, as well as for these resulting geons to displace themselves through a surface along a non-specified path.

There are two Dutch verbs that refer to a removing of protrusions and indentations in a surface: *strijken* 'to iron' and *egaliseren* 'to level'. The lexical structure of the first verb can be represented as in (60).

(60)

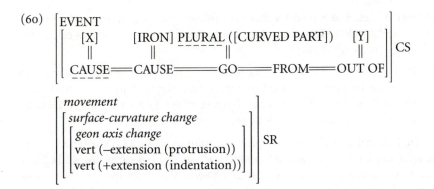

The CS component encodes that *strijken* refers to some Agent causing an iron to cause one or more curved parts to go out of a Patient. The SR component informally describes that this corresponds to a geon axis change, involving protrusions to be indented, and indentations to be protruded. The lexical structure of *egaliseren* 'to level' is similar. *Egaliseren* just does not explicitly encode the instrument in the LCS of the verb, but the Patient (the Patient is the ground level).

Sections 7.8 and 7.9 considered Dutch verbs that refer to object or surface-curvature change. The lexical structure of both verb groups has some interesting general properties, which can be captured by another hypothesis about the SR/CS interface:

(61) Hypothesis about the SR/CS interface with respect to the lexical structure of verbs that refer to object or surface-curvature change: if the LSS of a lexical item is represented as follows:

$$\begin{bmatrix} movement \\ \begin{bmatrix} geon\ axis\ change \\ \cdots\cdots\cdots \end{bmatrix} \end{bmatrix}$$

then the corresponding LCS in this lexical item is represented as:

⟨PLURAL⟩
$$\begin{bmatrix} \text{PART } ([Y]^i) \\ | \\ \text{1D/2D/3D} \\ \\ +/-/\pm\text{MATERIAL} \\ \text{ENTITY} \end{bmatrix} \qquad \begin{bmatrix} +/-/\pm\text{MATERIAL} \\ \text{ENTITY} \end{bmatrix}^i$$

[X]
‖
⟨CAUSE⟩══════════ GO=PATH-FUNCTION=IN/OUT OF

where / indicates a possible choice, and ⟨. . .⟩ presence or absence of the function

The level of detail at which we have considered the LCS of the verbs in Sections 7.8 and 7.9 also allows us to formulate a semi-productive lexical rule at the level of CS (Jackendoff 1997):

(62) If N is a Dutch noun referring to some curved part, and V a Dutch verb referring to object- or surface-curvature change, than the curved parts encoded in the LCS of N must be part of the LCS of V, and V must be represented in agreement with (61)

Rule (62) describes an important generalization over the LCS's of Dutch verbs that refer to object or surface deformation, while also not capturing all LCS's of those verbs. There are, e.g., no deformation verbs that accompany the nouns *lus* 'loop' and *hoek* 'angle'/'corner'. And, as we have seen before, the LCS of *golven* 'to wave' is described more like a path-curvature verb. Furthermore, the stative verb *meanderen* 'to meander' shows that its LCS cannot be described by (63) (argument 'j' can be fused only with the lexical structure of a word referring to a river, stream, etc.):

(63)   PLURAL ([BOCHT])

Let us now consider Dutch adjectives and adverbs that refer to curvature distinctions.

7.10. Adjectives and Adverbs that Refer to Curvature Distinctions

The curvature adjectives in the odd numbered sentences are based on the past-participle form of the verbs in the even numbered sentences:

(64)   Het blad spiraalde de tafel op.
        'The leaf spiraled onto the table.'

(65)   Een op de tafel gespiraald blad.
        'A leaf that has spiraled onto the table.'

(66)   Het blad spiraalde voor mijn neus.
        'The leaf spiraled in front of my nose.'

(67)   ??Een voor mijn neus gespiraald blad.
        ??An in front of my nose spiraled leaf.

(68)   Jan boog de staaf.
        'John bent the bar.'

(69)   Een door Jan gebogen staaf.
        'A bar that was bent by John.'

Example (69) is representative for all past-participle forms of verbs that refer to object- or surface-curvature deformation. It is possible to have an adjective that is derived from the verb, where this adjective expresses the same property as described by the verb. This is not the case for the path-curvature adjective *gespiraald* in (67). This adjective refers to a shape property of the leaf, but not of the path.

Classic situation-types do not allow us to explain the distinction between (65) and (67). For example, C. S. Smith (1991: 28, in Saeed 1997) would treat the path verb *spiralen* 'to spiral' as both an accomplishment verb and an action verb (its atelic and telic features, respectively, following from either an obligatory Path or Place PP). This distinction, however, needs explanation itself. Why is the verb *spiralen* an accomplishment verb in one context, but an action verb in the other context? What is more, a uniform treatment of verbs referring to object and surface curvature would not be possible on the basis of situation types, since, e.g., *krommen* 'to curve' is an accomplishment verb and *strijken* 'to iron' an activity verb, whereas both verbs allow the curvature adjectives *gekromd* 'curved' and *gestreken* 'ironed'.

A different approach would be to consider the role of the sentence context in the derivation of a path-curvature adjective from a path-curvature verb. It appears that if a sentence allows Inferred Eventual Position or State of an entity (IEPS), then the adjective that is derived on the basis of the sentence can be interpreted as we interpreted the verb (the idea of taking into account IEPS is based on Lieber and Baayen 1997, but also differs in some important respects from their ideas).[2] The difference between (64) and (66) is that the Path PP in (64) allows us to infer the eventual position of the leaf, whereas the Place PP in (66) does not (no end point is specified, only that the entire path is 'in front of my nose'). Example (68) allows us to infer the eventual state of the bar, which is why the adjective in (69) expresses the same idea as the verb in (68). IEPS does not only explain the derivation of curvature adverbs, but the derivation of all Dutch adverbs of the past-participle form type from Dutch verbs. Consider the examples in (70).

(70) Jan zette het glas neer.
      'John put down the glass.'

(71) Een neergezet glas.
      'A glass that has been put down.'

---

[2] Lieber and Baayen (1997) assume that the feature Inferred Eventual Position or State (IEPS) applies to the highest argument in a conceptual structure. However, this is not the case in causative constructions, or in the constructions under consideration here. Here the entity in the main conceptual structure of which the IEPS can be determined is a bar in *John bent the bar*, or John in *John zigzagged down the road*, etc.

In (70) the eventual position or endpoint of the glass can be determined, which is why the derived adjective in (71) has a similar meaning as that of the verb in (70).

The LCS of the adjective *gebogen* 'bent' in (69) can be described as follows:

(72)

The structure in (72) describes that X has the property of being bent. The argument of AT_{ident} carries that part of the LCS of the verb of which the adjective is derived.

Structure (72), in combination with the aforementioned observations, allows us to formulate the following principle with respect to the derivation of path-curvature adjectives from path-curvature verbs:

(73)   There seem to be no lexical constraints on deriving Dutch adjectives of the past-participle form from Dutch verbs. There is an extra lexical constraint, however, which says that only if a Dutch sentence allows Inferred Eventual Position or State (IEPS) can an adjective of the past-participle form be derived from the main verb. The meaning of this adjective is similar to that of the verb from which it is derived (the LCS of such adjectives is described here as in (72))

There are some apparent exceptions to (73). The path verbs *draaien* 'to turn/ rotate' and *rollen* 'to roll', which in their transitive use do not give rise to IEPS sentences, allow the past-participle forms *gedraaid* and *gerold*. But, although it is possible to use these adjectives when talking about the property of tops and cigarettes (*een gedraaide tol* 'a turned top' and *een gerolde cigaret* 'a rolled cigarette') it is not possible to use these adjectives when talking about the property of a ball (??*een gedraaide bal* 'a rotated ball' or *een gerolde bal* 'a rolled ball'). It seems that in the former examples readings are coerced that describe how these objects have been brought about, but not how they have moved, as we would expect from (73). The derivation of an adjective may thus be due to a specific property of the object described by the noun (see Pustejovsky 1995). Two other apparent exceptions are *meanderen* 'to meander' and *rechten* 'to straighten'. These verbs refer to object or surface deformation but cannot have a past participle that functions as an adjective. However, *meanderen* is accounted for by its not being an event verb (as seen in Section 7.9). And *rechten* 'to straighten' cannot have a past participle, because such a form is lexically encoded as a noun, referring to a court of justice. Finally, there is the adjective *omwikkeld* 'wrapped around'. This adjective has only a different morphology than the other adjectives that are derived from verbs. Let us now consider Dutch adverbs that refer to curvature.

The following distribution is representative for path-curvature adverbs:

(74) Jan rijdt zigzaggend.
      'John is driving in a zigzag like manner.'

(75) *Jan zigzagt rijdend.
      *John is zigzagging while driving.

Apparently it is possible for a path-curvature adverb to modify an event verb, but not for an event adverb to modify a path-curvature verb. And, as we have seen in (39) and (40) it is also possible to combine path-curvature adverbs with path-curvature verbs. Let us again consider the LCS of the verb *zigzaggen*:

(76)
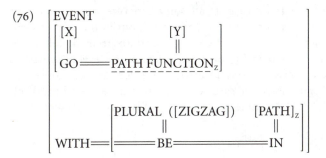

Let us consider a possible representation of the conceptual structure of (75) by using (76). *Zigzagt* in (75) is the main verb and the adverb *rijdend* is optional. Syntactic constraints thus demand that *rijdend* must be represented in adjunct position in the sentential conceptual structure, but semantic constraints demand that its LCS is fused with that of GO in the main CS structure. So, it seems that normal structure-preserving rules account for the unacceptability of (75). There is no clash if a general movement verb is the main verb and a path-curvature adjunct is the adverb, as in (74). In such cases the LCS of the main verb is fused with GO. And there are no clashes either if there is both a path-curvature verb and a path-curvature adverb, as in (39) and (40). In such cases there is one main CS structure describing global path-curvature, and two adjunct structures describing local path-curvature. These ideas allow us to formulate the following principle with respect to Dutch adverbs referring to path curvature:

(77) There seem to be no lexical constraints on deriving Dutch adverbs referring to path curvature from Dutch verbs referring to path curvature. Only normal structure preserving principles prevent such derivations.

Let us now consider adverbs that refer to object axis deformation and surface curvature deformation:

(78) *De rivier buigt zich/gaat kronkelend.
    *The river bends (itself)/goes wriggingly.

(79) De rivier buigt zich/gaat kronkelend door het landschap.
    'The river bends (itself)/goes wriggingly through the landscape.'

(80) *Het haar krult/gaat opgerold.
    *The curls/goes rolled up.

(81) Het haar krult/gaat opgerold terug.
    'The hair curls/goes back rolled up.'

It is difficult to find examples in Dutch in which adverbs referring to an object or surface deformation can be used to modify Dutch verbs. However, in the few cases where this is possible a PATH seems to be required as part of the sentential conceptual structure. In the case of path-curvature verbs this requirement is automatically fulfilled by a non-specified path at CS, but in the case of verbs referring to object or surface curvature there is no such unspecified path at CS. In the latter case, therefore, a path PP must be present at the level of syntax, as indicated above. These considerations mean that the lexical structure of all Dutch adverbs referring to object or surface curvature can be described as follows (where PATH FUNCTION indicates that a Path PP must be present at the level of syntax):

(82)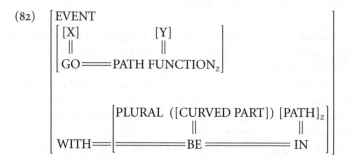

Example (82) makes it clear that the LCS of Dutch curvature adverbs is eventually based on the LCS of Dutch nouns referring to the corresponding curvature distinctions. Let us formulate this in more general terms:

(83) Dutch curvature adverbs can be derived from Dutch curvature nouns, either (1) by deriving the lexical structure of such adverbs from the lexical structure of the corresponding verb, which contains the lexical structure of a curvature noun (as is the case for Dutch adverbs referring to path curvature), or (2) by deriving the lexical structure of such adverbs from the lexical structure of a curvature noun plus (82) (as is the case for Dutch adverbs referring to object or surface curvature)

And, of course, (83) allows us to formulate an even more general principle:

(84) The lexical structure of Dutch curvature verbs, adjectives and adverbs can be derived from the lexical structure of Dutch curvature nouns, plus some extra principles

7.11. Concluding Discussion

This chapter considered the lexical structure of Dutch nouns, verbs, adjectives, and adverbs that refer to path curvature, object curvature, and surface curvature. It was shown that part of the meaning of these words must be described in terms of spatial features referring to axis and contour curvature. It was shown in particular that although Dutch words referring to axis curvature may refer to a whole range of curvature values, they preferably refer to a set of schematized curvature values. For example, *rechten* 'to straighten' preferably refers to an object-axis deformation to o degrees. The set of schematized curvature values describing axis curvature also appeared to be more constrained in Dutch than in Finnish.

At the end of this chapter it was observed that the lexical structure of Dutch curvature verbs, adjectives, and adverbs can be derived from the lexical structure of Dutch curvature nouns (see (84)). This evaluation was based on a more detailed analysis of these words. In particular, the lexical analysis of Dutch path-curvature verbs and nouns in Sections 7.5, 7.6, and 7.7 revealed:

(a) that the representation of global path-axis curvature at the level of spatial representation corresponds to an encoding of path-axis curvature in the main conceptual structure (see (42));

(b) that in Dutch syntax, local path-curvature can be expressed without referring to global path-curvature;

(c) that the representation of local path-axis curvature at the level of spatial representation corresponds to an encoding of path-axis curvature in a modifying conceptual structure (introduced here by 'WITH'; see (43));

(d) that the representation of intrinsic path-axis curvature at the level of spatial representation corresponds to an encoding of path-axis curvature in the main conceptual structure (by using the function 'AROUND' here), except when also global path-curvature is described. In the latter case extrinsic path-axis curvature is described in the main conceptual structure, and intrinsic path-axis curvature is described in a modifying conceptual structure (introduced here with the function 'BY'; see (44));

(e) that a semi-productive lexical rule describes the lexical structure of Dutch path-curvature verbs, based on the lexical structure of Dutch curvature nouns, and the structural rules in (a), (c) and (d) above (see (45)).

The lexical analysis of Dutch verbs that refer to object or surface curvature in Sections 7.8 and 7.9 showed:

(*a*) that an encoding of axis change at the level of spatial representation systematically corresponds to the lexical conceptual structure of these verbs (see (61));

(*b*) that a semi-productive lexical rule describes the lexical structure of these verbs, on the basis of the lexical structure of Dutch curvature nouns (see (62)).

The lexical analysis of Dutch curvature adjectives and adverbs in Section 7.10 demonstrated:

(*a*) that there seem to be no lexical constraints on deriving Dutch adjectives of the past-participle form from Dutch verbs. There is an extra lexical constraint, however, which says that only if a Dutch sentence allows Inferred Eventual Position or State (IEPS) can an adjective of the past-participle form be derived from the main verb. The meaning of this adjective is similar to that of the verb from which it is derived (the LCS of such adjectives is described here as in (72))

(*b*) Dutch curvature adverbs can be derived from Dutch curvature nouns, either (1) by deriving the lexical structure of such adverbs from the lexical structure of the corresponding verb, which contains the lexical structure of a curvature noun (as is the case for Dutch adverbs referring to path curvature), or (2) by deriving the lexical structure of such adverbs from the lexical structure of a curvature noun plus (82) (as is the case for Dutch adverbs referring to object or surface curvature) (the LCS of all curvature adverbs can be represented as in (82))

This evaluation not only shows that the lexical structure of Dutch nouns is central to talking about curvature in Dutch, but also that there is a systematic correspondence between spatial and conceptual representations in the lexical interface of a Dutch speaker.

At this moment more perception research is required to investigate the special status of certain axis and contour curvatures at the level of spatial structure, and more semantic research is necessary to investigate the number of schematized curvature distinctions available for different languages or for language development. This chapter has attempted to show, however, that a systematic study of language referring to curvature distinctions is possible and also necessary for a better understanding of the language-to-space interface.

Appendix I[3]

(A) *Nouns that refer to curvature distinctions*

bocht	'bend'	krul	'curl'
breuk	'breach'	lus	'loop'
bult	'bump'	rol	'roll'
hoek	'angle'	plooi	'pleat'
knik	'kink'	rimpel	'wrinkle'
kom	'basin'	rechte	'straight line'
kreukel	'crumple'	vouw	'fold'
kromming	'curve'	winding	'winding'
kronkel	'twist'		

(B) *Verbs that refer to extrinsic path-curvature*

biggelen	'to trickle along something'
cirkelen	'to circle'
dwarrelen	'to whirl/to flutter'
slingeren	'to swing/wind'
spiralen	'to spiral'
zigzaggen	'to zigzag'
zwenken	'to go left/right'

(C) *Verbs that refer to intrinsic path-curvature*

buitelen	'to tumble/ to somersault'	tollen	'to spin, to twirl'
		tuimelen	'to tumble/to pivot'
draaien	'to turn/to spin'	waggelen	'to waggle'
duikelen	'to turn somersaults'	wippen	'to seesaw'
kantelen	'to topple'	wentelen	'to turn/flip over'
kolken	'to swirl'	wervelen	'to whirl'
rollen	'to roll'	zwaaien	'to wave'
schommelen	'to swing'	zwermen	'to swarm'

---

[3] It is impossible to list all Dutch curvature verbs here. This set does not contain verbs describing curvature changes that are a consequence of stretching transformations, like *een gezicht trekken* 'to pull a face', *opstropen* 'to make folds by pushing/pulling', and *uitstrekken* 'to stretch/extend' (see Talmy 1988 for force dynamic features), or verbs that refer to more than only curvature change, like *zich wurmen* 'to worm one's way' and *zich weven door* 'to weave/thread oneself through', which also refer to 'betweenness', and *zich welven* 'to vault oneself', which also refers to 'being across something else'.

(D) *Verbs that refer to object (axis) deformation*

buigen	'to bend'
knikken/knakken	'to kink'
kreuken/kreukelen	'to crumple'
krommen	'to curve'
kronkelen	'to wind/to wriggle/to twist'
krullen	'to curl'
meanderen	'to meander'
oprollen	'to roll up'
rechten	'to straighten (out)/to bend straight'
vouwen	'to fold'
welven, zich	'to arch/to vault itself'
wikkelen	'to wind/to wrap'
winden	'to wind/to twist'

(E) *Verbs that refer to surface-curvature change*

bollen	'to bulge/to balloon'
bobbelen	'to become bumpy'
egaliseren	'to level'
fronsen	'to frown'
golven	'to undulate/to wave'
instulpen	'to get a concave part'
indeuken	'to dent'
plooien	'to pleat'
rimpelen	'to wrinkle'
strijken	'to iron'
uitstulpen	'to get a convex part'

Part Four

Constraints on 'Interfaces' From a Connectionist Perspective

8

Developing Relations

MICHAEL GASSER, ELIANA COLUNGA, and
LINDA B. SMITH

Relations lie at the center of humankind's most intellectual endeavors and are also fundamental to any account of linguistic semantics. Despite the importance of relations in
understanding cognition and language, there is no well-accepted account of the origins
of relations. What are relations made of? How are they made? In this chapter we address
these questions. First, we consider past proposals of how relations are represented and the
implications of these representational ideas for development. Second, we review the developmental evidence in the context of five psychological facts about relations that must be
explained by any account of their origin. This evidence suggests that relational concepts
are similarity based, influenced by specific developmental history, and influenced by
language. Third, we summarize Gasser and Colunga's Playpen model of learning relations.
This connectionist model instantiates a new proposal about the stuff out of which relations are made and the experiences that make them. Finally, we outline how the model
explains the five psychological facts and consider the implications of this model or one
of the questions addressed in this volume, the interface between conceptual structure and
spatial representation.

8.1. Introduction

Relations lie at the center of humankind's most intellectual endeavors—science,
mathematics, poetry. Relations are also fundamental to any account of linguistic
semantics. Indeed, a fundamental psychological distinction between objects and
relations may be reflected in the universal linguistic distinction between nouns
and verbs (Gentner 1982; Langacker 1987). Despite the importance of relations
in understanding cognition and language and despite the dogged and continuing
work of psychologists, linguists, and philosophers on the problem, there is no
well-accepted account of the origins of relations. What are relations made of?
How are they made? This chapter addresses this question by considering the
psychological evidence on how children acquire relations and relational language
and by proposing a computational model.

The plan of the chapter is as follows. First, we consider past proposals of how
relations are represented and the implications of these representational ideas for
development. Second, we review the developmental evidence in the context of

five psychological facts about relations that must be explained by any account of their origin. This evidence suggests that relational concepts are similarity based, influenced by specific developmental history, and influenced by language. Third, we summarize Gasser and Colunga's Playpen model of the learning of relations. This connectionist model instantiates a new proposal about the stuff out of which relations are made and the experiences that make them. Finally, we outline how the model explains the five psychological facts and consider the implications of this model for the question addressed in this volume, the interface between conceptual structure and spatial representation.

8.2. Representing Relations

Symbolic and connectionist theories seem at loggerheads throughout much of cognition, but in the domain of theories of relations, they are remarkably similar. Both classes of theories start with the same founding premise: objects are prior to relations and atomic in the definition of relations. This is reasonable: after all, ABOVE means two objects in a particular relation, one to the other. To make sense of the idea of ABOVE one should first have the idea of OBJECT. The starting problem, then, for all classes of relational theories, has been how to represent the connection between related objects that specifies the relation. Two components have been taken as critical to these representations: (1) an element that characterizes the content and arity of the relation—for example, that it is ABOVENESS for example and not BETWEENNESS that is being represented, and (2) a set of bindings that map the object arguments onto roles in the relation (Halford, Wilson, and Phillips forthcoming). The binding of objects to roles is crucial in order to conceptually keep separate distinct situations, for example, BOOK ABOVE TABLE and TABLE ABOVE BOOK.

A brief consideration of the kinds of solution offered to the binding problem suffices to make clear the uniformity of solutions to this representational problem. We begin with Figure 8.1, which offers a symbolic representation of ABOVE in which the relation term is represented by an explicit symbol—that is, the sequence of characters A, B, O, V, E. Binding is implemented by assigning par-

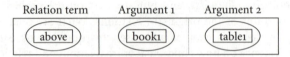

FIGURE 8.1. A relation represented using symbolic argument-style representation. The relation term and the arguments are symbols; the bindings are represented by the positions of the arguments

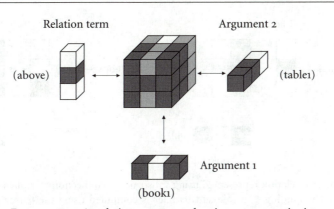

Relation term   Argument 2

(above)   (table1)

Argument 1

(book1)

FIGURE 8.2. A relation represented using a connectionist argument-style representation. The arguments are fed to dedicated banks of units, and their bindings are represented using the tensor product

ticular positions in the representation to the roles of the relation and then by inserting representations of objects into these positions. This is the approach used in standard predicate-calculus notation: *Above (Book, Table)*.

Halford *et al.* (1994) have proposed a connectionist version of the same kind of representation. We illustrate this in Figure 8.2: the relation term and the related objects are all activation vectors. They are fed into separate banks of units, places in the network, each of which is dedicated to representing a particular component. The tensor product of these three vectors (for a binary relation) is computed to complete the binding process.

Another solution to the binding problem involves pairing the objects with explicitly labelled role names (slots), rather than with places. A symbolic version of a slot-filler representation is illustrated in Figure 8.3. Here objects and roles are paired by concatenating the role-name symbol and the object symbol. One

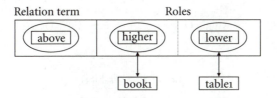

Relation term   Roles

above   higher   lower

book1   table1

FIGURE 8.3. A relation represented using the symbolic explicit-role representation. The binding is achieving by concatenating the role-name symbol and the filler object symbol

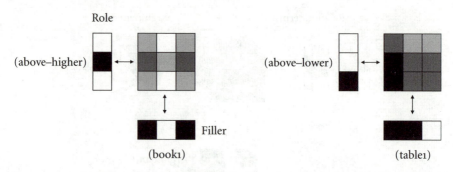

FIGURE 8.4. A relation represented using a distributed connectionist explicit-role representation. The binding of a role and its filler is computed using the tensor product or convolution

connectionist version of a slot-filler representation has been offered by Smolensky (1990). For each role-filler pair, a role-name vector and an object vector are fed into banks of role and filler units respectively and the tensor product of these vectors is calculated. Note that the relation term may be left out if it is completely specified by the role names; e.g., in place of ABOVE we have ABOVE-HIGHER and ABOVE-LOWER. This approach is illustrated in Figure 8.4.

In other connectionist approaches, separate role and filler units are somehow marked as belonging together rather than being placed on special purpose banks of units. In this approach, each unit in the network has an associated value (as well as an activation). When this value matches the value of another unit, they are bound together. In the dynamic binding approach (Sporns *et al.* 1989; Hummel and Biederman 1992; Shastri and Ajjanagadde 1993; Hummel and Holyoak 1997), units 'fire' at particular times, and those whose firings are syn-

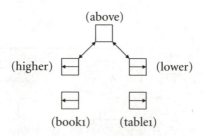

FIGURE 8.5. A relation represented using a localist connectionist explicit-role representation. Binding is achieved through a value that is shared by the bound role and filler (arrows in the figure)

chronized are considered bound. This localist approach is illustrated in Figure 8.5.

Even if not reducible one to the other, all of these ways of representing relations comprise a highly similar class. Table 8.1 summarizes the various approaches. All assume that the specification of how the objects in a relation are related is by explicitly labelling them as being in that relation. But where does this labelling come from? How do labelled representations interface with perception and actions on objects such that the experience of a particular book and particular table manages to engage the BOOK ABOVE TABLE representation? In all of the proposals about relational representation, the relations are just there, presumed a priori abstractions. This might be acceptable if there were a universal set of innate relations hardwired some way into biology. But the developmental and cross-language evidence on this point is clear: relations are learned. Their course of development is protracted and highly influenced by language learning.

TABLE 8.1. *Approaches to the representation of relational knowledge*

	Relation term	Bindings
Symbolic		
Predicate calculus	Symbol	Symbols in argument positions
Slot-filler	Symbol	Role symbol + filler symbol
Argument style	Vector	Tensor product of relation and filler vectors
Connectionist		
Distributed, explicit role	(Implicit in bindings)	Sum of tensor product of role and filler vectors
Localist	Unit	Role and filler units, synchronized

8.3. Five Facts About Relations

There are several extensive reviews of the development of relations (L.B. Smith 1989; Gentner and Rattermann 1991; Bloom, Tinker, and Margulis 1993; Gentner *et al.* 1995). We do not attempt to duplicate these reviews here. Instead, we highlight five facts about development, facts about which there is remarkably little dispute in the usually contentious subfield of cognitive development. We take these as the facts that must be explained in an account of how and out of what relations are made.

8.3.1. *Fact 1: Language Matters*

Languages look very different from one another with respect to relations (Gentner 1982; Choi and Bowerman 1992; Bowerman 1996). Even a cursory examination of the spatial relation expressions in a subset of languages reveals the variety of relational concepts possible. Consider some of the possibilities for encoding relations of CONTACT, SUPPORT, and CONTAINMENT between two objects (Landau 1996). The roles (or slots) for these spatial concepts are the **trajector**— the thing being related, and the **landmark**—the thing to which the trajector is being related. Thus, in *the ball is in the cup* the ball is the trajector and the cup the landmark.

Figure 8.6 presents four possible arrangements of a trajector (indicated by black) and a landmark (indicated by grey). Spanish uses a single word *en* for all of them. English uses one word, *on*, for the two situations in which containment is not involved and another, *in*, for situations in which the trajector is (at least partially) contained in the landmark. German distinguishes two kinds of situations for which English uses *on*: *auf* when the landmark is under the trajector and *an* when the trajector is fixed to a vertical surface of the landmark. Korean distinguishes two kinds of CONTAINMENT (and CONTACT) situations, those in which the trajector fits tightly with the landmark, for which *sok* is used, and those in which there is a loose fit, for which *ahn* is used. Clearly, languages 'slice up' the relational space in different ways. This means at the least that the human capacity to represent and learn relations is a flexible one.

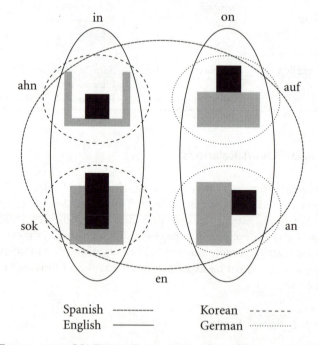

FIGURE 8.6. CONTAINMENT, SUPPORT, and CONTACT in four languages. Trajectors are indicated in black, landmarks in grey

Of course, to be more accurate, languages do not 'slice up' anything. Languages do not actually do anything at all; it is people that do. Each individual human being develops relational representations as a product of that individual's own activity—perceiving, acting, learning language. In learning the spatial categories that matter in their language, children could either be starting out with a universal set of fundamental categories (Pinker 1994; Jackendoff 1996) from which they select depending on their linguistic environment or learning the linguistic categories without the benefit of pre-existing knowledge. In either case, it is clear that the language being learned has much to do with the course of learning. Work by Bowerman and colleagues (Choi and Bowerman 1992; Bowerman 1996) on the acquisition of spatial terms by children learning different languages makes this clear. For children learning English (and many other languages as well), the ideas of CONTAINMENT and SUPPORT, the ideas conveyed by the words *in* and *on*, seem fundamental and early (Johnston and Slobin 1979). But Korean children seem to make no use of these ideas in any obvious way in learning spatial terms (Choi and Bowerman 1992). The global semantic categories of CONTAINMENT and SURFACE CONTACT/SUPPORT are not expressed in Korean in a transparent way and they are not used by Korean children. Instead, Korean children learn early and readily a distinction between TIGHT and LOOSE FIT, a distinction pertinent to their language. Any account of the development of relational representation must account for this diversity among developmental progressions.

But Korean children seem to make no use of these ideas in any obvious way in learning spatial terms (Choi and Bowerman 1992). The global semantic categories of CONTAINMENT and SURFACE CONTACT/SUPPORT are not expressed in Korean in a transparent way and they are not used by Korean children. Instead, Korean children learn early and readily a distinction between TIGHT and LOOSE FIT, a distinction pertinent to their language. Any account of the development of relational representation must account for this diversity among developmental progressions.

8.3.2. *Fact 2: Object Categories are Easier and Earlier Than Relational Categories*

Children's early vocabularies of their first 50–100 words provide one line of evidence suggesting that object categories are more easily learned than relational categories (see Gentner 1982 and Gentner and Boroditsky in press for reviews and discussion). Indeed, for a long time, object names were considered privileged at the start of word-learning. Certainly common nouns dominate in English-speaking children's early vocabularies; relational terms (verbs and spatial terms) are rare (Nelson 1973; Gentner 1982; Macnamara 1982). The universality of the noun advantage across languages is currently under attack (L. Bloom *et al.* 1993; Gopnik and Choi 1995; Tardif 1996). In particular, it has been suggested that in certain languages, such as Korean (Gopnik and Choi 1995) and Mandarin (Tardif

1996), verbs are as or more prevalent in early vocabularies. There are many controversies in this literature and studies contradicting the claim of a verb advantage in Korean and Mandarin (Gentner 1982; Au, Dapretto, and Song 1994; Tardif 1996). The controversies and ambiguities all revolve around how to measure the words in children's vocabularies. However, the best summary at present is that when proper nouns are included in the counts, the noun advantage over relational terms varies from a 4:1 noun advantage in early vocabulary by some measures in some languages (Au, Dapretto, and Song 1994) to near 1:1 parity by other measures in other languages (Tardif 1996; see Gentner and Boroditsky in press for a more detailed discussion.) All in all, there would seem to be a bias toward learning nouns over relational terms in early word learning, but just as clearly this advantage depends to some degree on the language being learned and on parents' usual means of talking to their children.

The evidence on early vocabularies concerns the words children say without consideration of how they understand them. Stronger evidence for the claim that object concepts are easier and earlier than relational concepts derives not from children's word productions but from their comprehension of common nouns versus relational terms. There is extensive literature in both areas, although they are difficult to compare because of differing methods, ages of subjects, and empirical questions. These differences derive directly from the apparent ease with which children learn object categories as opposed to their difficulty in learning relational categories. The key question for researchers who study early noun acquisition is how it is that children learn so many nouns so rapidly and with so few errors. The only errors consistently studied in this literature are the overextension errors in production typically noticed around the time productive vocabulary growth begins to accelerate. However, these errors may not be category errors per se. Instead, these overextensions (for example, calling a zebra 'doggie') may reflect pragmatic strategies or retrieval errors (Huttenlocher 1974; Gershkoff-Stowe and Smith 1997). Consistent with this idea is the rarity of overextensions in comprehension (see, for example, Naigles and Gelman 1995); if production overextensions result from overly broad representations of noun-meaning categories, those representations should enter into the comprehension of those nouns as well.

In contrast, the key question for researchers who study the acquisition of relational terms is why they are so difficult to learn. The central phenomena are comprehension errors. Long after children begin to use relational terms, when they are as old as three, four, or even five years, their interpretations are full of errors. Preschool children make such mistakes as misinterpreting *in front of* to mean 'near,' *put* to mean 'give,' *higher* to mean 'on top' (Clark, 1971; Gentner 1975; Kuczaj and Maratsos 1975; Johnston and Slobin 1979; Smith, Cooney, and McCord 1986; Bowerman 1994). Simply, common object-categories are for the most part trivially easy for children to acquire whereas relational terms exhibit a protracted and errorful course of development.

This difference is also evident in artificial word-learning studies. In these studies researchers present children with a novel object or event and label it. Children's interpretation of the label is measured by the kinds of other objects to which they generalize the newly learned label. Considerable evidence indicates that by 18 months (and quite possibly before), children systematically generalize novel nouns to new instances that are in the same taxonomic category (Markman 1989; Waxman 1994; L. B. Smith 1995). There are fewer studies of children's generalizations of novel relational terms and most involve children at least three years of age and older. But the results of these studies are markedly different from those concerning object terms. First, young children's judgements are more variable and less systematic (Landau 1996); they sometimes err by interpreting relational terms as labels for one of the objects entering in the relation (Kersten and Smith, submitted; Ryalls, Winslow, and Smith, in press); and they are much more conservative in their generalizations (Tomasello *et al.* 1997).

In sum, one major fact to be explained in developing a theory of relational representations is the relative difficulty in acquiring words to talk about relations as opposed to words to talk about objects.

8.3.3. *Fact 3: Understanding Relations is Dependent on the Specific Objects Entering into Those Relations*

The developmental evidence indicates that there is not some magical point in development at which children become able to use relations. Rather, relational development appears to progress domain by domain—with children understanding relations in domains in which they are knowledgeable and reasoning poorly in domains in which they are relative novices (see Gentner and Rattermann 1994 for a review). Thus, one sees in development the same developmental trend over and over in different domains—first children center on objects, then as they know more about the specific relational domain, they attend to relations presented in known contexts and with known objects, and ultimately, they attend to and/or reason about the relation across diverse kinds of objects and settings. That is, they progress from a more similarity-based to a more abstract understanding of relations within each domain.

This trend, for example, is evident in 4- to 7-month-old babies' attention to the relations of OVER and UNDER. In one study, Quinn (1994) used a familiarization paradigm. This paradigm makes use of the increased attention to novelty of infants. During familiarization trials, the infant is presented repeatedly with stimuli from one category and then on test trials is presented with novel stimuli that are either in that category or not. The reasoning is this: if infants perceive the within-category test stimulus to be like (in the same category as) the familiarization set, then they should find it boring in post-familiarization. In contrast, if infants see the out-of-category test stimulus as unlike (not in the same category

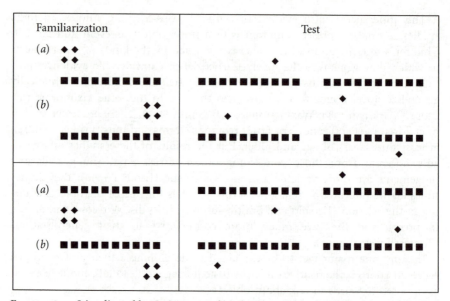

FIGURE 8.7. Stimuli used by Quinn to study infants' notions of OVER and UNDER. The infant is familiarized with patterns like those on the left and then presented patterns like those on the right. The subject should attend more to test stimuli which are perceived as novel

as) the familiarization set, they should show increased attention to this stimulus because it will be perceived as novel. Figure 8.7 (top) shows one familiarization and test set used by Quinn. The infants were repeatedly shown the (*a*) and (*b*) familiarization sets—sets which depict the relation of OVER. On test they were presented four novel test stimuli, two of which also depicted the relation of OVER and two the relation of UNDER.

Quinn found that 4-month-old infants looked longer at the UNDER test set, indicating that they saw these two stimuli as more different from the familiarization stimuli than the OVER test set. Analogously, when infants were presented the familiarization stimuli depicting UNDER (bottom of Figure 8.7), they looked more at test events depicting OVER than test events depicting UNDER. These results show that 4-month-olds, at least in this context, are able to attend to the relations among the line and dots and not to just the individual objects.

In a subsequent study, Quinn *et al.* (1996) varied the shapes of the components of the stimulus displays from familiarization to test. This variation among the objects involved in the relational display disrupted the performance of 4-month-olds. When the objects changed, all the test displays apparently looked new and therefore were attended to. In contrast, older infants, 7-month-olds, looked less at the test displays presenting the same relational configuration and more at the test displays presenting the different configurations even when the component

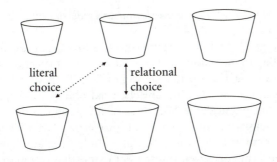

FIGURE 8.8. Stimuli used by Ratterman, Gentner, and DeLoache to study children's understanding of relations. The child's task is to select the object in the lower set which corresponds to the object in the upper set that has been selected by the experimenter

objects in the displays varied. Thus, 7-month olds but not younger infants were able to generalize over different kinds of objects involved in the relation. The developmental trend is from object-centered conservative generalizations to ones apparently based on a more abstract representation of the relation.

Gentner and Rattermann (1991) review a number of other studies of infants' attention to relations that make the same point: attention to relations is at first highly dependent on the objects involved and becomes less so with development. They also review numerous studies of relational concepts and reasoning in much older children that again show the same trend from more object-based relations to more abstract ones. In an unpublished study by Rattermann, Gentner, and DeLoache (cited in Gentner and Rattermann 1991) 3- and 4-year-olds were presented with the following task. The experimenter and child were each given three objects, as illustrated in Figure 8.8. The experimenter selected one from her set as the 'winner' and the child's task was to select the corresponding object. Young children had considerable difficulty choosing relationally and tended to choose the object from their set that matched the experimenters in actual size or in other object properties. However, in a subsequent experiment, it was shown that young children could respond relationally if the task was presented in a domain that they understood—specifically, if the objects in each set were presented as 'the daddy one', 'the mommy one', and 'the baby one'. This result, along with that of a study by Kotovski and Gentner (1996), in which infants were progressively trained to make more and more abstract relational inferences, demonstrates that the developmental change is driven more by experience than by maturation or age.

8.3.4. *Fact 4: Object Properties are Relevant to Understanding Relations*

It is probably a good thing that infants and children begin learning about relations by attending to the objects and context in which they encounter a relation. Consider, for example, real-world instances of CONTAINMENT and SUPPORT. What objects can go 'inside' other objects, what objects can support other objects, and how one physically realizes these relations; all this depends very much on the specific objects and their perceptible properties. Titzer, Thelen, and Smith (1998) recently demonstrated this point in a study of infants understanding of containment and support given transparent or opaque landmarks. The experimental procedure built on an earlier study by Diamond (1990). She showed that infants are more successful in retrieving desired toys from opaque rather than transparent containers. From one perspective, this is a perplexing result: an object in an opaque container cannot be seen and must be remembered, whereas the desired object in a transparent container can be continuously seen. However, from the perspective of a concept of containment, Diamond's results are not surprising. Transparent containers present unique perceptual cues to surfaces and openings. And, indeed, the babies in Diamond's study seemed not to understand where the openings were in the transparent containers as they tried to reach through the transparent surface to retrieve the toy. Titzer *et al.* (1998) tested the idea that specific experience with transparent containers may be essential to successful object-retrieval from such containers. In a two-month training study, they exposed 8-month-old infants to transparent containers; control infants were given opaque containers for the same period. The containers were identical in both cases except for opaqueness and varied in shape and size from small cups to buckets large enough for a baby to put over his or her head or even to sit on. The infants were given no special training; parents were simply asked to give the infants the containers to play with daily for at least 10 minutes over the two-month experiment. When the infants were brought back to the laboratory at ten months and tested in Diamond's procedure, the infants experienced with transparent containers and the control infants performed differently. Specifically, only the infants who had played with transparent boxes knew how to rapidly retrieve objects from transparent boxes. Two months of perceiving and acting on transparent containers taught these infants the unique perceptual cues relevant for containment in a transparent receptacle.

The infants generalized their learning about transparent containers to problems concerning SUPPORT. Titzer *et al.* (1998) tested both the infants trained with transparent containers and those trained with opaque containers on an apparatus known as the 'visual cliff'. This is a highly studied device invented by Gibson and Walk (1960) to test infants' sensitivity to depth cues. In traditional testing, the apparatus is a transparent tabletop that sits over a substantial drop. Infants are placed on the shallow side near the drop and their behaviour is observed. And the traditional result is that 10-month-old infants avoid the cliff and the deep end, crawling away from the visual cliff to a secure position on the shallow side. Titzer *et al.* (1998) observed the infants in the control condition, the ones who had only played with opaque containers, also retreat from the visual cliff, apparently believing—despite the solid transparent surface below them—that they might fall. In contrast, infants trained with the transparent containers acted unlike infants in any other study of the visual cliff; they confidently and happily crawled right over the visual cliff. These infants had apparently learned the visual cues to transparent surfaces and knew what typically developing infants with limited experiences with transparent surfaces do not: solid transparent surfaces support just as do opaque ones. Clearly, real-word experiences and specific object properties matter in understanding SUPPORT and CONTAINMENT in the context of transparency. We suspect that this is the same for understanding of SUPPORT and CONTAINMENT in the context of opacity. The real-world use and recognition of relations requires their grounding in specific object properties.

Indeed, object properties are integral to all spatial concepts. For example, when shown a block on a box while being told 'the block is acorp the box' English speakers interpret *acorp* to mean 'on'. In contrast, when shown a stick on a box, English speakers interpret *acorp* to mean 'across' (Landau 1996). The shape of the trajector and the shape of the landmark matter. The relevance of object properties is also apparent in judgements of containment. Consider, for example, Panels (*a*) and (*b*) in Figure 8.9. Most people judge the apple not to be in the bowl in Panel (*a*) but to be in the bowl in Panel (*b*). An apple on top of other fruit that is contained in a vessel is IN. The relevant properties are not just spatial ones; object categories matter as well. For example, the apple is in the bowl when sitting on other apples but is not in the bowl in Panel (*c*) when sitting on blocks that are in the bowl.

Feist and Gentner (1998) showed in a recent study of adults' judgements of *in* and *on* that the way in which the very same object was categorized determined relational judgement. They varied the curvature of the landmark, as illustrated in Figure 8.10. In some conditions, the displays were unlabelled; in others the trajector was labelled as an animate fly and the landmark as a bowl, plate, or

FIGURE 8.9. Effect of the properties of the trajector and landmark on judgements of a relation. An apple is construed as *in* a vessel when it is supported by other fruit which is in the vessel (*b*) but not when it is not supported by anything in the vessel (*a*) or even when it is supported by objects other than fruit (*c*)

FIGURE 8.10. Stimuli used by Feist and Gentner to study adults' judgements of *in* and *on*. Curvature of the landmark was varied

dish. All variables mattered. Inanimate trajectors were more likely to be judged *in* than animate ones, more curved landmarks yielded more *in* judgements than less curved ones, and labelling the landmark as a bowl rather than as a plate yielded more *in* judgements. Clearly, object labels—not just their spatial properties—matter when adults make relational judgements. Thus, relational development must not consist so much of stripping away all object information, but must instead consist of learning the particular kinds of object properties relevant to particular relations.

8.3.5. *Fact 5. Relational Concepts have a Category Structure*

Other research indicates that relational concepts seem to be like object concepts in having a graded similarity structure. For example, Logan and Sadler (1996) asked adults to rate the goodness of representations such as those shown in Figure 8.11 as instances of the spatial terms *above, below, over, under, left of,* and *right of.* The judgements of the adults were highly organized and consistent, and as shown in Figure 8.12. Various instances of trajector–landmark relatedness are better and worse instances of the concepts.

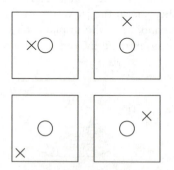

FIGURE 8.11. Stimuli used by Logan and Sadler to study adults' ratings of the goodness of spatial terms. The crosses represent trajectors, the circles landmarks

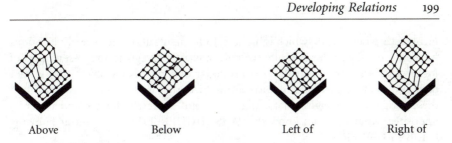

| Above | Below | Left of | Right of |

FIGURE 8.12. Average ratings for *above, below, left of, right of* in Logan and Sadler's goodness rating task

Children's acquisition of relational terms also exhibits a graded category structure. Smith, Cooney, and McCord (1986; see also Ryalls, Winslow, and Smith in press) investigated children's understanding of the words *higher* and *lower*. 3- and 4-year-old children were presented with two objects at a time and asked to indicate 'which is higher?' or on other trials 'which is lower?' The objects were discs about a foot in diameter that were positioned (above the ground) at 1 ft vs. 2 ft, 3 ft vs. 4 ft or 5 ft vs. 6 ft. The results are shown in Figure 8.13. When presented with the discs at the two highest locations (5 ft vs. 6 ft), young children chose correctly when asked, 'which is higher?' but chose incorrectly when asked, 'which is lower?' Conversely, when presented with the discs at the two lowest locations (1' vs. 2'), young children chose correctly when asked, 'which is lower?' but chose

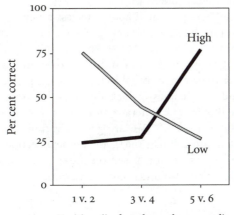

Position (in feet above the ground)

FIGURE 8.13. Children's accuracy in selecting the *lower* or *higher* of two discs placed at different heights (Smith, Cooney, and McCord 1986)

incorrectly when asked, 'which is higher?' Judgements at the mid-height locations were intermediate. These results strongly suggest a categorical representation of *higher* and *lower* in which the best exemplar of *higher* is an object that is very high and the best exemplar of *lower* is an object that is very low. Notice also that these judgements suggest that children do not represent higher and lower as opposites—that they can know that A IS HIGHER THAN B without knowing that B IS LOWER THAN A.

It is not only children's representations that are categorical in this way. In comparative judgement tasks, adults show the same pattern in reaction time that children show in errors (Petrusic 1992). For both children and adults, some instances of a relation are better instances.

8.3.6. *Summary and Implications*

These five facts are not easily alignable with the kinds of relational representations summarized in Table 8.1. What kind of system can develop different relational concepts depending on its linguistic experiences in the world? Why does development go from being more object centered to more relational as a function—not of maturation or age—but of experience with that specific relation? How are the relevant object properties discovered and represented for different relations and how do these yield a graded category structure?

Past approaches all concentrate on the specification of how the objects in a relation are related to one another, and all accomplish this by some explicit relation term (or explicit role name) together with a mechanism for binding the objects to the roles of the relation. But none of these approaches tells us where the relation term or roles come from.

The five empirical facts presented above suggest a new approach, one which seeks an explanation of the substrate and processes out of which relational categories such as ABOVE are formed. At the center of this approach is the question of how specific relation instances are handled. A relation instance is an explicit association of a particular pair of objects, for example, the spatial relation between a book and a table above which the book is suspended. Just as object categories such as BOOK are generalizations over instances of the category, relational categories such as ABOVE are generalizations over instances of the category (see Kersten and Billman 1997). In the next section, we present a new model of relational representation based on these ideas: Gasser and Colunga's Playpen model (Gasser and Colunga 1997; Gasser and Colunga 1998).

8.4. A New Proposal About Relational Representations

We propose that relations are represented in terms of directly accessible relational associations which specify how objects are related to one another in terms of object features and inter-relations associations. In this approach, relation categories are built up from relational feature correlations learned on the basis of relation instances, much as object categories are built up from object feature correlations on the basis of object instances.

8.4.1. *Representing Objects*

Objects are crucial in our account of relations just as they are in all accounts. For our purposes, object instances are cognitive entities (rather than entities in the external world) consisting of values on dimensions such as colour, size, extent, material. Object categories such as BOWL take the form of ranges of values on each dimension. They are developed from repeated experiences with individual instances.

Playpen's representation of objects is illustrated in Figure 8.14. Each rectangle represents the pattern of activation on a single object dimension (for example, vertical extent, horizontal extent, colour). The particular values on these dimensions presented by this single object-instance are indicated by the blackened region. Thus, Figure 8.14a might represent a particular object that is 8 inches tall, 20 inches long, and blue. The presented values on the three illustrated dimensions are associated by the illustrated connections among them. Figure 8.14b illustrates an object category which consists of a range of values (features) on the different dimensions defined by the correlations among features found over multiple instances. Thus, object-feature correlations begin with the inter-value connections that are created (or strengthened) with the presentation of an object instance.

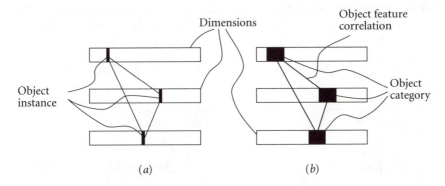

FIGURE 8.14. An object instance (*a*) consists of values on each of a set of dimensions. An object category (*b*) consists of *ranges* of values on the different dimensions defined by the correlations (bold lines) found over multiple instances

8.4.2. *Representing Relations*

When two objects are experienced simultaneously, there is the potential for an explicit connection between features of different objects. An explicit connection between features of different objects is a relation instance. Imagine for example the experience of a small round object on a flat surface. The connection between small and round would be created (or strengthened) within the object instance (and the object category) representation but the connection between small and flat could also be created (or strengthened); this would be a connection between features in different object instance representations. With the presentation of multiple-relation instances with similar values for different dimensions, a relational correlation is created.

Consider first the case of a single dimension. Each of the two objects in a relation instance has a value on that dimension; one object, for example, may be big and the other little. Multiple-relation instances of this sort, if repeated sufficiently, may lead to a one-dimensional relational correlation. Figure 8.15 illustrates a relation instance (left) and a one-dimensional relational correlation (right). For example, the relation instance might be a small object and a large object represented by the specific values on the input dimension, the small object by the white region, for example, and the large object by the black region. If such instances are experienced with regularity, a relational correlation would develop, consisting of the ranges of correlated values, as illustrated on the right. For this kind of a system to work, the relational correlations between distinct objects must be represented in ways that are distinguished from those used to represent the feature correlations presented by a single object instance or object category. We propose that these relational correlations are represented not by simple connections as feature correlations, but by separate micro-relation units (MRUs). In the figures, these units appear as diamonds. Note that these units need have no built-in meaning, but are analogous to units in distributed representations of objects in PDP networks. That is, MRUs take on their significance as the weights connecting them to object feature units and other MRUs evolve in response

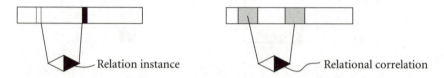

FIGURE 8.15. A relation instance (left) is two objects presented simultaneously. If the values of the two objects along a particular dimension correlate over several relation instances, a one-dimensional relational correlation can be created (right)

to correlations in input events. In this way, the relational meaning of an event is similarity-based and object-based: a generalization across multiple experiences of bundles of object features that co-occur.

With experience, a learner may generalize from narrow regions of values for the two objects as instances of a relation to relative values across the whole dimension. For example, NEAR does not refer to two objects located in a range of specific absolute locations, but rather to the proximity of objects located anywhere. One way to represent such a relation is through the association of more specific absolute relational correlations with each other through a relational category unit, as shown in Figure 8.16 for NEAR. The category unit must point to each of the relational correlations rather than to the correlated values; each relational correlation must thus take the form of an explicit unit rather than a simple connection. Notice that both the correlations and the category unit are MRUs.

As with a single dimension, a learner can generalize from absolute values to relative values across one or more of the dimensions. For example, the knowledge about the relationship between SIZE and LOUDNESS could take the form of the knowledge that relative size, wherever on the size scale, correlates with relative loudness, wherever on the loudness scale. We believe that many familiar spatial relational categories (such as ON) are actually learned in terms of cross-dimensional relational correlations of this type. Thus, for ON, the relative location of the upper and lower boundaries of two objects, which seems to define the relation for us, correlates with the relative size and movability of the objects.

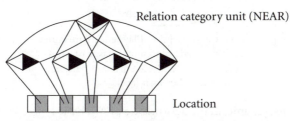

FIGURE 8.16. An example of how a relational category unit can be used to represent a relational category (NEAR) by connecting several units representing specific absolute relational correlations along a dimension (LOCATION)

8.4.3. *Playpen*

In this section we summarize the main features of Playpen, focusing on those that are relevant for this chapter. For technical details see Gasser and Colunga (1998).

8.4.3.1. *Architecture*

Playpen (Gasser and Colunga 1997; Gasser and Colunga 1998) is a connectionist model of the acquisition of word meaning. The network itself is a generalization of a continuous Hopfield network; that is, it consists of symmetrically connected simple processing units which respond by updating their activations when certain units are 'clamped' to a particular input pattern. The long-term knowledge in the network is encoded in the weights on the connections; these are either hard-wired or learned as the network is presented with training patterns.

We divide the units into three layers (Figure 8.17); a VISION layer, a SPATIAL CONCEPTS layer, and a WORDS layer. In our work to date, we have treated the VISION and WORDS layers as input/output layers, and the SPATIAL CONCEPTS layer as a hidden layer. That is, when we present a pattern to the network for training or testing, it is the VISION or WORDS units which are clamped to the values in that pattern, and then it is the VISION and WORDS units which we treat as the network's response to the input pattern. The SPATIAL CONCEPTS units are hidden in the sense that they are not directly accessible 'from the outside' (though we can of course observe their activations as the network runs).

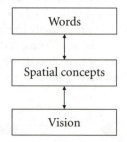

FIGURE 8.17. Basic Playpen architecture. Each rectangle represents a layer of MOUs and/or MRUs and each arrow a pattern of connectivity between layers

As discussed above, units in the network are of two basic types. *Micro-object units* (MOUs) represent primitive features of objects. These are just the familiar processing units in networks of this general type except that in addition to an activation, each has a *phase angle*. Phase angles provide a solution to the *binding problem*; activated MOUs with similar phase angles represent features of a single object. MOUs which are in phase with one another affect each other's activation more strongly—units connected by positive weights tend to attract each other's phase angles, and units connected by negative weights tend to repel them.

Micro-relation units (MRUs) represent features of relations. While each MRU is a single unit in the sense that it has a single activation, it has two separate *micro-roles*, and separate connections from each micro-role to other MOUs and MRUs. Each micro-role has its own phase angle, corresponding to the phase angle of one of the objects that is being related. All else being equal, an MRU tends to be activated to the extent that it receives inputs on its two micro-roles which are maximally out-of-phase—that is, inputs representing two distinct objects.

Relational correlations take the form of connections between MRUs. Each connection is really a pair of connections, mapping the micro-roles of one MRU to those of the other. Positive connections cause one MRU to tend to activate the other and align its phase angles with it. Negative connections cause one MRU to tend to inhibit the other.

8.4.3.2. *Processing*

As noted above, the model is run on a pattern by clamping (fixing the activations and phase angles of) some of the units on the VISION or WORDS layers. The units in the network are then updated repeatedly—that is, their activations and phase angles are updated—until the changes have stabilized. The pattern of activation of the units on the VISION and WORDS layers at this point represents the network's response to the input pattern. Note that the model can be run in both the 'comprehension' and the 'production' directions, or even in combinations of the two, by clamping units on different layers.

8.4.3.3. *Learning*

Weights on the connections joining units are learned as the network is trained on a set of patterns. Learning is through a variant of Hebbian learning, known as *Contrastive Hebbian Learning* (Movellan 1990). Learning takes place in two phases. During the positive phase, an input pattern and the appropriate pattern are both clamped, the network is allowed to stabilize, and the weights are adjusted in proportion to the correlation between the activations of the connected units. During the negative phase, only an input pattern is clamped, the network is again allowed to stabilize, and the weights are adjusted in proportion to the *anti-correlation* between the activations of the connected units. When the patterns have been learned, the two changes cancel each other out because the network's behaviour in the two phases is identical. That is, the network produces the desired output for a given input during the negative phase.

8.4.4. *Simulation*

In this section we illustrate the behaviour of the model with a simple simulation.[1] In this simulation a network learns both inter-MRU correlations across different dimensions and also simple relational categories. The simulation also illustrates how the ease of learning particular words can depend on the match between the words and the relational correlations that the system has already picked up on.

We first defined a set of correlations among non-linguistic dimensions and a

---

[1] For details of this and two other related simulations, see Colunga and Gasser (1998).

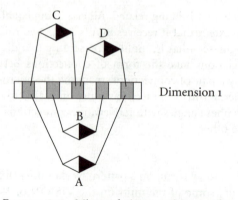

FIGURE 8.18. Micro-relations used in simulation. A, B, C, and D represent possible micro-relations between features within Dimension 1. (Relations on Dimension 2, E, F, G, and H, are not shown. They are isomorphic to the relations on Dimension 1.)

set of correlations between the non-linguistic dimensions and words. There were two non-linguistic dimensions and four possible micro-relations within each of these dimensions. For example, micro-relation A represented a relation between a very low value for one object and a very high value for another object on Dimension 1, and micro-relation E represented a similar micro-relation on Di-

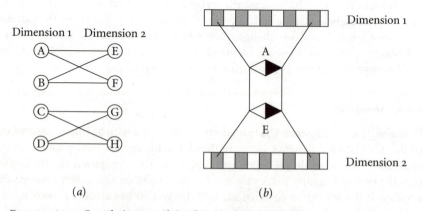

FIGURE 8.19. Correlations used in the simulation. (*a*) The micro-relations on Dimensions 1 and 2 correlate with each other across the dimensions in the two clusters shown. (*b*) Illustration of one of the correlations

mension 2. The micro-relations within Dimension 1 are shown in Figure 8.18. Keep in mind that each micro-relation is a relation between values on a particular dimension for two different objects.

Across the dimensions there were correlations between particular micro-relations. That is, a pair of objects with a particular relation between their values on one dimension tended to have one or another of a set of relations between their values on the other. For example, micro-relation A on Dimension 1 correlated with micro-relations E and F, but not with micro-relations G and H, on Dimension 2. The relational correlations are shown in Figure 8.19*a*. Figure 8.19*b* illustrates one of the correlations, that between micro-relation A on Dimension 1 and micro-relation E on Dimension 2.

We defined two 'languages', an *Easy* language, which agrees with the non-linguistic correlations, and a *Hard* one, which disagrees with the non-linguistic correlations, as shown in Figure 8.20. Each language consists of two relational words. In the figure, the two words are indicated by the boxes with either solid (Word 1) or dashed (Word 2) borders. The two words in the Easy language are indicated by boxes with thick borders (the two vertical boxes); the two words in the Hard language are indicated by boxes with thin borders (the two diagonal boxes). All four words are relational; that is, they represent relations between two separate objects. Each word is associated with a cluster of four possible situations, each characterized by a pairing of a micro-relation on Dimension 1 and a micro-relation on Dimension 2. As can be seen in Figure 8.19*a*, each of these situations corresponds to an actual correlation of micro-relations in the real world. The two languages differ in terms of how these situations are grouped for the two words.

Consider first the choice of one word over the other in the *Easy* language. In this language, Word 1 (the vertical box on the left in Figure 8.20) is associated with situations AE, AF, BE, and BF, whereas Word 2 (the vertical box on the right) is associated with situations CG, CH, DG, and DH. On Dimension 1, dis-

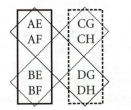

— Easy language
---- Hard language

······· Word 1
— Word 2

FIGURE 8.20. Possible pairings of micro-relations on the two dimensions are associated with one or the other of two words. In the Easy language, the words agree with the non-linguistic correlations; in the Hard language, the words correlate only with micro-relations on Dimension 1

tinct sets of micro-relations are associated with distinct words: A and B for Word 1, C and D for Word 2. Therefore, given a pair of related objects, we can select the appropriate word if we know their relation on Dimension 1 only; for example, objects related by A on Dimension 1 will be referred to with Word 1. The same holds for Dimension 2. E and F are associated with Word 1, G and H with Word 2. Given a pair of objects, we can select the appropriate word if we know their relation on Dimension 2 only. More importantly, each of the two words in this language agrees with the clusters of correlations in the world. Given these correlations and the relation for a pair of objects on Dimension 1, we know something about their relation on Dimension 2, and both of these relations are associated with the same word. For example, if we know that a pair of objects is associated by relation C on Dimension 1, the correlations in the world tell us that those objects are likely to be associated by relation G or H on Dimension 2 (Figure 8.19*a*). But in the Easy language, both of these features of the objects (C on Dimension 1, G or H on Dimension 2) call forth the same word, Word 1. The same holds when we start with the Dimension 2 and predict the value on Dimension 1. Thus the words in the Easy language 'make sense'. They should be relatively easy to learn because they are supported by the correlations in the world; inferences about uncertain values on one or the other dimension only help in the selection of the word.

Now consider the *Hard* language. Word 1 in the Hard language (the solid diagonal box in Figure 8.20), is associated with four possible pairings of relations on the two dimensions: AE, AF, DG, and DH. For Dimension 1, the situation is as with the Easy language. If we know that an input pair of objects has relation D on Dimension 1, we know that Word 1 is the appropriate word. However, unlike for the Easy language, Dimension 2 is of no help in selecting the word. Each word can take all four possible values on Dimension 2. In and of itself, the irrelevance of Dimension 2 for the Hard language does not make the language difficult. The learner could simply come to ignore that dimension and attend only to Dimension 1. On some accounts, this could actually make the learning task simpler. But consider how this language relates to what goes on in the world around the learner. Again, because of the correlations in the world, knowing the relation between a pair of objects on Dimension 1 allows one to make predictions about the relation on Dimension 2. But, unlike for the Easy language, this prediction is of no help; the relation on Dimension 2 is irrelevant for word selection. Similarly, knowing the relation between two objects on Dimension 2 allows predictions to be made about Dimension 1. But for the Hard language, these predictions are of no use; the two relations on Dimension 1 correlated with a relation on Dimension 2 (for example, C and D with G) are associated with different words. Thus the Hard language does not make as much 'sense' as the Easy language because it fails to capitalize on the clusters of correlations occurring in the world. The architecture of the network used in the simulation is shown in Figure 8.21.

The goal of the experiment is to see how the different correlational patterns (both between dimensions and with the words) affect the difficulty of learning the two languages. The network was trained and tested on two different tasks. Training began with a Pre-linguistic Phase in which the task was *Non-linguistic Pattern Completion*. That is, for each trial the network was presented with a pattern on one of the visual dimensions, representing values for two different objects on that dimension, and expected to produce an appropriate pattern on the other, representing the values for those objects on that dimension. (Note that there are always two possibilities for the appropriate pattern.) The network can learn to solve this task using the connections joining the VISION and SPATIAL CONCEPTS layers or the connections between the two SPATIAL CONCEPTS layers. This phase continued for 30 repetitions of the relevant training patterns (epochs). Next, during a Linguistic Phase, Pattern Completion training was discontinued, and the networks were trained on *Production* for seven epochs. For this task, the network was presented with a pattern on the VISION layer, representing the values for two objects on both dimensions, and expected to output a word.

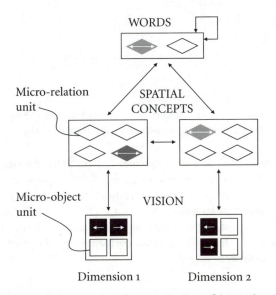

FIGURE 8.21. Network architecture. Micro-object units are represented by squares, micro-relation units by diamonds. Arrows indicate complete connectivity between layers. Each MRU in the SPATIAL CONCEPTS layer is associated with a pair of VISION MOUs. A possible pattern across the network is shown. Darkness indicates activation, and arrow direction indicates relative phase angle

Training in the Linguistic Phase began with weights of 0.0 connecting the SPA-TIAL CONCEPTS to the WORDS units, so the network was initially unable to produce any words.

We predicted that the Easy language would be learned faster than the Hard language during the Production phase because the Easy language categories agreed with the non-linguistic categories. That is, the correlations learned during the Pre-linguistic Phase should support the selection of words in the Easy language but should provide no support for the selection of words in the Hard language.

During the Pre-linguistic Phase, the networks mastered the Pattern Completion task by learning weights between the two Hidden layers representing the non-linguistic correlations. Results for the Linguistic Phase are shown in Figure 8.22, starting with performance after one epoch.

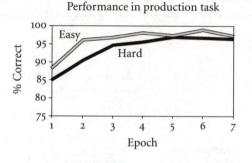

FIGURE 8.22. Results for simulation. The Easy language is learned faster than the Hard language

The data were submitted to a 2 (Language) × 7 (Epoch) analysis of variance for a mixed design. This analysis revealed a main effect of epoch, indicating that the networks get better as they receive more training. More importantly, as predicted, there is a main effect of language ($p < .001$). Thus, as predicted, the Easy language is learned faster than the Hard language, although by the end of the training the two networks have comparable performance. No interactions between language and epoch were found.

8.4.5. *How Playpen Fits the Five Facts*

8.4.5.1. *Language Matters*

In Playpen, language is crucially involved in the learning of spatial concepts. Spatial concepts are learned as the network picks up on correlations between spatial features of pairs of objects in the world. When spatial terms are presented, these take part in the correlations as well. Because spatial terms in different languages correlate differently with spatial features, the particular language being learned will affect the way spatial concepts are learned in the network. Particular correlations in the world may or may not agree with the words being learned, and this can result in two sorts of effects. Words that match the correlations in the world are learned faster than those that do not. When words agree with the values on a particular visual/spatial dimension, the network can use the language to help it process visual scenes, even in ostensibly non-linguistic tasks.

8.4.5.2. *Object Categories are Easier and Earlier than Relational Categories*

Learning a category in Playpen means learning the correlations among a set of features. For both objects and relations, this presupposes the preprocessing required for extracting the features, for example, for detecting the edges that are the boundaries of objects. For the learning of an object category all that is then required is that two or more object features be activated simultaneously. The co-occurrence of a particular texture and a particular colour may be the beginning of a category such as YOGURT. For the learning of a relational category, there must also be a set of activated units, in this case relation units, but now there is the additional constraint that the phase angles of the corresponding micro-roles of the relation units match one another. That is, the relation units need to have been activated in response to the features of two objects, which the system must have distinguished from one another.

Note that the network can treat a scene consisting of more than one object as a single object, activating object units and learning feature correlations, but learning nothing relational about the scene because no relation units have been activated.

Because they do not presuppose the object segregation that is required for the learning of relational categories, object categories are easier and earlier than relational categories in Playpen.

The fact that each relation unit brings together two features or sets of features also means that, all else being equal, more relation units than object units are required to cover the space of possibilities. Thus, given the same amount of resources in the network for objects and relations, the space will be covered more sparsely by relation units. This should lead to slower learning of relations.

8.4.5.3. *Understanding Relations is Dependent on the Specific Objects Entering into Those Relations*

Learning in Playpen, as in neural networks in general, starts from specific instances. For objects, the first (weak) correlations that are learned correspond to individual objects or small sets of objects—a particular cup or the three cups most often presented. Only after the presentation of a number of exemplars does the pattern of connectivity come to reflect the more general associations we expect for categories such as CUP. This does not mean that specific associations are lost; as long as the network continues to be presented frequently with specific cups, those cups will continue to exist as 'micro-categories' within the network.

For relations the same context-specificity applies, but now it is the specific objects entering into the relation that are relevant. Given repeated presentation of the same doll in the same basket, the network's early representation of CONTAINMENT will be specific to that doll and that basket. When the basket is presented with different dolls in it, the relational concept becomes more general in one way. When different baskets are presented, it becomes more general in another way. Only after considerable variation among both the container and the contained objects would the network come to represent the set of associations characterizing CONTAINMENT (if ever). But the more specific subtypes of CONTAINMENT would not be lost.

Thus, in their development and in their endstate, relations in Playpen are bound to the specific objects that were presented during training.

8.4.5.4. *Object Properties are Relevant to Understanding Relations*

Rather than directly associating full-blown objects, relation units in Playpen associate the features of two objects. Relations in Playpen can therefore 'look into' their component objects in a way that is not possible in approaches where the components of relations are essentially symbolic, labels representing already categorized objects.[2] In the learning of the SUPPORT relation, for example, the shape and even the colour of the supported object is potentially relevant to the relational associations that develop in Playpen, but this is independent of how the supported object is categorized by the system, that is, what word unit it turns on.

However, because relational categories involve correlations of all sorts, the categories of the component objects may also be relevant. If the objects in a spatial relation instance are categorized by the network (that is, they activate category label units), these categories may play a role in the particular relation units that are activated, just as primitive object features are.

8.4.5.5. *Relational Concepts Have Category-Structure*

In Playpen, both object categories and relational categories have a graded similarity structure. As in other neural networks, a category *is* the instances that make it up. When an instance is presented, it results in changes in the weights between units representing correlations between features. Each of these weights is the combined result of all of the instances the network has seen, and each category is realized as a pattern of weights among a number of units. When a new object is presented to the network, it activates object units. To the extent that these units are strongly associated with others through a pattern of learned weights, the

---

[2] Note, however, that the approach we are proposing does not exclude a representational system in which the primitive features of objects are built into the system and each input object unit has an inherent meaning and each relation unit associates a fixed set of these object units.

object is a good instance of the category represented by those weights and will tend to activate the category label unit.

In the same way, relation instances are better or worse instances of relational categories to the extent that they activate the relation units which are associated with others through the learned weights that make up the relational category. A network trained on instances of HIGHER in which one object is far from the other will fail to activate the HIGHER unit when presented with two objects which are close together.

8.5. Concluding Discussion

In this chapter we have adopted a very different perspective on the relationship between language and spatial cognition than have the other authors in this book. We have focused on the *emergence* of relations and language rather than the end-state. In doing so, we have been concerned with the very nature of relations and have presented an account of the 'stuff' out of which relations are constructed. We believe that this groundwork is essential if we are to understand the fully-fledged adult system because we believe the adult system is the product of more of the same sort of process we have proposed for the early emergence of relations, the learning of more and more abstract relational correlations.

In taking this low-level, developmental approach, we have ignored most of the data that are of interest to the other authors in the book, data that have led people such as Jackendoff to posit separate representational modules for spatial concepts, conceptual representations, and language, as well as interface modules connecting them. Thus it should not be surprising that the picture we offer is considerably simpler than the one offered by others. In a sense our picture is one in which WORDS and VISION are mediated by a single 'interface module', which we have called SPATIAL CONCEPTS, a layer of micro-object and micro-relation units which is simultaneously under the influence of units in the WORDS and VISION layers.

However, we are aware that the mapping from visual/spatial representations to words and syntax is not a simple one. The SPATIAL CONCEPTS layer in our model is not meant to be taken as a layer of completely connected relation units and object units. Rather we expect this layer in the adult system to consist of multiple sublayers, each performing some form of transformation on the patterns it receives from above or below, each connected to its neighbours by an 'interface' in the form of a simple pattern of connectivity. As yet we have nothing specific to say about the ultimate internal structure of the SPATIAL CONCEPTS layer nor about how much of this structure is built in and how much develops as spatial categories and words are learned. The point is that our proposals are not incompatible with accounts in which different levels of representation reside in different architectural layers. Our contribution to the question of the putative modules and interfaces joining visual and linguistic representations is twofold. (1) The modularity may be a matter of degree; that is, the representations may simply be more and more linguistic (under the influence of words and syntax) as they appear closer to the strictly linguistic portion of the neural network and more and more visual (under the influence of specifically visual patterns) as they appear closer to the visual portion of the network. (2) Modularity (to whatever degree) can *develop*, and the interface between language and vision is a place where we might expect this. Therefore, a major goal should be elucidating the mechanisms by which development takes place in response to the visual and linguistic patterns it is exposed to.

Spatial cognition and spatial language are fundamentally relational. In fact, given the importance of space in the young child's world, space may be the place to look for the emergence of relational knowledge. A range of well-attested data are consistent with the view that we have proposed: relational categories, like object categories, take shape as the child picks up on the rich set of correlations available to her in the world and in language, and, like object categories in neural network models, they are built up of primitive connectionist units.

9

Temporal Bounds on Interfaces

JON M. SLACK

The cognitive architecture implemented in the brain is built on a common neural platform and it can be argued that the nature of the human cognition is heavily determined by the characteristics of its computational foundations. This chapter promotes this view by deriving some of the structural properties of language from the assumption that the brain's cognitive subsystems employ a common currency of representations based on distributed patterns, or vectors. The derivation focuses on a neural network implementation of the computational architecture proposed within Chomsky's Minimalist program. Each syntactic object generated by the computational procedure must have both synchronic (defined at the same time) and diachronic (defined over time) components. The constituent tokens of anti-symmetric relations can only be differentiated by their type and this leads to a bound on synchronically tokened structure that emerges within language as the characteristic features of phrasal structure. The two key levels of linguistic representation, Phonetic Form and Logical Form, are shown to employ different distributions of synchronic and diachronic components, with Logical Form being more dependent on synchronic representations.

9.1. Introduction: The Architecture of Language

Language is sound with meaning—this traditional view of language underlies the architecture of the human language faculty as proposed in Chomsky's (1995) most recent theoretical framework, the Minimalist program. Within this approach, the language system is regarded as interfacing with both the articulatory–perceptual system (the sound part), and the conceptual–intentional system (the meaning part). Each interface comprises a level of representation; Phonetic Form (PF) at the sound interface and Logical Form (LF) at the meaning interface. A linguistic expression thus consists of a pair of objects, (π, λ), where π is the PF representation of the expression and λ is the LF representation. The system that generates these objects, the language system, comprises a lexicon and a computational procedure, denoted C_{HL}, that computes the PF and LF of a generated linguistic expression, as shown in Figure 9.1. Chomsky (1995) conceptualizes C_{HL} as a mapping from an array of elements selected from the lexicon to a pair (π, λ), a procedure that recursively builds syntactic objects out of elements from the lexical array and already formed syntactic objects. The derivation of an expression is complete when a syntactic object is created corresponding to the pair (π, λ).

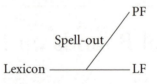

FIGURE 9.1. The architecture of C_{HL}

A basic assumption of Chomsky's approach is that an architecture of the sort shown in Figure 9.1 must underlie the human language faculty and must, therefore, be implemented in the brain. However, it is not clear to what extent the basic tenets of Chomsky's theory (1995) are compatible with the types of computational processes that characterize the higher cognitive centres in the brain. In particular, the neural machinery that instantiates language within the brain is likely to process representations which are quite different in form from the syntactically-structured symbols posited by linguists. In connectionist networks, or brain-style modelling, mental representations correspond to distributed patterns over sets of units enabling different patterns to be superposed on the same set of units.[1] In some models, the distributed representations correspond to patterns of activation across the units, while in other models, they correspond to the patterns of weights on connections. In either case, the patterns are formalized as vectors, or points in a vector space, V. Some connectionists have argued that mental representations are specified on two levels; they have the abstract structure characteristic of complex, syntactically-structured objects, but are realized physically as distributed patterns over networks of neurons (Smolensky 1988).[2]

In this chapter, I want to explore whether or not anything interesting can be derived from the assumption that Chomsky's theoretical framework captures something important about the way language is represented and processed in the brain. To achieve this I need to make some assumptions about the way in which cognitive architecture, of which the language system forms a part, relates to brain structures. The key assumptions are that both language processing and brain structures are modular (Fodor 1983) and that some form of one-to-one correspondence exists between the two (localization). Language processing can be functionally decomposed and Chomsky's architecture suggests one such decomposition. Similarly, at one level of description, the brain can be analyzed

---

[1] Connectionist models have employed various representational schemes, but only distributed, superpositional representations differ in a fundamental way from classical symbolic representations.

[2] This view of mental representations is tantamount to the implementational connectionism position that regards neural networks as the computational medium in which classical symbolic processing runs (Pinker and Prince 1988).

into interconnected modules. The form of the modules depends on the chosen level of description. I shall focus on the level of neural networks. At this level, the brain is viewed as a collection of neurons which are interconnected to form a massively complex network comprising subnetworks, subsubnetworks, and so on. Each network computes an input–output function and the localization assumption requires the elemental modules of language to be localized in the brain as neural networks computing elemental input–output functions.

My other key starting assumption is that distributed patterns, or vectors, are the common currency of the brain's networks, at least, those associated with language. That is, the neural networks that implement our language capacities communicate through passing vectors. These vectors must correspond in some meaningful way to the modular functionality Chomsky proposes for language. If this is not the case, then my explorations will lead nowhere. Specifically, PF and LF must be vectors that are generated by the neural network that instantiates C_{HL} and passed to the networks implementing the articulatory–perceptual and conceptual–intentional systems, respectively. I want to explore the extent to which the properties of the language system can be derived from the properties of the underlying neural hardware. To do this I shall focus on the network, C_{HL}, that maps an array of vectors encoding lexical elements onto a pair of vectors corresponding to (π, λ). To give you some idea of where all this might be leading, one of the main conclusions is that π is a complex object, or vector, whose structure unfolds over time, whereas λ is a complex object in which the constituents are encoded as synchronically defined chunks.

9.2. Diachronic Structure and PF

At the heart of the classical explanation of human language is a compositional operator that creates complex syntactic objects from simpler ones—in Chomsky's framework this is the Merge operator (1995). The operator is applied recursively to the array of lexical elements and partially constructed syntactic objects to form more complex objects. Clearly, a neural network instantiating C_{HL} must implement some form of compositional mechanism of this type. So I want to begin by considering how neural networks might compose and encode linguistic strings.

A number of connectionist researchers have proposed equivalent forms of compositionality functioning on neural networks (Hinton 1990; Smolensky 1990; Pollack 1990). As an example, consider Pollack's (1990) SRAAM (Sequential Recursive Auto-Associative Memory) encoding of symbol strings. A string such as 'wxyz' can be characterized as a left-branching tree $(((((\#w)x)y)z)$, where # denotes an empty string. The network is based on two mechanisms, a compressor, and a reconstructor. A vectorial representation is first assigned to each atomic symbol in the string. The compressor encodes the tree from the bottom up by merging the vectors of two constituents to form a new pattern over a fixed-size vector that represents the resulting composite object. For example, the vectors encoding # and w are merged to generate a new vector R_1 of the same fixed size. To encode arbitrarily long strings the compressor is applied recursively merging R_1 with the pattern for x to form R_2, and so on, through the string finally generating R_4 that encodes the complete string. The reconstructor operates in the opposite direction, decomposing vectors into their constituent patterns—R_4 would decompose into R_3 and the pattern for z, for example. The SRAAM architecture provides a method for building vector representations of complex structured objects from the representations of their constituents and has a reliable operation for decomposing such representations.

The problem with this method of encoding complex objects is that vectors do not support co-tokening (Fodor and Pylyshyn 1989; Fodor and McLaughlin 1990). This problem relates to a key distinction in any theory of cognitive representations, the type/token distinction, originally introduced by Peirce (1958). As this distinction is generally understood, types are abstract entities and tokens are concrete instantiations of types. For example, in the sentence *My dog ate my dinner* there are two 'my's, each corresponding to an individual constituent of the sentence. On the other hand, as Peirce claimed, there is a sense in which the English language contains just one word *my*. The two *my*s in the sentence are concrete realizations, or tokens, of the English word *my* which is itself an abstract entity, or type. The distinction applies not only to the words of a language but to all forms of representational elements. When a complex object is encoded as a vector, the object's constituent structure is not apparent within the pattern. That is, the vector token for the complex object does not comprise tokens of its constituents. For example, the vector tokens assigned to λ and w are not discernable within the vector R_1. This inaccessibility of constituent tokens has been identified by Fodor and his colleagues (Fodor and Pylyshyn 1989; Fodor and McLaughlin 1990) as a reason for dismissing distributed representations as an adequate representational basis for cognition. This is because in the classical explanation of cognition, processes are sensitive to the structure of representations and so the structure must be accessible to them. As a classical framework, the same argument would hold in Chomsky's architecture. The PF and LF vectors are interpreted within the articulatory–perceptual system and the conceptual–intentional system, respectively, and the structure they encode would need to be accessible to these systems. However, Butler (1995) has argued convincingly that connectionist representations have their structure laid out in time rather than in space. This suggests that PF and LF might be complex objects encoded in both space and time in the brain.

9.2.1. *Synchronic and Diachronic Objects*

Butler's (1995) argument draws on the distinction between synchronic and diachronic structure. Synchronic structure is characterized as being defined in parallel, that is, all the structural elements, along with their configuration, are present at the same time. Complex syntactically structured symbols, for example, are synchronic in that their syntactic constituents are regarded as being present, or accessible, in parallel. In contrast, the structure of a complex event is diachronic in that it is laid out in time. Butler (1995) has suggested that, while it is difficult to identify the synchronic structure of connectionist representations, the constituents implicit in such representations can be differentiated diachronically in the temporal and causal history of a network's patterns of activation.

An immediate problem with this distinction relates to the definition of synchronic. The meaning of the phrase *at the same time* is open and dependent on a chosen level of temporal resolution. However, in the context of neural networks, it can be given a more precise meaning in terms of the distinction between the states of a network, and the network's state-space, defined as the set of all possible sequences of states the network might achieve. Synchronic structure must be defined within a state of a network, while diachronic structure is defined over the state-space. Butler argues that the constituents of a 'complex' connectionist representation can be identified within the state-space of a network even though they may not be simultaneously identifiable within any given state.

As concrete entities, tokens must occupy unique space-time locations. Accordingly, the constituent tokens of synchronic structures, that is, synchronic tokens, occupy unique spatial locations, as their temporal position must be the same by definition. In contrast, diachronic tokens can occupy the same spatial location but at unique points in time. A vectorial encoding of a complex structured object cannot support differentiated synchronic tokens, and hence, co-tokening, because the spatial extent of a distributed pattern is unarticulated. Thus, by definition, a vector corresponds to an individual synchronic token. However, synchronic tokens are differentiated within the state of a network as it necessarily distinguishes the input and output vectors of the function it computes. For example, the SRAAM compressor network differentiates two inputs and an output, and as the input–output function is applied recursively both input and output vectors are defined over the same vector space.

Armed with these key distinctions, I want to consider again the SRAAM encoding of strings. The architecture of the network is based on the fact that symbolic strings can be generated by linear grammars with productions of the form A→ωB and A→ω where A and B are strings and ω is a terminal symbol or a string of such symbols. The first production expresses the fact that a string can be decomposed into its first element followed by the rest of the string. The SRAAM network instantiates these productions within the synchronic–diachronic distinction in that A and B are diachronic objects, whereas ω is a synchronic object. To demonstrate why, I shall focus on the reconstructor mechanism such that A corresponds to the input vector, ω to the output vector encoding the first string element, and B to the output vector encoding the rest of the string. As A is recursively decomposed, successive synchronic tokens are instantiated in the ω output slot. They are synchronic tokens because as terminal elements they cannot be further decomposed. As a form of functional compositionality (van Gelder 1990), the network 'unpacks' composed vectors into their constituent vectors and, within any given state, two output vectors are tokened that are differentiated by their type. The ω output vector is a terminal, or synchronic token, while the **B** output vector is a diachronic object that can be further decomposed.

The SRAAM network composes a diachronic object, encoded as a vector, whose structure unfolds over time, that is, as the successive states of the network. In this way, the network preserves the order of the elements in a linguistic string encoded as a non-differentiable token. This type of vector token is compatible with the requirements of the articulatory–perceptual system and would seem to be a perfect candidate for the PF vector. The articulatory system might incorporate SRAAM reconstructor networks that could 'unpack' the PF vector and pass the successive synchronic tokens to networks that translate them into patterns of articulation. However, it is questionable whether the LF vector encodes an equivalent diachronic object.

9.3. Synchronic Structure and LF

Chomsky has argued that the ordering of linguistic elements is irrelevant to LF, as evidenced below:

There is no clear evidence that order plays a role at LF or in the computation from N to LF. [. . .] It seems natural to suppose that ordering applies to the output of Morphology, assigning a linear (temporal, left-to-right) order to the elements it forms. [. . .] If correct, these assumptions lend further reason to suppose that there is no linear order in the N→LF computation, assuming that is has no access to the output of Morphology.   (Chomsky 1995: 334–5)

In this quote, N refers to the numeration specified on the array of chosen lexical elements that forms the starting point for the generation of a linguistic expression. In generating LF from N, the C_{HL} must encode significant relationships between elements of N. After all, the cognitive–intentional system is interested in who did what to whom and this requires the appropriate predicate–argument relations to be encoded in the LF vector. However, these relationships are not going to be captured through the simple temporal ordering of the lexical elements. The cognitive–intentional system needs to 'unpack' vectors that synchronously token relationships between constituents. Is this a problem for neural networks or not?

To realize the potential problems, consider the SRAAM reconstructor network again but this time implementing the alternative interpretation of ω as a synchronic string of more than one element. This would require a network with multiple output vectors for differentiating the terminal elements such as the network shown in Figure 9.2. In this figure, both ω_1 and ω_2 are terminal vectors, and as such, synchronic tokens. The problem is, how would the network distinguish the ω-string $\omega_1\omega_2$ from the string $\omega_2\omega_1$? The general problem characterized here is that of individuating synchronic token vectors. In Figure 9.2, the terminal outputs are not differentiated by the topology of the network—we could transpose the output connections and the output would be unchanged. On the other hand, the network's topology does differentiate the B output from the ω-string because of the feedback loop required for implementing recursion. Thus, in recursive networks, only two output or input vectors can be individuated, the ω-vector and the B-vector.

This would seem to be a very serious bound on synchronic token individuation, so is there any way of getting around it? A general solution would be to find a way to index the individual vector tokens just as the elements of the ω-string are individuated by numerical indices. Such indices would, of course, have to be realized as vectors, as they are the only representational elements available. A way of binding the index vectors to the output or input vectors would also have to be implemented. This is variable-binding in a slightly different guise and the problems of 'cross-talk' are well documented (Pinker and Prince 1988; Shastri and Ajjanagadde 1993). If a workable binding system can be identified that allows multiple individuated, that is, indexed, synchronic vector-tokens to be realized, then the computational nature of neural networks should not restrict the form of LF, and hence, language, in any way. However, the current state of connectionist research would suggest that the term 'multiple, indexed, synchronic vector-tokens' is an oxymoron. Neural networks can bind index vectors to other vectors but multiple bindings cannot be tokened synchronously by a single network. The only other possible solution to the problem of individuating synchronic vector-tokens is to differentiate them by their type.

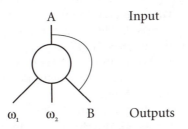

FIGURE 9.2. A neural-network architecture for composing/decomposing 'complex' vectors

9.3.1. *Type Theory and Representations*

A theory of types imposes an organization upon the set of objects posited within a given computational system (see, for example, Mendelson 1987). In type theory, types are defined either as basic in that they cannot be analysed into more fundamental types or constructed. The latter types are generated from basic types through the application of constructors such as function space and product space. Applying these concepts to neural networks requires certain representational types to be classed as basic; these are the types that can be considered as primitive representational elements. In the N→LF computation, lexical elements are specified as basic and as such can only be generated by a scheme of enumeration. The enumerated set corresponds to the listing of the lexical entries. In the implementation domain of neural networks, vectors are considered a basic type and their enumerated set comprises the vector space, V. All other representational types derived within the N→LF computation must be functions defined over these basic types.

A type scheme consists of a hierarchy of levels of types. At the first level are the basic types, type (o), in this case, comprising lexical elements in the content domain and vectors in the implementation domain. At the next level of a functional hierarchy are the functional types, which take the lower level types as variables, type level (o→o).[3] Thus, in type theory, if a and b are types, then so is (a→b), which stands for functions taking an argument of type a and returning a result of type b. The two basic types, denoted LEX (lexical items) and v (vectors) support the functional type, (LEX→v), which assigns vector values to the lexical elements. A crucial property of this mapping is that it is faithful which means that it is one-to-one where no item lexical element maps onto the zero vector. This property ensures that the mapping is invertible allowing 'simple' vectors in the codomain of (LEX→v) to be interpreted within the language domain.

We can apply the same ideas to the SRAAM network, which encodes strings of lexical elements as diachronic objects. In this case, arbitrarily complex objects are generated through the recursive composition of vectors implementing simpler objects. The input–output function of the network instantiates a form of functional compositionality, denoted *cf*, and its type is ((v→v)→v), such that the function is faithful so that a complex vector can be decomposed back into its constituent vectors, (v→?v→v)). This is also the type of diachronic objects. Thus, we have two functional types, (LEX→v) and diachronic objects, and no other types can be constructed at this point. This type scheme formalizes the basic conclusion stated above that recursive networks individuate, at most, two input/output vector tokens synchronously.

The type scheme seems to get us no further in overcoming the bound on individuating synchronous tokens. However, more functional types can be

---

[3] In general, the functional types at a given level of the hierarchy take lower level types as variables.

constructed by increasing the number of basic types. This would be necessary in any case in order for LF to encode relationships. LF encodes significant relationships between constituents, including lexical elements. The relations are not lexical elements, but they must be explicitly encoded as vectors as they cannot be implicit to the neural networks. Thus, a new basic type, REL, needs to be defined which allows the functional type, (REL→v), to be constructed. But where does the type, REL, come from?

9.3.2. *Kayne's Linear Correspondence Axiom (LCA)*

Linear order plays little part in Chomsky's formalization of phrase structure (1995). However, he has suggested that Kayne's ideas on linear order (1993, 1994) can be successfully incorporated into the Minimalist program (1995). Kayne has suggested that a precise relationship holds between dominance and linear order in well-formed phrase structures. The relationship is referred to as the linear correspondence axiom and can be expressed as (1).

(1)   Asymmetric c-command imposes a linear ordering on the terminal elements of a well-formed phrase marker.

To clarify the concept of asymmetric c-command, consider the phrase marker shown in (2). Let me begin by reminding you of the relation of c-command. In (2), the node W c-commands the node N and all the nodes that N dominates, because every node that dominates W also dominates N, but W does not itself dominate N. Given this definition, it is clear that N also c-commands W, which means that c-command is symmetric.

(2) A phrase marker consistent with the LCA

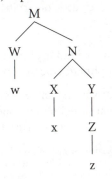

Kayne's crucial insight is that because linear order is an antisymmetric relation the key dominance relation is asymmetric c-command. In (2) W c-commands X but X does not c-command W, hence an asymmetric c-command relation holds between them. In fact, W asymmetrically c-commands X, Y, and Z, and X asymmetrically c-commands Z. These asymmetric relations holding between the non-terminals impose a linear order on the terminals, w, x, and z, that they dominate. Kayne's bold claim is that this correspondence between asymmetric c-command and the linear ordering of the terminals characterizes all well-formed phrase markers. The argument to be made here is that Kayne's LCA is an accurate descriptor of phrase markers which derives from a fundamental property of neural networks that requires order to be used to encode significant relationships at LF.

The LCA is an axiom of Kayne's theoretical framework from which he derives some of the key properties of phrase structure as delineated within X-bar theory. This theory describes the structure common to all natural language phrases and is regarded as a component of UG (Jackendoff 1977; Chomsky 1986b). As such, it was taken as primitive within syntactic theory, but it has recently been stripped down to its most essential form within the Minimalist program (Chomsky 1995). According to the theory, phrasal constituents are built upon a central structure based on a head item, X, that fixes the type of the phrase, XP.[4] For example, NPs are headed by nouns. In addition, the theory specifies how a 'head' relates to its complements (the arguments of the phrase) and its specifiers (the elements that 'front' and modify the phrase). This skeletal structure, re-ferred to as an X-bar skeleton, becomes instantiated by assigning values to the 'head', 'complement', and 'specifier' roles. The most important features of the standard version of the theory (Stowell 1981) are:

- a phrase must be headed but cannot have more than one 'head';[5]
- a phrasal structure comprises a hierarchy of phrasal constituents, X, X', X", such that, for English, X' is the constituent comprising X followed by its com-plements, and X" is the constituent comprising a specifier followed by X'.[6] In addition, the X' constituent permits recursion allowing it to accommodate, for example, strings of prenominal adjectives and relative clauses of arbitrary length;
- a phrase can have no more than one 'specifier';
- only maximal projections can appear as non-head terms within a phrase;
- only information relating to the 'head' is accessible to phrasal constituents.

Different versions of X-bar theory have been proposed, varying in terms of (i) the number of phrasal levels (Jackendoff 1977; Kornai and Pullum 1990), (ii) whether nodes have binary or multiple branching (Kayne 1984), (iii) the

---

[4] For English, X can correspond to the lexical classes noun, verb, adjective, or preposition. It can also include functional categories such as tense, aspect, complementizer, and so on (Chomsky 1986b).

[5] In linguistics, the property that a phrase can have only one head is controversial. For example, the syntactic categories N (noun) and Det (determiner) are both unique to NPs and could thus function as heads of the phrase. Abney (1987) has argued that each category is a head generating its own phrase, that is, an NP and a DetP, respectively. An alternative analysis by Ernst (1991) argues for N being the head of an NP and Det being a specifier rather than a head. The derivation of X-bar theory to be proposed clarifies what it means for a head to be unique within a phrase.

[6] In some versions of the theory a X''' constituent has been proposed (Jackendoff 1977), but the existence of such a constituent remains controversial. The present derivation of the theory rules out this possibility.

number of heads for a given phrase (Dryer 1992), and (iv) whether or not both lexical and functional categories can head phrases (Chomsky 1986*b*). Kayne (1993) derives the first four of the above listed components of X-bar theory from the LCA but in doing so he is forced to modify the X-bar hierarchy such that a head with its complements constitutes the maximal projection, XP, and specifiers are viewed as a form of adjunct. According to this version of X-bar theory, the two phrase decomposition rules are as shown in (3), where YP and ZP are maximal projections.

(3) XP → YP XP &
     XP → X ZP

Kayne's (1993) key insight into the nature of syntax is his identification of asymmetry as a fundamental property. The property is also fundamental to Chomsky's stripped-down version of X-bar theory as embodied in his definition of Merge (1995). The complex object created by Merge(α, β), K = {H(K), {α, β}}, differentiates the operands by projecting the head of one of them as the label of the new object. This asymmetry underlies the X-bar property of 'headedness'. What I want to argue is (*a*) that 'headedness' is essentially an asymmetric property required to differentiate the operands of a binary operator and (*b*) that Kayne's asymmetric c-command reflects the same underlying characteristic.

In Kayne's analysis, the problem of symmetry is that sister nodes cannot be differentiated. In (2), the nodes W and N can only be ordered if they can first be differentiated. However, asymmetric c-command can be re-interpreted as differentiating the sisters by type, where one sister is a synchronous, or terminal, type and the type of the other is diachronic object. In other words, Kayne's analysis is consistent with my main argument that recursive networks implementing C_{HL} differentiate only two input/output vector tokens within a given state. Moreover, his work suggests that linear order may be the source of the REL type that is missing in the N→LF computation.

In some languages, for example Japanese, predicate–argument relations are indicated by case affixes, and this requires REL to be an explicit type within the N→LF computation. In the absence of such an explicit type, order is the only other type of relational information available within C_{HL} in that it is implicitly encoded within PF. To encode synchronic relationships requires the order relations implicit in PF to be encoded explicitly as vectors. The key characteristics of linear order relations is that they are antisymmetric and arbitrarily complex relations can be generated through the composition of simple relations holding between adjacent elements. For example, a relation such as SUCCESSOR_OF, denoted a, can be defined over the elements in PF and complex relations can be derived through building chains of this simple relation—SUCCESSOR_OF (SUCCESSOR_OF( )), denoted aa. Given that REL is the type of *a*, we can now define the simple functional type, (REL→v), that assigns a vector value to *a*.

9.3.3. *A Bound on Synchronic Structure*

A neural network can encode structural relationships by composing two argument vectors and a relation vector of the type (REL→v). However, for anti-symmetric relationships to be defined, the argument vectors must be of different types. Anti-symmetry can be defined only on individuated token vectors requiring them to be differentiated by their type. One argument must be of the type (LEX→v) and is referred to as the head of the relationship, denoted X. The other argument must be a complex vector, as this is the only other type available within the network, referred to as X_{com}. Arbitrarily complex relationships can be encoded by composing relation vectors through applying *c* to the type (REL→v) producing the type in (4).

(4) *cf*[REL→v]: (((REL→v)*cf*[RELv]) *cf*[REL→v])

Arbitrarily complex structural relationships can now be defined with the type in (5).

(5) (((X_{com}→(LEX→v)) *cf*[REL→v])→v)

This latter type can be implemented as a neural network with the structure depicted in Figure 9.3.

In this network, the two sets of feedback connections, the two loops, support the recursive generation of complex vectors, in one case encoding several instances of X_{com}, and in the other, complex chains of relations, *cf*[REL→v]. A chain of relations is composed via one loop to create a *cf*[REL→v], which is then composed with an X and a X_{com} to create an order relationship. This type of network can be implemented in terms of RAAMs (Pollack 1990) or networks based on tensor product operators (Smolensky 1990). Regardless of the precise form of the network, the key idea it realizes is that synchronic structure is bounded by the limited number of input/outputs instantiated within the state of the network. Complex structure can be laid out in time through recursive composition and decomposition, but synchronic structure is limited to the types shown in Figure 9.3. However, an additional encoding operation, superposition, allows multiple relationships to be defined relative to the same head and superposed to form a complex vector (Hinton 1990; Pollock 1990; Smolensky 1990; Shastri and Ajjanagadde 1993). Both composition and superposition operators generate complex vectors from simpler ones, but superposition can be defined within the state of a network as it does not require the recursion (Slack 1994). Moreover, composition operators are invertible while superposition is not reversible, although superposed vectors can be regarded as being synchronously addressable. Most importantly, composition is distributive over superposition. This means that (6) holds.

(6) $v_1 \otimes v_2 \oplus v_1 \otimes v_3 = v_1 \otimes (v_2 \oplus v_3)$

where $\otimes$ and $\oplus$ denote the operations of composition and superposition, respec-

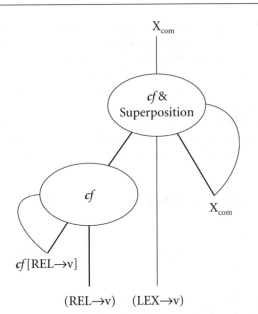

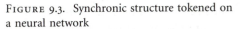

FIGURE 9.3. Synchronic structure tokened on
a neural network

tively, and v_1–v_3 are vectors. This property is particularly important in explaining
the nature of synchronic structure. The limits on differentiating input/output
tokens within the state of a network imposes a severe bound on synchronic
structure. The limit relates to the number of types that can defined as inputs/
outputs. Figure 9.3 shows only four types, namely, (LEX→v), X_{com}, (REL→v),
and cf[REL→v]. These four types are generated from the three basic types, and
because REL is a type of anti-symmetric relations each input/output must be of
a unique type for them to be differentiated. Thus, synchronic structure comprises the order relationship holding between a simple and a complex constituent. However, many such relationships can be encoded relative to the same
simple constituent and these encodings can be superposed to form a single network state. This implies that synchronic structure is not bounded by the number
of relationships that can be encoded, but rather by the number that can be interpreted within a given state, and this is determined by the number of types
and the range of values of each type.

To illustrate the nature of the bound, consider the two relationships,
aaaX–X_{com} and aaX–X_{com}, where 'aaa' is the composition of three relations. The
first relationship cannot be defined synchronically because the elements of the
relation string cannot be differentiated by their type within a given state. The
first relation has the type, (REL→v), but the value of the cf[REL→v] type is the

complex constituent [a,a] and this cannot be interpreted under the inverse of (REL→v). However, the complex constituent could be decomposed diachronically as temporally differentiated tokens. In contrast, all the components of the second relationship can be differentiated by type; the head, X, and the first and second relation are of the types (LEX→v), (REL→v), and cf[RELv], respectively, where the latter type is interpreted under the inverse of (REL→v). To sum up, the type-scheme incorporates an inherent bound on the length of relationships that can be tokened synchronically and this bound is independent of the nature of the computational mechanism that generates complex representational objects.

9.4. Synchronicity—Two, Three, or Four Relationships?

Experimental psychologists have identified a relatively small bound on parallel processing in a range of cognitive tasks. For example, Fisher (1984) has shown that in visual search tasks only a limited number of items can be processed in parallel—the number of parallel channels has a mean of four, with a range of three to five, the exact number being dependent on the individual subject. He suggests that the channels identified and quantified in his model are multipurpose conduits which can be used for comparing visual inputs as in the visual search paradigm, for enumerating items as in subitizing (that is, the ability to enumerate a small number of items in parallel), or for reporting items from iconic memory. However, I want to argue that the limits reflect the bounds on tokening synchronic structure.

To this point, the input/output types have taken constant values, namely, X and 'a', and in this case, the bound on synchronically defined relationships is two corresponding to the relations 'a' and 'aa'. However, the basic types of relation could take a range of values. In particular, both immediately after and immediately before, denoted r and l, respectively, can be defined resulting in the relation set, {r, l}. In this case, the full set of synchronically bounded relations that can be generated is {r, l, rr, ll, lr, rl}. This set of relations implies that a maximum of six relationships can be encoded in parallel. However, not all addresses correspond to unique relationships. It is important that there is a one-to-one correspondence between relations and relationships as the mapping between them needs to be fully invertible. For example, the relations lr and rl correspond to the same ordinal position, that of the head, under the normal configural interpretations of r and l. This means that these two relations must be ruled out in order to maintain the one-to-one correspondence. It follows that the absolute maximum number of relationships that can be encoded relative to a given head is four. However, there is a cost involved in increasing the amount of synchronic structure.

Two relationships can be encoded by assigning the input/output types constant values. Three relationships, on the other hand, require one of the types to be variable. For example, by assigning two values, r and l, to the type cf[a→v] we can generate the symmetrical relation sets {r, rr, lr} and {l, rl, ll}. In this case, the type (REL→v) has a constant value, namely, r or l. Under the standard structural interpretation of the relation values, the relation lr, or (rl), corresponds to the position of the head and so ought to be ruled out. However, in this case, the key property of a one-to-one correspondence between ordinal positions and relationships can be maintained by interpreting the values of the type, *cf*[REL→v], relative to the substring, (X ?), where '?' denotes the position immediately to the right of the head. This maps the relation lr onto the string position immediately to the left of the substring, that is, to the left of the head, and the relation rr onto the position to the right of the substring. This is allowable because the two types taking constant values generate the relation, r (or l), corresponding to the substring, (X ?), which is common to all synchronically defined relationships. To illustrate this, consider the string, (W X Y Z), where X is taken as the head position. This string can be composed as a single vector through the superposition of a set of three relationships, {rX–Y, rrX–Z, lrX–W}. Because *cf* is distributive over superposition, this vector-encoding can be factored as [rX] [Y ⊕ r–Z ⊕ l–W], where ⊕ denotes the superposition operator. This means that the relationships corresponding to the outer string-positions can be defined relative to the substring, XY. Thus, the item Z is at the relationship corresponding to the position immediately to the right of XY, and the item W is at the relationship immediately to the left of XY. Most importantly, this interpretation-mapping preserves the one-to-one correspondence. A symmetrical set of addresses can be defined in the case where the type (REL→v) takes the constant value l.

Finally, four relationships can be encoded by creating relations which re-bind both relation values r and l to the input/output types (REL→v) and *cf*[REL→v]. Keeping only the head constant generates the full set of bounded relations of which two, the pair lr and rl, are eliminated under the criterion of maintaining a one-to-one correspondence between ordinal positions and relationships. In this case, the only element common to all the relationships is the constant type, a head, that is, X. All four relationships are defined relative to this position. In sum, two relationships require no typed variables; three require one typed variable, namely, *cf*[REL→v]. The maximum number of synchronic relationships, four, requires two typed variables, (REL→v) and *cf*[REL→v]. Assuming that there is a cost associated with each level of variable binding then this should be reflected in the extent to which synchronic structure is employed in the generation of complex syntactic objects.

9.5. X-Bar Theory and Synchronic Structure

I want to argue that phrase structure reflects the temporal organization of the mental representations of complex syntactic objects. Put simply, a phrase is a chunk of synchronically defined structure and constituency relations arise from recursively embedding such chunks within each other. Embedded phrases unfold over time, but the interpretable contents of a given phrase are tokened synchronically and the properties of phrase structure reflect this synchronic nature. Constituency relates to the 'packing' or 'unpacking' of complex objects/vectors, whereas X-bar theory describes the structure of the contents of an 'unpacked' vector.

Different versions of X-bar theory have been proposed, but I shall derive the properties proposed in the standard version of the theory (Stowell 1981). The one concept maintained in all version of X-bar theory and preserved within the Minimalist program (Chomsky 1995) is that of 'headedness'. Phrases must be headed by only one head. This property is crucial to the nature of synchronic structure. All relations underlying the order relationships comprising synchronic structure are defined relative to a head, and, moreover, they must be defined relative to the same head. This is because synchronic structures are based on unique input/ output types and the value of the type—head—is held constant within a phrase, ensuring that a total order is defined on its constituents.

As synchronic structure cannot be defined across constituency levels, it is not clear how the hierarchical organization of phrasal levels in X-bar theory can be explained. However, I want to argue that this organization is illusory and derives from the existence of relations such as lr. Above, I have argued that relations of this form are defined relative to a constant relationship, rX, corresponding to the substring $(X \ ?)$ where '?' denotes the position immediately to the right of the head. Thus, the string, $(W \ X \ Y)$, is encoded as $[rX][Y \oplus l{-}W]$, which means that the component, $[rX]$, makes the relationship, $rX{-}Y$, into a quasi-constituent as other elements are configured relative to it resulting in an illusory $(W(XY))$ structure. However, $rX{-}Y$ cannot be isolated as a true constituent and hence cannot be moved.

The only elements that can be moved are those corresponding to individual types such as X and X_{com}, as these are instantiated as differentiated vectors within the network. Order relationships are defined across a number of types and cannot be accessed as individual, coherent vectors, which means that they cannot be copied or re-located within a structure. This explains the peculiar nature of the X' level, a category that is invisible at the interface and for computation (Chomsky 1995: 242). The category does not exist; rather X' is the common component of all the relationships comprising synchronic structure based on, at most, one type variable.

The significance of the $[rX]$ component also provides support for the existence of a directional parameter hypothesized for human languages (Chomsky 1982; Koopman 1984; Travis 1989). The $[rX]$ component characterizes the head-initial languages, such as English, in which the head of a phrase is to the left of its complements. In contrast, head-final languages, such as Navajo, in which the head is to the right of its complements, employ the similarly defined $[lX]$ component. Other languages, such as German, use both components depending on the syntactic category of the phrase.

The use of the relation lr also explains why phrases have only one specifier. For a language like English, the specifier precedes the head and is encoded synchronically using the relation lr. This address is within the bound on synchronic structure but the position preceding it, corresponding to llr, lies beyond it, which means that it cannot be interpreted as a specifier position. On the other hand, a language which makes use of two typed variables, generating four possible relationships, can have up to two specifiers based on the relations l and ll. Chomsky (1995) has suggested that the use of multiple specifiers is an option that some languages may employ for certain constructions. However, the present theoretical approach would strongly imply that such a possibility is rare, due to the increased mental costs of coordinating two typed variables. Evidence for this claim comes from two sources. First, the use of two typed variables rules out any form of directional parameter. Some researchers have argued that languages of this type are more difficult to learn (Berwick 1985). Secondly, such languages may also be more difficult to recognize and generate (Hawkins 1994). The property that all non-head terms within a phrase are X_{com} (XPs) results from two constraints of synchronic structure. First, each component of an order relationship must be of a different type, and second, only Xs and instances of X_{com} are defined as constituent terms. If a constituent term within a phrase is not an X then it must be an X_{com}. This property also explains why only information relating to the head of a phrase is accessible to the phrasal constituent. As all the non-head constituent terms are instances of X_{com} the information relating to them can only be accessed through decomposition. The only terms interpreted within synchronic structure are the components of relationships, including the head. As the relations do not carry any feature information, the only information available within a phrase must relate to the head.

Another obvious consequence of the bound on synchronic structure for the nature of phrase structure is that the maximum number of complements a head can take is two, associated with the relations r and rr. This limit is not a stated property of X-bar theory. However, I would argue that it has the same origins as the bound on the number of specifiers within a phrase. Support for this maximum comes from the observation that there are no verbs that take more than two obligatory internal arguments (Hale and Keyser 1993). Such arguments fill complement positions and only two such positions correspond to interpretable relationships within synchronic structure.

It is important to be clear that synchronically defined order relationships are the only relationships that can be interpreted as grammatical functions within a phrase. A phrase may contain other constituents that have no identifiable syntactic role, as in the case of adjuncts. For this reason we need to distinguish two classes of relationship, phrasal and synchronic. A network that implements composition can generate addresses of arbitrary length relative to a given head and all such relationships are referred to as phrasal. The only constraint that such relationships must satisfy is that they are unique. Each phrasal element must

occupy a unique phrasal relationship. Synchronic relationships are phrasal relationships that can be tokened, or defined, within the bounds on synchronic
structure. The recursion allowable at the X′ level in X-bar theory is the recursive
generation of phrasal relationships. For example, the constituents of a string of
prenominal adjectives are not associated with grammatical functions, but correspond to unique phrasal relationships.[7]

Languages that do not use linear order to differentiate argument positions are
not constrained by the bounds on synchronic structure. This allows a language
like Japanese to use recursion to generate phrasal relationships of arbitrary complexity. In Japanese, predicate–argument relations are indicated by case affixes,
rather than by linear order, and so the bound on synchronic relationships is
irrelevant as there is no requirement for them to be tokened as arguments
(Kuno 1973). For example, the sentence in (7a) has the alternative grammatical
forms in (7b–e).

(7) (a) Marikoga Naokini sono hono watasita.
          'Mariko handed Naoki that book.'
     (b) Naokini Marikoga sono hono watasita.
     (c) Naokini sono hono Marikoga watasita.
     (d) Sono hono Marikoga Naokini watasita.
     (e) Sono hono Naokini Marikoga watasita.

These are all very similar, if not identical, in meaning. Japanese employs case
affixes to signal who did what to whom as shown in (8).

(8) Mariko-ga   Naoki-ni sono hon-o   watasita.
     Mariko-SUBJ Naoki-IO that book-DO handed

Each phrasal element needs to correspond only to a unique relationship—the
case affixes do the rest of the work in determining the predicate–argument relations. The analysis of this class of language has led some linguists to argue that
the X-bar configuration for lexical categories such as verbs has no bound on the
number of iterations of X′ with a sister phrase (Fukui 1986). This is consistent
with the recursive generation of phrasal relationships at the X′ level.

9.6. Dual System of Representation

The main conclusion of the arguments presented in this chapter is that C_{HL}
computes two syntactic representations. One underlies PF and is consistent with
Kayne's (1993) LCA. The other encodes the structural relationships on which

---

[7] In this case, any determiner phrase fronting such a string, as in the phrase *The big . . . red house*,
would be analyzed as a DetP taking an NP as its argument—that is, [The [big . . . red house]$_{NP}$]$_{DetP}$.
This means that the determiner would not function as the specifer of the NP (Abney 1987).

LF is founded and incorporates a natural bound on the complexity of such relationships. The two representations are composed using the same neural network; the first representation is generated from one basic type, lexical elements, while the second representation contains two basic types, lexical elements and relations. Implementing syntactic objects on neural networks results in the PF representation being laid out in time whereas the LF representation also makes use of synchronic structure. One of the key proposals is that the chunks of synchronic structure correspond to phrases consistent with the properties of X-bar theory.

A similar dual system of syntactic representation has been proposed by Pesetsky (1995). He argues that the range of phenomena that a theory of grammar needs to explain can only be accommodated within a dual-representation system. The two forms of representation he proposes are concordant with those proposed here. His cascade-structures are binary trees similar to the diachronic structures proposed for PF. His second form of representation, layered structures, are *n*-ary trees encoding semantically contentful relations equivalent to the synchronic chunks claimed to be necessary for LF. He arrives at his dual system from linguistic evidence—layered syntax provides a good account of XP movement and ellipsis, whilst cascade syntax provides the basis for explaining everything else. I have arrived at a dual system from a very different starting point— how composed syntactic objects might be implemented within the brain, given the characteristics of its neural network architecture. Interestingly, we seem to be converging on the same solution to two very different sets of problems. If the computational nature of the human brain has influenced the nature of the theory of grammar it instantiates then this is only to be expected. However, cognitive science has, in general, not delivered such coherent results.

This chapter started from the approach of the Minimalist program, but the conclusion is clearly not minimalist. If the aim is to generate the simplest conceivable theory of grammar then a single form of syntactic representation is always preferable to a dual form. However, I want to argue that because the language system has two interfaces, two representations are required which are consistent with the different space-time characteristics of the interfaces. The perceptual–articulatory system employs diachronic structure, that is, temporal strings and the corresponding interface, PF, must be consistent with this. The conceptual–intentional system is also partially diachronic but it attempts to maximize the size of synchronically defined units. As a subsystem of the brain it is limited by the bound on synchronic structure as mediated through the corresponding interface, LF. The wider implication of this is that wherever order is encoded on distributed patterns within the brain, the limit on synchronicity will apply. If order is important in encoding meaning, albeit in terms of constituency, then something similar to X-bar theory should characterize the structural properties of the meaningful 'chunks' resulting in something like an X-bar semantics (Jackendoff 1990; Braine 1992).

The dual nature of syntactic objects does not imply that PF and LF are completely unrelated representations. One problem that they can only solve conjointly is the preservation of type–token distinctions within the language system. Within PF, the tokens of individual lexical items are realized through a temporal sequence, each item occupying a unique temporal location. However, LF does not necessarily preserve the same temporal identities. In synchronic structure, all non-head constituents are located relative to their phrasal head with a one-to-one correspondence between constituents and relationships. Heads, by contrast, are not located relative to any space-time framework within LF, although their vector tokens are ordered and occupy unique temporal locations when recovered through full decomposition. The question that requires investigation is whether or not heads of the same type need to be individuated at LF. If the answer is no, this would imply that the conceptual–intentional system also encodes and processes diachronic objects. If heads are differentiated by type and temporal location in LF, then this differentiation must be preserved within the conceptual–intentional system. Equally important for C_{HL} is the question of the relationship of the different temporal positions of the lexical items with PF and LF.

References

ABNEY, S. (1987). *The English Noun Phrase in its Sentential Aspect.* Ph.D. thesis, MIT.

ALEXIADOU, A., and ANAGNOSTOPOULOU, E. (1998). 'Parametrizing AGR: Word Order, V-Movement and EPP-Checking'. *Natural Language and Linguistic Theory*, 16: 491–539.

ARAD, M. (1996). 'A Minimalist View of the Syntax-Lexical Semantics Interface'. *University College of London Working Papers in Linguistics*, 8: 215–42.

ARNOLD, M. (1995). *Case, Periphrastic* do, *and the Loss of Verb Movement in English.* Ph.D. thesis, University of Maryland.

ASHER, N. (1993). *Reference to Abstract Objects in Discourse.* Dordrecht: Kluwer Academic Publishers.

ATTNEAVE, F., and REID, K.W. (1968). 'Voluntary Control of Frame of Reference and Slope Equivalence under Head Rotation'. *Journal of Experimental Psychology*, 78: 153–9.

AU, T.K., DAPRETTO, M., and SONG, Y.K. (1994). 'Input vs. Constraints: Early Word Acquisition in Korean and English'. *Journal of Memory and Language*, 33: 567–82.

BAKER, M. (1996). *The Polysynthesis Parameter.* Oxford: Oxford University Press.

BEHRMANN, M., and TIPPER, S.P. (1999). 'Attention Accesses Multiple Reference Frames: Evidence from Visual Neglect'. *Journal of Experimental Psychology: Human Perception and Performance*, 25(1): 83–101.

BENNETT, D. (1975). *Spatial and Temporal Uses of English Prepositions: An Essay in Stratificational Semantics.* London: Longman.

BERWICK, R.C. (1985). *The Acquisition of Syntactic Knowledge.* Cambridge, Mass.: MIT Press.

BESTEN, H. DEN (1983). 'On the Interaction of Root Transformations and Lexical Deletive Rules'. In W. Abraham (ed.), *On the Formal Syntax of the Westgermania, Papers from the 3rd Groningen Grammar Talks.* Amsterdam and Philadelphia: John Benjamins, 47–121.

BIEDERMAN, I. (1987). 'Recognition by Components: A Theory of Human Image Understanding'. *Psychological Review*, 94(2): 115–47.

—— and GERHARDSTEIN, P.C. (1993). 'Recognizing Depth Rotating Objects: Evidence and Conditions for Three-dimensional Viewpoint Invariance'. *Journal of Experimental Psychology: Human Perception and Performance*, 19: 1162–82.

—— —— (1995). 'Viewpoint-dependent Mechanisms in Visual Object Recognition: Reply to Tarr and Buelthoff (1995)'. *Journal of Experimental Psychology: Human Perception and Performance*, 2(6): 1506–14.

BIERWISCH, M., and LANG, E. (1989). 'Somewhat Longer—Much Deeper—Further and Further'. In M. Bierwisch and E. Lang (eds.), *Dimensional Adjectives: Grammatical Structure and Conceptual Interpretation.* Heidelberg: Springer, 471–514.

BIZZI, E., ACCORNERO, N., CHAPPLE, W., and HOGAN, N. (1984). 'Posture Control and Trajectory Formation during Arm Movement'. *Journal of Neuroscience*, 4: 2738–44.

BLOOM, L., TINKER, E., and MARGULIS, C. (1993). 'The Words Children Learn: Evidence against a Noun Bias in Early Vocabularies', *Cognitive Development*, 8: 431–50.

BLOOM, P., PETERSON, M.A., NADEL, L., and GARRETT, M.F. (eds.) (1996). *Language and Space*. Cambridge, Mass.: MIT Press.

BLOOMFIELD, L. (1933). *Language*. New York: Holt, Reinhard & Winston.

BOECKX, C. (1998). 'Agreement Constraints in Icelandic and Elsewhere'. *Working Papers in Scandinavian Syntax*, 62: 1–35. To be published in *Studia Linguistica* 54 (2000).

BORER, H. (1993). 'The Projection of Arguments'. In E. Benedicto and J. Runner (eds.), *Functional Projections. University of Massachusetts Occasional Papers*, 17. Amherst: University of Massachusetts, 19–47.

BOWERMAN, M. (1994). 'Learning a Semantic System: What Role Do Cognitive Predispositions Play?'. In P. Bloom (ed.), *Language Acquisition: Core Readings*. Cambridge, Mass.: MIT Press, 329–63.

—— (1996). 'Learning How to Structure Space for Language: A Crosslinguistic Perspective'. In Bloom *et al.* (eds.), 385–436.

BRAINE, L.G., PLASTOW, E., and GREENE, S.L. (1987). 'Judgments of Shape Orientation: A Matter of Contrasts'. *Perception and Psychophysics*, 41: 335–44.

BRAINE, M.D.S. (1992). 'What Sort of Innate Structure is Needed to "bootstrap" into Syntax?' *Cognition*, 45: 77–100.

BRANIGAN, P. (1996). Verb-Second and the A-Bar Syntax of Subjects. *Studia Linguistica*, 50: 50–79.

BRANSFORD, J.D., BARCLAY, J.R., and FRANKS, J.J. (1972). 'Sentence Memory: A Constructive versus Interpretive Approach'. *Cognitive Psychology*, 3: 193–209.

BRODY, M. (1995). *Lexico-logical Form. A Radically Minimalist Theory*. Cambridge, Mass.: MIT Press.

—— (1997). 'Perfect Chains'. In Haegeman (ed.), 139–67.

BRUCE, V., and YOUNG, A. (1985). 'Understanding Face Recognition'. Revised version of a paper presented at the Workshop on Functional Models of Face and Person Recognition, Grange over Sands.

BRYANT, D.J., and TVERSKY, B. (1992). 'Assessing Spatial Frameworks with Object and Direction Probes'. *Bulletin of the Psychonomic Society*, 30: 29–32.

—— —— (1999). 'Mental Representations of Spatial Relations from Diagrams and Models'. *Journal of Experimental Psychology: Learning Memory and Cognition*, 25: 137–56.

—— and WRIGHT, W.G. (1999). 'How Body-asymmetries Determine Accessibility in Spatial Frameworks'. *Quarterly Journal of Experimental Psychology*, 52A: 487–508.

—— TVERSKY, B., and FRANKLIN, N. (1992). 'Internal and External Spatial Frameworks for Representing Described Scenes'. *Journal of Memory and Language*, 31: 74–98.

BUB, D., BLACK, S., HAMPSON, E., and KERKESY, A. (1988). 'Semantic Encoding of Pictures and Words: Some Neuropsychological Observations'. *Cognitive Neuropsychology*, 5: 27–66.

BURZIO, L. (1986). *Italian Syntax. A Government-Binding Approach*. Dordrecht: Reidel.

BUTLER, K. (1995). 'Content, Context and Compositionality'. *Mind and Language*, 10: 3–24.

CARDINALETTI, A. (1990). 'Subject/object Asymmetries in German Null-topic Constructions and the Status of SpecCP'. In Mascaró and Nespor (eds.), 75–84.

—— and STARKE, M. (1999). 'The Typology of Structural Deficiency: A Case Study of the Three Classes of Pronouns'. In van Riemsdijk (ed.), 145–233.

CARLSON-RADVANSKY, L.A., and IRWIN, D.E. (1993). 'Frames of Reference in Vision and Language: Where Is Above?' *Cognition,* 46: 223–44.

—— —— (1994). 'Reference Frame Activation During Spatial Term Assignment'. *Journal of Memory and Language,* 33: 646–71.

—— and JIANG, Y. (1998). 'Inhibition Accompanies Reference Frame Selection'. *Psychological Science,* 9: 386–91.

—— and LOGAN, G.D. (1997). 'The Influence of Reference Frame Selection on Spatial Template Construction'. *Journal of Memory and Language,* 37: 411–37.

—— and RADVANSKY, G.A. (1996). 'The Influence of Functional Relations on Spatial Term Selection'. *Psychological Science,* 7: 56–60.

—— and TANG, Z. (in press). 'The Influence of Function on Reference Frame Selection'. *Memory and Cognition.*

—— COVEY, E., and LATTANZI, K. (1999). '"What" Effects on "Where": Functional Influences on Spatial Relations'. *Psychological Science,* 10: 516–21.

CHERTKOW, H., and BUB, D. (1990). 'Semantic Memory Loss in Dementia of Alzheimer's type'. *Brain,* 113: 397–417.

CHOI, S., and BOWERMAN, M. (1992). 'Learning to Express Motion Events in English and Korean: The Influence of Language-specific Lexicalization Patterns'. *Cognition,* 41: 83–121.

CHOMSKY, N. (1957). *Syntactic Structures.* Cambridge, Mass.: MIT Press.

—— (1965). *Aspects of the Theory of Syntax.* Cambridge, Mass.: MIT Press.

—— (1970). 'Remarks on Nominalizations'. In R. Jacobs and P. Rosenbaum (eds.), *Readings in English Transformational Grammar.* Waltham, Mass.: Guinn.

—— (1972). *Studies on Semantics in Generative Grammar.* The Hague: Mouton.

—— (1977). 'On Wh-Movement'. In P. Culicover *et al.* (eds.), *Formal Syntax.* New York: Academic Press, 71–132.

—— (1981). *Lectures on Government and Binding.* Dordrecht: Foris.

—— (1982). *Some Concepts and Consequences of the Theory of Government and Binding.* Cambridge, Mass.: MIT Press.

—— (1986*a*). *Barriers.* Cambridge, Mass.: MIT Press.

—— (1986*b*). *Knowledge of Language.* New York: Praeger.

—— (1995). *The Minimalist Program.* Cambridge, Mass.: MIT Press.

—— (1998). 'Minimalist Inquiries: The Framework'. *MIT Optional Papers in Linguistics,* 15. To appear in R. Martin, D. Michaels, and J. Uriagereka (eds.), *Step by Step: Essays in Honor of Howard Lasnik.* Cambridge, Mass.: MIT Press.

CINQUE, G. (1997). 'Adverbs and Functional Heads. A Cross-linguistic Perspective'. Venice: *Working Papers in Linguistics,* 7: 1–2.

CLARK, E.V. (1971). 'On the Acquisition of the Meaning of *Before* and *After*'. *Journal of Verbal Learning and Behavior,* 10: 266–75.

CLARK, H.H. (1973). 'Space, Time, Semantics, and the Child'. In T. Moore (ed.), *Cognitive Development and the Acquisition of Language.* San Diego: Academic Press.

—— and HAVILAND, S.E. (1974). 'Psychological Processes as Linguistic Explanation'. In D. Cohen (ed.), *Explaining Linguistic Phenomena.* Washington, D.C.: Hemisphere Publishing, 91–124.

CLARK, H.H., and WILKES-GIBBS, D.L. (1986). 'Referring as a Collaborative Process'. *Cognition,* 22: 1–39.

CLEMENTS, G. (1975). 'The Logophoric Pronoun in Ewe: Its Role in Discourse'. *Journal of West African Languages,* 2: 141–77.

COLUNGA, E., and GASSER, M. (1998). 'Linguistic Relativity and Word Acquisition: A Computational Approach'. *Annual Conference of the Cognitive Science Society,* 20: 244–9.

CORBALLIS, M.C., and CULLEN, S. (1986). 'Decisions about the Axes of Disoriented Shapes'. *Memory and Cognition,* 14: 27–38.

—— NAGOURNEY, B.A., SHETZER, L.I., and STEFANATOS, G. (1978). 'Mental Rotation under Head Tilt: Factors Influencing the Location of the Subject Reference Frame'. *Perception and Psychophysics,* 24: 263–73.

COVENTRY, K.R. (1992). *Spatial Prepositions and Functional Relations: The Case for Minimally Specified Lexical Entries.* Unpublished doctoral dissertation. University of Edinburgh.

—— (1998). 'Spatial Prepositions, Functional Relations, and Lexical Specification'. In Olivier and Gapp (eds.), 247–62.

—— CARMICHAEL, R., and GARROD, S.C. (1994). 'Spatial Prepositions, Object-specific Function, and Task Requirements'. *Journal of Semantics,* 11: 289–309.

—— and PRAT-SALA, M. (1998). 'Geometry, Function, and the Comprehension of Over, Under, Above and Below'. In M.A. Gernsbacher and S.J. Derry (eds.), *Proceedings of the Twentieth Annual Conference of the Cognitive Science Society.* Mahwah, N.J.: Lawrence Erlbaum, 261–6.

DAVIS, A. (1996). *Linking and the Hierarchical Lexicon.* Ph.D. thesis, Stanford.

—— and KOENIG, J.-P. (1998). *Linking as Constraints on Word Classes in a Hierarchical Lexicon.* Manuscript, Cycorp, Inc. Austin, Texas, and SUNY at Buffalo.

DEKKER, P. (1997). 'The Values of Variables in Dynamic Semantics'. *Linguistics and Philosophy.*

DELSING, L.-O. (1993). *The Internal Structure of Noun Phrases in the Scandinavian Languages. A Comparative Study.* Ph.D. dissertation, Lund University.

DENIS, M., and COCUDE, M. (1989). 'Scanning Visual Images Generated from Verbal Descriptions'. *European Journal of Cognitive Psychology,* 1: 293–307.

—— —— (1992). 'Structural Properties of Visual Images Constructed from Well- or Poorly-structured Verbal Descriptions'. *Memory and Cognition,* 20: 497–506.

—— GONCALVES, M.-R., and MEMMI, D. (1995). 'Mental Scanning of Visual Images Generated from Verbal Descriptions: Toward a Model of Image Accuracy'. *Neuropsychologia,* 33: 1511–30.

—— and ZIMMER, H.D. (1992). 'Analog Properties of Cognitive Maps Constructed from Verbal Descriptions'. *Psychological Research,* 54: 286–98.

DIAMOND, A. (1990). 'Developmental Time Course in Human Infants and Infant Monkeys, and the Neural Bases of Inhibitory Control in Reaching'. In A. Diamond (ed.), *The Development and Neural Bases of Higher Cognitive Functions.* New York: National Academy of Sciences, 637–76.

DIESING, M., and JELINEK, E. (1993). 'The Syntax and Semantics of Object Shift'. *Working Papers in Scandinavian Syntax,* 51.

DIJK, T.A. van, and KINTSCH, W. (1983). *Strategies of Discourse Comprehension.* New York: Academic Press.

DORR, B. (1993). *Machine Translation: A View from the Lexicon.* Cambridge, Mass.: MIT Press.

—— and VOSS, C. R. (1996). 'A Multi-level Approach to Interlingual MT: Defining the Interface between Representational Languages'. *International Journal of Expert Systems*, 9(1): 15–51.

DRYER, M. S. (1992). 'The Greenbergian Word Order Correlations'. *Language*, 68: 81–138.

EISENKOLB, A., MUSTO, A., SCHILL, K., HERNANDEZ, D., and BRAUER, W. (1998). 'Representational Levels for the Perception of the Courses of Motion'. In Freksa *et al.* (eds.), 129–55.

ELMAN, J. L., BATES, E. A., JOHNSON, M. H., KARMILOFF-SMITH, A., PARISI, D., and PLUNKETT, K. (1996). *Rethinking Innateness: A Connectionist Perspective on Development*. Cambridge, Mass.: MIT Press.

ENGDAHL, E. (1998). 'Integrating Pragmatics into the Grammar'. To appear in Lunella Mereu (ed.), *Boundaries of Morphology and Syntax*. Amsterdam and Philadelphia: John Benjamins.

ERNST, T. (1991). 'A Phrase Structure Theory for Tertiaries'. In S. Rothstein (ed.), *Perspectives on Phrase Structure. Syntax and Semantics*, 25. New York: Academic Press.

ESCHENBACH, C., HABEL, C., KULIK, L., and LESSMOELLMANN, A. (1998). 'Shape Nouns and Shape Concepts: A Geometry for Corner'. In Freksa *et al.*, 177–202.

ESSEGBEY, J. (1994). *The Anaphoric Phenomena of Ewe*. Hovedoppgave, University of Trondheim.

FARAH, M. J. (1988). 'Is Visual Imagery Really Visual? Overlooked Evidence from Neuropsychology'. *Psychological Review*, 95: 307–17.

—— BRUNN, J. L., WONG, A. B., WALLACE, M. A., and CARPENTER, P. A. (1990). 'Frames of Reference for Allocating Attention to Space: Evidence from the Neglect Syndrome'. *Neuropsychologia*, 28: 335–47.

FARKAS, D. (1981). 'Quantifier Scope and Syntactic Islands'. *Papers from the Seventeenth Regional Meeting of the Chicago Linguistic Society*. Chicago Linguistic Society. Chicago: University of Chicago Press, 59–66.

FARRELL, W. S. J. (1979). 'Coding Left and Right'. *Journal of Experimental Psychology: Human Perception and Performance*, 5: 42–51.

FEIST, M. I., and GENTNER, D. (1998). 'On Plates, Bowls, and Dishes: Factors in the Use of English *In* and *On*'. *Annual Conference of the Cognitive Science Society*, 20: 345–9.

FILLMORE, C. J. (1971). *Santa Cruz Lectures on Deixis*. Bloomington, Ind.: Indiana University Linguistics Club.

FINKE, R. A. (1980). 'Levels of Equivalence in Imagery and Perception'. *Psychological Review*, 87: 113–32.

—— and SHEPARD, R. N. (1986). 'Visual Functions of Mental Imagery'. In K. R. Boff, L. Kaufman, and J. P. Thomas (eds.), *Handbook of Perception and Performance*, ii: *Cognitive Processes and Performance*. New York: John Wiley and Sons.

FISHER, D. L. (1984). 'Central Capacity Limits in Consistent Mapping, Visual Search Tasks: Four Channels or More?' *Cognitive Psychology*, 16: 449–84.

FLASH, T., and HOGAN, N. (1985). 'The Coordination of Arm Movements: An Experimentally Confirmed Mathematical Model'. *Journal of Neuroscience*, 5: 1688–703.

FODOR, J. (1983). *Modularity of Mind*. Cambridge, Mass.: MIT Press.

—— and MCLAUGHLIN, B. P. (1990). 'Connectionism and the Problem of Systematicity: Why Smolensky's Solution Doesn't Work'. *Cognition*, 35: 183–204.

FODOR, J., and PYLYSHYN, Z. (1988). 'Connectionism and Cognitive Architecture: A Critical Analysis'. *Cognition*, 28: 3–71.

—— FRANKLIN, N., and TVERSKY, B. (1990). 'Searching Imagined Environments'. *Journal of Experimental Psychology: General*, 119: 63–76.

—— TVERSKY, B., and COON, V. (1992). 'Switching Points of View in Spatial Mental Models Acquired from Text'. *Memory and Cognition*, 20: 507–18.

—— HENKEL, L.A., and ZANGAS, T. (1995). 'Parsing Surrounding Space into Regions'. *Memory and Cognition*, 23: 397–407.

FREKSA, C., HABEL, C., and WENDER, K.F. (eds.) (1998). *Spatial Cognition: An Interdisciplinary Approach to Representing and Processing Spatial Knowledge*. Berlin: Springer Verlag.

FRIEDERICI, A.D., and LEVELT, W.J.M. (1990). 'Spatial Reference in Weightlessness: Perceptual Factors and Mental Representations'. *Perception and Psychophysics*, 47: 253–66.

FUKUI, N. (1986). 'A Theory of Category Projection and its Applications'. Ph.D. thesis, MIT.

GARDNER, H. (1983). *Frames of Mind: The Theory of Multiple Intelligences*. London: Granada Publishing Ltd.

GARFIELD, J.L. (1987). *Modularity in Knowledge Representation and Natural Language Understanding*. Cambridge, Mass.: MIT Press.

GARNHAM, A. (1989). 'A Unified Theory of Meaning of Some Spatial Relational Terms'. *Cognition*, 31: 45–60.

GARROD, S., and ANDERSON, A. (1987). 'Saying What You Mean in Dialogue: A Study in Conceptual and Semantic Co-ordination'. *Cognition*, 27, 181–218.

GASSER, M., and COLUNGA, E. (1997). *Playpen: Toward an Architecture for Modeling the Development of Spatial Cognition*. Technical Report 195, Indiana University Cognitive Science Program, Bloomington, Ind.

—— —— (1998). *Where Do Relations Come From?* Technical Report 221, Indiana University, Cognitive Science Program, Bloomington, Ind.

GELDER, T. VAN (1990). 'Compositionality: A Connectionist Variation on a Classical Theme'. *Cognitive Science*, 14: 355–84.

GENTNER, D. (1975). 'Evidence for the Psychological Reality of Semantic Components: The Verbs of Possession'. In D.A. Norman and D.E. Rumelhart (eds.), *Explorations in Cognition*. San Francisco: Freeman, 211–46.

—— (1982). 'Why Nouns Are Learned before Verbs: Linguistic Relativity versus Natural Partitioning'. In S.A. Kuczaj (ed.), *Language Development*, ii: *Language, Thought, and Culture*. Hillsdale, N.J.: Lawrence Erlbaum, 301–34.

—— and STEVENS, A.L. (1983). *Mental Models*. Hillsdale, N.J.: Lawrence Erlbaum.

—— and RATTERMANN, M.J. (1991). 'Language and the Career of Similarity'. In S.A. Gelman and J.P. Byrnes (eds.), *Perspectives on Language and Thought: Interrelations in Development*. Cambridge: Cambridge University Press, 225–77.

—— RATTERMANN, M.J., MARKMAN, A., and KOTOVSKY, L. (1995). 'Two Forces in the Development of Relational Similarity'. In T.J. Simon and G.S. Halford (eds.), *Developing Cognitive Competence: New Approaches to Process Modeling*. Hillsdale, N.J.: Lawrence Erlbaum, 263–313.

—— and BORODITSKY, L. (in press). 'Individuation, Relativity, and Early Word Meaning'. In M. Bowerman and S. Levinson (eds.), *Language Acquisition and Conceptual Development*. Cambridge: Cambridge University Press.

GERSHKOFF-STOWE, L., and SMITH, L.B. (1997). 'A Curvilinear Trend in Naming Errors as a Function of Early Vocabulary Growth'. *Cognitive Psychology*, **34**: 37–71.

GIBSON, E.J., and WALK, R.D. (1960). 'The "Visual Cliff"'. *Scientific American*, **202**: 64–71.

GLENBERG, A.M., MEYER, M., and LINDEM, K. (1987). 'Mental Models Contribute to Foregrounding During Text Comprehension'. *Journal of Memory and Language*, **26**: 69–83.

GOLDBERG, A. (1995). *Constructions*. Chicago: University of Chicago Press.

GOPNIK, A., and CHOI, S. (1995). 'Names, Relational Words, and Cognitive Development in English and Korean Speakers: Nouns Are Not Always Learned Before Verbs'. In M. Tomasello and W.E. Merriman (eds.), *Beyond Names for Things: Young Children's Acquisition of Verbs*. Hillsdale, N.J.: Lawrence Erlbaum, 63–80.

GRAY, R., and REGAN, D. (1996). 'Accuracy of Reproducing Angles: Is a Right Angle Special?' *Perception*, **25**: 531–42.

GRAY, W.S., RINCK, M., MCNAMARA, T.P., BOWER, G.H., and MORROW, D.G. (1993). 'Mental Models and Narrative Comprehension: Some Qualifications'. *Journal of Memory and Language*, **32**: 141–54.

GREWENDORF, G. (1989). *Ergativity in German*. Dordrecht: Foris.

GRIMSHAW, J., and MESTER, A. (1988). 'Light verbs and θ-marking'. *Linguistic Inquiry*, **19**: 205–32.

GROHMANN, K. (in progress). *Prolific Peripheries: A Radical View from the Left*. Doctoral Dissertation, University of Maryland, College Park. [Planned for December 1999].

GRUBER, J. (1965). *Studies in Lexical Relations*. Ph.D. dissertation, MIT. Reprinted as part of Gruber (1976).

—— (1976). *Lexical Structures in Syntax and Semantics*. Amsterdam: North Holland.

GULLA, J.A. (1996). 'A Proposal for Linking LFG F-structures to a Conceptual Semantics'. *University of Trondheim Working Papers in Linguistics 26*.

HAEGEMAN, L. (1990). 'Non-overt Subjects in English Diaries'. In Mascaró and Nespor (eds.), 167–74.

—— (ed.) (1997). *Elements of Grammar: Handbook in Generative Syntax*. Dordrecht: Kluwer.

HALASZ, F.G., and MORAN, T.P. (1983). 'Mental Models and Problem Solving in Using a Calculator'. In A. Janda (ed.), *CHI'83 Conference on Human Factors in Computing Systems*. New York: ACM, 212–16.

HALE, K.L., and KEYSER, S.J. (1993). 'On Argument Structure and the Lexical Expression of Syntactic Relations'. In K. Hale and S. Keyser (eds.), *The View from Building 20*. Cambridge, Mass.: MIT Press.

HALFORD, G.S., WILSON, W.H., GUO, J., GAYLER, R.W., WILES, J., and STEWART, J.E.M. (1994). 'Connectionist Implications for Processing Capacity Limitations in Analogies'. In K.J. Holyoak and J. Barnden (eds.), *Advances in Connectionist and Neural Computation Theory, Vol. 2: Analogical Connections*. Norwood, N.J.: Ablex, 363–415.

HALFORD, G.S., WILSON, W.H., and PHILLIPS, S. (forthcoming). 'Processing Capacity Defined by Relational Complexity: Implications for Comparative, Developmental, and Cognitive Psychology', *Behavioral and Brain Sciences*.

HAWKINS, J.A. (1994). *A Performance Theory of Order and Constituency*. Cambridge: Cambridge University Press.

HAYWARD, W.G., and TARR, M.J. (1995). 'Spatial Language and Spatial Representation'. *Cognition*, 55: 39–84.

HEIM, I. (1982). *The Semantics of Definite and Indefinite Noun Phrases*. Ph.D. thesis. University of Massachussetts, Amherst.

HELLAN, L. (1988). *Anaphora in Norwegian and the Theory of Grammar*. Dordrecht: Foris.

—— (1991). 'Containment and Connectedness Anaphors'. In J. Koster and E. Reuland (eds.), *Long-distance Anaphora*. Cambridge: Cambridge University Press, 27–48.

—— (1993). 'Minimal Signs'. *University of Trondheim Working Papers in Linguistics*, 16.

—— and DIMITROVA-VULCHANOVA, M. (1995). 'Criteriality and Grammatical Realization'. In P. Coopmans, M. Everaert, and J. Grimshaw (eds.), *Lexical Specification and Insertion*. Amsterdam and Philadelphia: John Benjamins, 165–94.

—— and PLATZACK, C. (1999). 'Pronouns in Scandinavian Languages: An Overview'. In van Riemsdijk (ed.), 123–42.

HERSKOVITS, A. (1986). *Language and Spatial Cognition: An Interdisciplinary Study of the Prepositions of English*. Cambridge: Cambridge University Press.

—— (1998). 'Schematization'. In Olivier and Gapp (eds.), 149–62.

—— (in press). 'Language, Spatial Cognition, and Vision'. In O. Stock (ed.), *Temporal and Spatial Reasoning*. Dordrecht: Kluwer Academic Publishers.

HIGGINBOTHAM, J. (1983). 'Logical Form, Binding and Nominals'. *Linguistic Inquiry*, 14: 395–420.

HINTON, G.E. (1990). 'Special Issue on Connectionist Symbol Processing'. *Artificial Intelligence*, 46, No. 1–2.

—— and PARSONS, L.M. (1988). 'Scene-based and Viewer-centered Representations for Comparing Shapes'. *Cognition*, 30: 1–35.

HINTZMAN, D.L., O'DELL, C.S., and ARNDT, D.R. (1981). 'Orientation in Cognitive Maps'. *Cognitive Psychology*, 13: 149–206.

HOEKSTRA, T., and MULDER, R. (1990). 'Unergatives as Copular Verbs: Locational and Existential Predication'. *The Linguistic Review*, 7: 1–79.

HÖHLE, T. (1988). 'VERUM-Fokus'. *Sprache und Pragmatik*, 5, 1–7. Arbeitsberichte, Germanistisches Institut der Universität Lund.

HOLMBERG, A. (1984). 'On Certain Clitic-like Elements in Swedish'. *Working Papers in Scandinavian Syntax*, 13.

—— (1999). 'Remarks on Holmberg's Generalization'. *Studia Linguistica*, 53: 1–39.

—— and PLATZACK, C. (1995). *The Role of Inflection in Scandinavian Syntax*. New York: Oxford University Press.

—— and U. NIKKANE (to appear). 'Expletives, Subjects and Topics in Finnish'. In P. Svenonius (ed.), *Subjects, Expletives and the EPP*.

HORNSTEIN, N. (1995). *Logical Form: From GB to Minimalism*. Oxford: Blackwell.

—— (1998). 'Movement and Chains'. *Syntax*, 1: 99–127.

HUANG, J.C.T. (1984). 'On the Distribution and Reference of Empty Pronouns'. *Linguistic Inquiry*, 15: 531–74.

HUMMEL, J.E., and BIEDERMAN, I. (1992). 'Dynamic Binding in a Neural Network for Shape Recognition'. *Psychological Review*, **99**: 480–517.

—— and HOLYOAK, K.J. (1997). 'Distributed Representation of Structure: A Theory of Analogical Access and Mapping'. *Psychological Review*, **104**: 427–66.

HUTTENLOCHER, J. (1974). 'The Origins of Language Comprehension'. In R. Solso (ed.), *Theories in Cognitive Psychology*. Potomac, Md.: Lawrence Erlbaum, 154–76.

—— HEDGES, L.V., and DUNCAN, S. (1991). 'Categories and Particulars: Prototype Effects in Estimating Spatial Location'. *Psychological Review*, **98**: 352–76.

JACKENDOFF, R. (1972). *Semantic Interpretation in Generative Grammar*. Cambridge, Mass.: MIT Press.

—— (1977). *X-bar Syntax*. Cambridge, Mass.: MIT Press.

—— (1983). *Semantics and Cognition*. Cambridge, Mass.: MIT Press.

—— (1987*a*). *Consciousness and the Computational Mind*. Cambridge, Mass.: MIT Press.

—— (1987*b*). 'On beyond Zebra: The Relation of Linguistic and Visual Information'. *Cognition*, **26**: 89–114.

—— (1987*c*). 'The Status of Thematic Roles in the Linguistic Theory'. *Linguistic Inquiry* 18: 369–411.

—— (1990). *Semantic Structures*. Cambridge, Mass.: MIT Press.

—— (1991). 'Parts and Boundaries'. *Cognition*, **41**: 9–45.

—— (ed.) (1992). *Languages of the Mind: Essays on Mental Representation*. Cambridge, Mass.: MIT Press.

—— (1996*a*). 'The Architecture of the Linguistic-spatial Interface'. In P. Bloom *et al.* (eds.), 1–30.

—— (1996*b*). 'The Proper Treatment of Measuring Out, Telicity, and Perhaps Even Quantification in English'. *Natural Language and Linguistic Theory*, **14**: 305–54.

—— (1997). *The Architecture of the Language Faculty*. Cambridge, Mass.: MIT Press.

—— and LANDAU, B. (1991). 'Spatial Language and Spatial Cognition'. In D. J. Napoli and J. Kegl (eds.), *Bridges between Psychology and Linguistics: A Swarthmore Festschrift for Lila Gleitman*. Hillsdale, N.J.: Lawrence Erlbaum.

—— —— (1992). 'Spatial Language and Spatial Cognition'. In R. Jackendoff (ed.), *Languages of the Mind*, Cambridge, Mass.: MIT Press.

JARVELLA, R.J., and KLEIN, W. (eds.) (1982). *Speech, Place and Action*. Chichester: Wiley.

JOHNSON, K. (1991). 'Object Positions'. *Natural Language and Linguistics Theory*, **9**: 577–636.

JOHNSON-LAIRD, P.N. (1983). *Mental Models: Towards a Cognitive Science of Language, Inference, and Consciousness*. Cambridge, Mass.: Harvard University Press.

—— and BYRNE, R.M.J. (1991). *Deduction*. Hillsdale, N.J.: Lawrence Erlbaum.

JOHNSTON, J.R., and SLOBIN, D.I. (1979). 'The Development of Locative Expressions in English, Italian, Serbo-Croatian, and Turkish'. *Journal of Child Language*, **6**: 529–45.

JOLICOEUR, P. (1985). 'The Time to Name Disoriented Natural Objects'. *Memory and Cognition*, **13**: 289–303.

—— INGLETON, M., BARTRAM, L., and BOOTH, K.S. (1993). 'Top-bottom and Front-behind Decisions on Rotated Objects'. *Canadian Journal of Experimental Psychology*, **47**: 657–77.

JOSEFSSON, G. (1992). 'Object Shift and Weak Pronominals in Swedish'. *Working Papers in Scandinavian Syntax*, **49**: 59–94.

JOSEFSSON, G., and PLATZACK, C. (1998). 'Short Raising of V and N in Mainland Scandinavian'. *Working Papers in Scandinavian Syntax*, **61**: 23–52.

KAMP, H., and REYLE, U. (1993). *From Discourse to Logic.* Kluwer Academic Publishers: Dordrecht.

KAPPERS, A.M.L., KOENDERINK, J.J., and OUDENAARDEN, G. (1997). 'Large Scale Differences between Haptic and Visual Judgements of Curvature'. *Perception*, **26**: 313–20.

KAYNE, R. (1984). *Connectedness and Binary Branching.* Dordrecht: Foris.

—— (1993). *The Antisymmetry of Syntax.* MS, Graduate Center, City University of New York.

—— (1994). *The Antisymmetry of Syntax.* Cambridge, Mass.: MIT Press.

KERSTEN, A., and BILLMAN, D. (1997). 'Event Category Learning'. *Journal of Experimental Psychology: Learning, Memory and Cognition*, **23**: 638–58.

—— and SMITH, L.B. (submitted). 'Attention to Novel Objects During Verb Learning'.

KIERAS, D.E., and BOVAIR, S. (1984). 'The Role of a Mental Model in Learning to Operate a Device'. *Cognitive Science*, **8**: 255–73.

KITA, S., and ÖZYÜREK, A. (1999). *Semantic Coordination between Speech and Gesture Cross-linguistically: Evidence for the Interface Representation of Spatial Thinking and Speaking.* MS, Max Planck Institute for Psycholinguistics, Nijmegen.

KITAHARA, H. (1997). *Elementary Operations and Optimal Derivations.* Cambridge, Mass.: MIT Press.

KOIZUMI, M. (1993). 'Object Agreement Phrases and the Split VP Hypothesis'. *MIT Working Papers in Linguistics*, **18**: 98–148.

KOOPMAN, H. (1984). *The Syntax of Verbs: From Verb Movement Rules in the Kru Languages to Universal Grammar.* Dordrecht: Foris.

KORNAI, A., and PULLUM, G.K. (1990). 'The X-bar Theory of Phrase Structure'. *Language*, **66**: 24–50.

KOSMEIJER, W. (1993). *Barriers and Licensing.* Ph.D. thesis, University of Groningen.

KOSSLYN, S.M. (1976). 'Can Imagery Be Distinguished from Other Forms of Internal Representation? Evidence from Studies of Information Retrieval Time'. *Memory and Cognition*, **4**: 291–7.

—— (1980). *Image and Mind.* Cambridge, Mass.: Harvard University Press.

—— (1987). 'Seeing and Imagining in the Cerebral Hemispheres: A Computational Approach'. *Psychological Review*, **94**: 148–75.

—— BALL, T.M., and REISER, B.J. (1978). 'Visual Images Preserve Metric Spatial Information: Evidence from Studies of Image Scanning'. *Journal of Experimental Psychology: Human Perception and Performance*, **4**: 47–60.

—— ALPERT, N.M., THOMPSON, W.L., MALJKOVIC, V., WEISE, S.B., CHABRIS, C.F., HAMILTON, S.E., RAUCH, S.L., and BUONANNO, F.S. (1993). 'Visual Mental Imagery Activates Topographically Organized Visual Cortex: Pet Investigations'. *Journal of Cognitive Neuroscience*, **5**: 263–87.

KOTOVSKI, L., and GENTNER, D. (1996). 'Comparison and Categorization in the Development of Relational Similarity'. *Child Development*, **67**: 2797–822.

KUCZAJ, S.A., and MARATSOS, M.P. (1975). 'On the Acquisition of *Front, Back,* and *Side*'. *Child Development*, **46**: 202–358.

KUNO, S. (1973). *The Structure of the Japanese Language.* Cambridge, Mass.: MIT Press.

LAKOFF, G. (1990). 'The Invariance Hypothesis'. *Cognitive Linguistics*, 1(1): 39–74.

LANDAU, B. (1996). 'Multiple Geometric Representations of Objects in Languages and Language Learners'. In P. Bloom *et al.* (eds.), 317–63.

—— and JACKENDOFF, R. (1993). 'What and Where in Spatial Language and Spatial Cognition'. *Behavioral and Brain Sciences*, 16: 217–65.

—— SMITH, L., and JONES, S. (1998). 'Object Shape, Object Function, and Object Name'. *Journal of Memory and Language*, 38: 1–27.

LANGACKER, R. (1986). *Foundations of Cognitive Grammar*, i. Stanford, Calif.: Stanford University Press.

—— (1990). *Concept, Image, and Symbol*. Berlin: Mouton de Gruyter.

LARSON, R. (1988). 'On the Double Object Construction'. *Linguistic Inquiry*, 18: 239–66.

LESSMOELLMANN, A. (1999). 'The World Is Round Again. How Shape Adjectives Get their Meanings'. Manuscript, GRKK, University of Hamburg.

—— (forthcoming). 'Der Ball ist rund: Formadjektive und Objektkonzepte'. In C. Habel and C. V. Stutterheim (eds.), *Raemliche Konzepte und Sprachliche Strukturen*. Tübingen: Niemeyer.

LEVELT, W. J. M. (1982). 'Cognitive Styles in the Use of Spatial Direction Terms'. In Jarvella and Klein (eds.), 251–68.

—— (1984). 'Some Perceptual Limitations on Talking about Space'. In A. J. van Doorn, W. A. van der Grind, and J. J. Koenderink (eds.), *Limits in Perception*. Utrecht: VNU Science Press, 323–58.

LEVINSON, S. (1996). 'Frames of Reference and Molyneux's Questions: Cross-linguistic Evidence'. In Bloom *et al.* (eds.), 109–69.

LEYTON, M. (1988). 'A Process Grammar for Shape'. *Artificial Intelligence*, 34: 213–47.

LIEBER, R., and BAAYEN, H. (1997). 'A Semantic Principle of Auxiliary Selection in Dutch'. *Natural Language and Linguistic Theory*, 15: 789–845.

LIN, E. L., and MURPHY, G. L. (1997). 'Effects of Background Knowledge on Object Categorization and Part Detection'. *Journal of Experimental Psychology: Human Perception and Performance*, 23: 1153–69.

LOGAN, G. D. (1995). 'Linguistic and Conceptual Control of Visual Spatial Attention'. *Cognitive Psychology*, 28: 103–74.

—— and SADLER, D. D. (1996). 'A Computational Analysis of the Apprehension of Spatial Relations'. In Bloom *et al.* (eds.), 493–530.

MCMULLEN, P., and JOLICOEUR, P. (1990). 'The Spatial Frame of Reference in Object Naming and Discrimination of Left-right Reflections'. *Memory and Cognition*, 18: 99–115.

MACNAMARA, J. (1982). *Names for Things: A Study of Human Learning*. Cambridge, Mass.: MIT Press.

MAKI, R. H. (1986). 'Naming and Locating Tops of Rotated Pictures'. *Canadian Journal of Psychology*, 40: 368–87.

—— and BRAINE, L. G. (1985). 'The Role of Verbal Labels in the Judgement of Orientation and Location'. *Perception*, 14: 67–80.

—— and JOHNSON-LAIRD, P. N. (1982). 'The Mental Representation of Spatial Descriptions'. *Memory and Cognition*, 10: 181–7.

—— and MAREK, M. N. (1997). 'Egocentric Spatial Framework Effects from Single and Multiple Points of View'. *Memory and Cognition*, 25: 677–90.

MANI, K., and JOHNSON-LAIRD, P.N. (1982). 'The Mental Representation of Spatial Descriptions'. *Memory and Cognition*, 10: 181–7.

MANNING, C., and SAG, I. (1998). 'Argument Structure, Valence, and Binding'. *Nordic Journal of Linguistics*, 21: 107–44.

MARANTZ, A. (1984). *On the Nature of Grammatical Relations*. Cambridge, Mass.: MIT Press.

MARKMAN, E.M. (1989). *Categorization and Naming in Children: Problems of Induction.* Cambridge, Mass.: MIT Press.

MARR, D. (1982). *Vision: A Computational Investigation into the Human Representation and Processing of Visual Information.* New York: W.H. Freeman and Company.

—— and NISHIHARA, H.K. (1978). 'Representation and Recognition of Three Dimensional Shapes'. *Proceedings of the Royal Society of London, Series B*, 200: 269–94.

MASCARÓ, J., and NESPOR, M. (eds.) (1990). *Grammar in Progress*. Dordrecht: Foris.

MAY, R. (1985). *Logical Form. Its Structure and Derivation*. Cambridge, Mass.: MIT Press.

MENDELSON, E. (1987). *Introduction to Mathematical Logic*. 3rd edn. Monterey, Calif.: Wadsworth & Brooks.

MERRIMAN, W., SCOTT, P., and MARAZITA, J. (1993). 'An Appearance-function Shift in Children's Object Naming'. *Journal of Child Language*, 20: 101–18.

MILLER, G.A. (1979). 'Images and Models, Similes and Metaphors'. In A. Ortony (eds.), *Metaphor and Thought*. Cambridge, Mass.: Cambridge University Press, 202–50.

—— and JOHNSON-LAIRD, P.N. (1976). *Language and Perception*. Cambridge, Mass.: Harvard University Press, 374–410.

MORROW, D.G., and CLARK, H.H. (1988). 'Interpreting Words in Spatial Descriptions'. *Language and Cognitive Processes*, 3: 275–91.

—— BOWER, G.H., and GREENSPAN, S.L. (1989). 'Updating Situation Models during Narrative Comprehension'. *Journal of Memory and Language*, 28: 292–312.

MOVELLAN, J. (1990). 'Contrastive Hebbian Learning in the Continuous Hopfield Model'. In D. Touretzky, J. Elman, T. Sejnowski, and G. Hinton (eds.), *Proceedings of the 1990 Connectionist Models Summer School*. San Mateo, Calif.: Morgan Kaufmann, 10–17.

NAIGLES, L.G., and GELMAN, S. (1995). 'Overextensions in Comprehension and Production Revisited: Preferential-looking in a Study of *Dog, Cat,* and *Cow*'. *Journal of Child Language*, 22: 19–46.

NELSON, K. (1973). 'Some Evidence for the Cognitive Primacy of Categorization and its Functional Basis'. *Merrill-Palmer Quarterly*, 19: 21–39.

NEWMEYER, F. (1998). *Language Form and Language Function*. Cambridge, Mass.: MIT Press.

NIKANNE, U. (1987). *Rajoittunut Mieli* [The Restricted Mind]. Master Thesis, Licentate of Philosophy thesis, University of Helsinki, Department of Finnish.

—— (1990). *Zones and Tiers: A Study of Thematic Structure*. Helsinki: Finnish Literature Society.

—— (1995). 'Action Tier Formation and Argument Linking'. *Studia Linguistica*, 49: 1–31.

—— (1997a). 'Lexical Conceptual Structure and Syntactic Arguments'. SKY, 1997 [The 1998 Yearbook of the Finnish Linguistic Society], 81–118.

—— (1997b). 'On Locative Case Adjuncts in Finnish', *Nordic Journal of Linguistics*, 20: 155–78.

—— (1998). 'The Lexicon and Conceptual Structure'. In: T. Haukioja (ed.) *Papers from the 16th Scandinavian Conference of Linguistics*. Turku, Finland: University of Turku, 305–18.

—— (1999). *From p-positions to axes*. Paper presented at the Twenty First Annual Conference of the Cognitive Science Society in Vancouver, Canada.

O'KEEFE, J. (1990). 'A Computational Theory of the Hippocampal Cognitive Map'. In J. Storm-Mathisen, J. Zimmer, and O. P. Ottersen (eds.), *Progress in Brain Research*, vol. 83. Elsevier Science Associates, 301–12.

OLIVIER, P., and GAPP, K.-P. (eds.) (1998). *Representation and Processing of Spatial Expressions*. Mahwah, N.J.: Lawrence Erlbaum.

PAIVIO, A. (1986). *Mental Representations: A Dual Coding Approach*. New York: Oxford University Press.

PEIRCE, C. S. (1958). *Collected Papers of Charles Sanders Peirce*, vol. iv. C. Hartshorne and P. Weiss (eds.). Cambridge, Mass.: Harvard University Press.

PERRIG, W., and KINTSCH, W. (1985). 'Propositional and Situational Representations of Text'. *Journal of Memory and Language*, 24: 503–18.

PESETSKY, D. (1995). *Zero Syntax*. Cambridge, Mass.: MIT Press.

PETERSON, M. A., NADEL, L., BLOOM, P., and GARRETT, M. F. (1996). 'Space and Language'. In P. Bloom *et al.* (eds.), 553–77.

PETRUSIC, W. (1992). 'Semantic Congruity Effects and Theories of the Comparison Process'. *Journal of Experimental Psychology: Human Perception and Performance*, 18: 962–86.

PINKER, S. (1980). 'Mental Imagery and the Third Dimension'. *Journal of Experimental Psychology: General*, 109: 354–71.

—— (1994). 'How Could a Child Use Verb Syntax to Learn Verb Semantics?' *Lingua*, 92: 377–410.

—— and PRINCE, A. (1988). 'On Language and Connectionism'. *Cognition*, 28: 73–195.

PITZ, A. (1994). *Nominal Signs in German*. Doctoral dissertation, University of Trondheim.

PLATZACK, C. (1998). 'A Visibility Condition for the C-domain'. *Working Papers in Scandinavian Syntax*, 61: 53–99.

—— (1999). 'A Complement-of-N° Account of Restrictive and Non-restrictive Relatives: The Case of Swedish'. In A. Alexiadou, P. Law, A. Meinunger, and C. Wilder (eds.), *The Syntax of Relative Clauses*. Dordrecht: Foris.

—— and ROSENGREN, I. (1998). 'On the Subject of Imperatives: A Minimalist Account of the Imperative Clause'. *The Journal of Comparative Germanic Linguistics*, 1: 177–224.

POLLACK, J. (1990). 'Recursive Distributed Representations'. *Artificial Intelligence*, 46: 77–107.

POLLARD, C., and SAG, I. (1994). *Head Driven Phrase Structure Grammar*. Chicago: University of Chicago Press.

POLLOCK, J.-Y. (1989). 'Verb Movement, UG, and the Structure of IP'. *Linguistic Inquiry*, 20: 365–424.

POSNER, M. I. (1989). *Foundations of Cognitive Science*. Cambridge, Mass.: MIT Press.

PUSTEJOVSKY, J. (1995). *The Generative Lexicon*. Cambridge, Mass.: MIT Press.

QUINN, P. C. (1994). 'The Categorization of *above* and *below* Spatial Relations by Young Infants'. *Child Development*, 65: 58–69.

QUINN, P.C., CUMMINS, M., KASE, J., MARTIN, E., and WEISSMAN, S. (1996). 'Development of Categorical Representations for *above* and *below* Spatial Relations in 3- to 7-month-old Infants'. *Developmental Psychology*, 32: 942–50.

REGAN, D., GRAY, R., and HAMSTRA, S.J. (1996). 'Evidence for a Neural Mechanism that Encodes Angles'. *Vision Research*, 36(2): 323–30.

REGIER, T. (1996). *The Human Semantic Potential: Spatial Language and Constrained Connectionism*. Cambridge, Mass.: MIT Press.

—— and CARLSON-RADVANSKY, L.A. (1999). *Grounding Spatial Language in Perception: An Empirical and Computational Investigation*. MS.

RICHARDS, N. (1998). 'The Principle of Minimal Compliance'. *Linguistic Inquiry*, 29: 599–629.

RIEMSDIJK, H. VAN (1978). *A Case Study in Syntactic Markedness: The Binding Nature of Prepositional Phrases*. Dordrecht: Foris.

—— (ed.) (1999). *Clitics in the Languages of Europe*. Berlin: Mouton de Gruyter.

—— and WILLIAMS, E. (1981). 'NP-structure'. *The Linguistic Review*, 1: 171–217.

RIESER, J.J. (1989). 'Access to Knowledge of Spatial Structure at Novel Points of Observation'. *Journal of Experimental Psychology: Learning, Memory, and Cognition*, 15: 1157–65.

RIZZI, L. (1997). 'The Fine Structure of the Left Periphery'. In Haegeman (ed.), 281–337.

ROCK, I. (1973). *Orientation and Form*. New York: Academic Press.

ROSCH, E., MERVIS, C., GRAY, W., JOHNSON, D., and BOYES-BRAEM, P. (1976). 'Basic Objects in Natural Categories'. *Cognitive Psychology*, 8: 382–439.

ROSENKVIST, H. (1995). *Discourse Identification of Non-canonical Empty Categories: An Inquiry into the Typology of Empty Categories*. MS, University of Lund, Department of Scandinavian Linguistics.

ROSS, J.R. (1968). *Constraints on Variables in Syntax*. Indiana University Linguistics Club Publication.

RYALLS, B., WINSLOW, E., and SMITH, L.B. (in press). 'A Semantic Congruity Effect in Children's Acquisition of *high* and *low*'. *Journal of Memory and Language*.

SAEED, J.I. (1997). *Semantics*. Oxford: Blackwell Publishers.

SAHOO, K., and HELLAN, L. (1998). *Multiple Co-relativization in Oryia*. MS, presented at meeting of SALA, York, and ConSOLE, Bergen.

SÆTHERØ, E., and HELLAN, L. (1996). *Minimal Verbs in Akan*. MS, presented at CALL 20 (Conference on African Languages, Leyden, the Netherlands).

SCHOBER, M. (1993). 'Spatial Perspective-taking in Conversation'. *Cognition*, 47: 1–24.

SEIBERT, A. (1993). 'Intransitive Constructions in German and the Ergative Hypothesis'. *The University of Trondheim Working Papers in Linguistics*, 14.

SELLS, P. (1987). 'Aspects of Logophoricity'. *Linguistic Inquiry*, 18: 445–80.

SHALLICE, T. (1996). 'The Language-to-object Perception Interface'. In P. Bloom *et al.* (eds.), 531–52.

SHASTRI, L., and AJJANAGADDE, V. (1993). 'From Simple Associations so Systematic Reasoning: A Connectionist Representation of Rules, Variables, and Dynamic Bindings Using Temporal Synchrony'. *Behavioral and Brain Sciences*, 16: 417–94.

SHEPARD, R.N. (1984). 'Ecological Constraints on Internal Representations: Resonant Kinematics of Perceiving, Imagining, Thinking, and Dreaming'. *Psychological Review*, 91: 417–47.

—— and COOPER, L.A. (1982). *Mental Images and their Transformations*. Cambridge, Mass.: MIT Press.

—— and HURWITZ, S. (1984). 'Upward Direction, Mental Rotation, and Discrimination of Left and Right Turns in Maps'. *Cognition*, 18: 161–93.

—— and PODGORNY, P. (1978). 'Cognitive Processes that Resemble Perceptual Processes'. In W.K. Estes (ed.), *Handbook of Learning and Cognitive Processes*. Hillsdale, N.J.: Lawrence Erlbaum, 189–237.

SHOLL, M.J. (1987). 'Cognitive Maps as Orienting Schemata'. *Journal of Experimental Psychology: Learning, Memory, and Cognition*, 13: 615–28.

—— and EGETH, H.E. (1981). 'Right-left Confusion in the Adult: A Verbal Labeling Effect'. *Memory and Cognition*, 9: 339–50.

SIGURÐSSON, H. (1988). *Verbal Syntax and Case in Icelandic in a Comparative GB Approach*. Ph.D. thesis, Lund University.

SLACK, J. (1994). 'Getting Structure from Subsymbolic Interactions'. In G. Adriaens and U. Hahn (eds.), *Parallel Models of Natural Language Computation*. New Jersey: Ablex Publishing Co.

SMITH, C.S. (1991). *The Parameter of Aspect*. Dordrecht: Kluwer.

SMITH, L.B. (1989). 'From Global Similarities to Kinds of Similarities: The Construction of Dimensions in Development'. In S. Vosniadou and A. Ortony (eds.), *Similarity and Analogy*. Cambridge: Cambridge University Press, 146–78.

—— (1995). 'Self-organizing Processes in Learning to Learn Words: Development Is Not Induction'. In C. Nelson (ed.), *Basic and Applied Perspectives on Learning, Cognition, and Development*, vol. 28. Mahwah, N.J.: Lawrence Erlbaum, 1–32.

—— COONEY, N.J., and McCORD, C. (1986). 'What Is "High"? Development of Implicit Reference Points for "High" and "Low"'. *Child Development*, 57: 583–602.

SMOLENSKY, P. (1988). 'On the Proper Treatment of Connectionism'. *Brain and Behavioral Sciences*, 11: 1–23.

—— (1990). 'Tensor Product Variable Binding and the Representation of Symbolic Structures in Connectionist Systems'. *Artificial Intelligence*, 46: 159–217.

SNIPPE, H.P., and KOENDERINK, J.J. (1994). 'Discrimination of Geometric Angle in the Fronto-parallel Plane'. *Spatial Vision*, 8(3): 309–28.

SPORNS, O., GALLY, J.A., REEKE, G.N., and EDELMAN, G.M. (1989). 'Reentrant Signaling among Simulated Neuronal Groups Leads to Coherency in their Oscillatory Activity'. *Proceedings of the National Academy of Sciences*, 86: 7265–9.

SRIVASTAV, V. (1991). 'The Syntax and Semantics of Correlatives'. *Natural Language and Linguistic Theory*, 9: 637–86.

STOWELL, T.A. (1981). *Origins of Phrase Structure*. Cambridge, Mass.: MIT dissertation.

SZABOLCSI, A. (1983). 'The Possessor that Ran Away from Home'. *The Linguistic Review*, 3: 89–102.

TALMY, L. (1983). 'How Language Structures Space'. In H.L. Pick and L.P. Acredolo (eds.), *Spatial Orientation: Theory, Research and Application*. New York: Plenum Press, 225–82.

—— (1988). 'Force Dynamics in Language and Thought'. *Cognitive Science*, 12: 49–100.

TARDIF, T. (1996). 'Nouns Are Not Always Learned before Verbs: Evidence from Mandarin Speakers' Early Vocabularies'. *Developmental Psychology*, 33: 492–504.

TAYLOR, H.A., and TVERSKY, B. (1992). 'Spatial Mental Models Derived from Survey and Route Descriptions'. *Journal of Memory and Language*, 31: 261–92.

——— —— (1996). 'Perspective in Spatial Descriptions'. *Journal of Memory and Language*, 35: 371–91.

TESNIÈRE, L. (1959). *Éléments de syntaxe structurale*. Paris: Klincksiek.

TITZER, B., THELEN, E., and SMITH, L.B. (1998). 'The Developmental Dynamics of Learning about Transparency: A New Interpretation of the Object Retrieval Task and the Visual Cliff'. MS.

TOMASELLO, M., AKHTAR, N., DODSON, K., and REKAU, L. (1997). 'Differential Productivity in Young Children's Use of Nouns and Verbs'. *Journal of Child Language*, 24: 373–87.

TRAVIS, L. (1989). 'Parameters of Phrase Structure'. In M.R. Baltin and A.S. Kroch (eds.), *Alternative Conceptions of Phrase Structure*. Chicago: University of Chicago Press.

TURVEY, M.T., and CARELLO, C. (1995). 'Some Dynamical Themes in Perception and Action', in R.F. Port and T. van Gelder (eds.), *Mind as Motion: Explorations in the Dynamics of Cognition*. Cambridge, Mass.: MIT Press, 373–401.

TVERSKY, B. (1989). 'Parts, Partonomies, and Taxonomies'. *Developmental Psychology*, 25: 983–95.

—— (1991). 'Spatial Mental Models'. In G.H. Bower (ed.), *The Psychology of Learning and Motivation: Advances in Research and Theory*, 27: 109–45.

—— and HEMENWAY, K. (1984). 'Objects, Parts, and Categories'. *Journal of Experimental Psychology: General*, 113: 169–93.

—— KIM, J., and COHEN, A. (in press). 'Mental Models of Spatial Relations and Transformations from Language'. In C. Habel and G. Rickheit (eds.), *Mental Models in Discourse Processing and Reasoning*. Amsterdam and Philadelphia: John Benjamins.

ULLMER-EHRICH, V. (1982). 'The Structure of Living Space Descriptions'. In Jarvella and Klein (eds.), 219–49.

UNGERLEIDER, L.G., and MISHKIN, M. (1982). 'Two Cortical Systems'. In D.J. Ingle, M.A. Goodale, and R.J.W. Mansfeld (eds.), *Analysis of Visual Behavior*. Cambridge, Mass.: MIT Press, 549–86.

URIAGEREKA, J. (1998). 'Multiple Spell-out'. To appear in S. Epstein and N. Hornstein (eds.), *Working Minimalism*. Cambridge, Mass.: MIT Press.

VALLDUVÍ, E. (1992). *The Informational Component*. New York: Garland.

VANDELOISE, C. (1991). *Spatial Prepositions: A Case Study from French*. Chicago: University of Chicago Press.

—— (1994). 'Methodology and Analyses of the Preposition'. *Cognitive Linguistics*, 5: 157–84.

VERSPOOR, C. (1997). *Contextually Dependent Lexical Semantics*. Ph.D. thesis, University of Edinburgh.

VULCHANOVA, M.D. (1996). *Verb Semantics, Diathesis and Aspect*. Doctoral dissertation, NTNU, University of Trondheim.

WAGENER-WENDER, M., and WENDER, K.F. (1990). 'Expectations, Mental Representations, and Spatial Inferences'. In A.G. Graesser and G.H. Bower (eds.), *Inferences and Text Comprehension: The Psychology of Learning and Motivation*. San Diego, Calif.: Academic Press, 137–57.

WAXMAN, S.R. (1994). 'The Development of an Appreciation of Specific Linkages between Linguistic and Conceptual Organization'. *Lingua*, **92**: 229–50.

WEERMANN, F. (1989). *The V2 Conspiracy*. Dordrecht: Foris.

WHITEHALL, H. (1964). 'Modification and Shift of Emphasis'. In P.C. Wermuth (ed.), *Modern Essays on Writing and Style*. New York: Holt, Rinehart & Winston.

WILSON, R.A., and KEIL, F.C. (1999). *The MIT Encyclopedia of the Cognitive Sciences*. Cambridge, Mass.: MIT Press.

WUNDERLICH, D. (1991). 'How Do Prepositional Phrases Fit into Compositional Syntax and Semantics?' *Linguistics*, **29**: 591–621.

ZANUTTINI, R. (1997). *Negation and Clausal Structure: A Comparative Study of Romance Languages*. Oxford: Oxford University Press.

ZEE, E. VAN DER (1996). *Spatial Knowledge and Spatial Language: A Theoretical and Empirical Study*. Utrecht: ISOR Publication, Utrecht University, the Netherlands.

—— (1999a). 'A Case Study in Conceptual Semantics: The Conceptual Structure of Dutch Curl Verbs, Fold Verbs and Crumple Verb'. In B. Kokinov (ed.), *Perspectives on Cognitive Science*, iv. Sofia: New Bulgarian University Press, 52–76.

—— (1999b). 'A Special Role for the 45°, 90° and 135° Angles and the Straight Line in Visual Processing?' *Proceedings of the 4th Fachtagung of the Gesellschaft für Kognitionswissenschaft* in Bielefeld, Germany.

—— (1999c). 'A Special Role for the 45°, 90°, 135° Angles and the Straight Line in Visual Memory'. *Proceedings of the 1999 European Cognitive Science Conference*. Siena, Italy.

—— (forthcoming). 'Zigzagging through the Lexicon: The Lexical Structure of Dutch Curvature Verbs'. In C. Lehmann (ed.), *Verbs and Situations: Verb Semantics in Linguistics and Connected Disciplines*.

—— and BERNI, J. (forthcoming). 'Are 45°, 90°, 135° Angles and the Straight Line Special in Visual Processing?' *Perception and Psychophysics*.

—— and ESHUIS, R. (1997). 'Spatial Language and Spatial Cognition: The Categorization of Sides and Regions'. *Proceedings of the Workshop in Spatial Cognition*. Rome, 73–4.

—— —— (2000). 'Directions from Shape: How Spatial Features Determine Reference Axis Categorization'. In E. van der Zee and J. Slack (eds.), *Proceedings of the Workshop on Axes and Vectors in Language and Space*. Lincoln, UK, 95–103.

—— and NIKANNE, U. (forthcoming). 'Curvature Verbs in Dutch and Finnish'.

Notes on Contributors

DAVID J. BRYANT is a human factors consultant specializing in human cognition and decision-making and works at Human Systems Inc., Ontario, Canada.

LAURA A. CARLSON is Associate Professor of Psychology at the University of Notre Dame.

ELIANA COLUNGA is a Ph.D. student in Computer Science and Cognitive Science at Indiana University.

MICHAEL GASSER is Associate Professor of Computer Science, Linguistics, and Cognitive Science at Indiana University.

LARS HELLAN is professor of linguistics at Trondheim University.

MARGARET LANCA is a postdoctoral fellow in clinical neuropsychology at Harvard University Medical School and works at the Massachusetts Health Center in Boston, MA.

URPO NIKANNE is Professor of Finnish in the Department of East European and Oriental Studies at the University of Oslo, Norway.

CHRISTER PLATZACK is Professor in Scandinavian Linguistics at Lund University in Sweden.

JON SLACK is the head of Psychology at the University of Lincolnshire and Humberside. He completed his Ph.D. at Manchester University in 1976 and has held lectureships at the Open University and the University of Kent. His main research interests are in neural network modeling and representational theory.

LINDA B. SMITH is Professor of Psychology and Cognitive Science at Indiana University.

BARBARA TVERSKY is Professor at the Department of Psychology, Stanford University.

EMILE VAN DER ZEE is senior lecturer in Psychology at the department of Psychology at the University of Lincolnshire and Humberside.

Subject Index

Akan 69
anaphora 40, 42, 54, 57–60, 70, 71, 74

binding:
  as connectionist notion 186–9, 204
  as linguistic notion 14–15, 36, 41, 42, 54,
    55, 58, 59, 70–4
  of variables 221, 229

chain 21, 26–30, 38–46
Conceptual Semantics 16, 77, 85, 143–5,
  162
correspondence (of information), *see*
  interface

Discourse Form (DF) 21, 24, 25, 38, 53
  as interface 33, 34
Dutch 10, 143, 144, 154, 155, 158–82

English 1, 5, 9, 10, 22, 31, 44, 45, 47, 48, 62,
  82, 91, 94, 96, 99, 143, 146, 190, 191,
  218, 224, 230, 231
Ewe 69

Figure 85–7, 92, 93, 156, 164
  conceptual constraints on 80–6
  and Ground 77, 85, 86
Finnish 48, 51, 90, 91
French 99
function (or object function) 15, 94–115

German 26, 60, 61, 63, 144, 154, 168, 190,
  230
Gestalt psychology 85
Grammatical Form (GF) 21, 24, 25
  as interface 32, 33, 37–9, 50, 52, 53

headedness 5–7, 10, 11, 225, 226, 228–31, 234
Hindi 71

Icelandic 28
imagery 1, 15, 117–18, 138, 139, 146
  see also spatial relations, physical
    transformation model
indexing:
  conceptual 54–74
  syntactic-structure-to-conceptual-
    structure 82
  track keeping 69–74
Indo-Aryan 71

interface:
  conceptual-structure-to-spatial-
    structure 4, 8–10, 16, 77–139, 155, 167,
    173, 179, 180, 185, 186, 189
  conceptual-structure-to-syntactic-
    structure 4, 8, 10–14, 16, 21–74, 167,
    174, 179, 180
  constituent linking 54–74
  level 21, 22
  multiple interfaces 21–53; conceptual
    arguments for 30–8
  from a connectionist perspective 183–234
  constraints on 1–17
  lexical 16, 79, 143–82
    curvature representation 143–82
  modules 4
  temporal bounds on 17, 215–34
intrinsic computation model, *see* spatial
  relations
Italian 28, 48, 51

Japanese 232

Korean 53, 190–2

Lexical Conceptual Structure (LCS) 82, 153,
  156, 157–9, 167, 169–71, 173, 174, 176–80
Lexical Spatial Structure (LSS) 153–5, 158,
  159, 169, 171, 172
linking rules, *see* interface
Logical Form (LF) 17, 22, 23, 25–7, 30, 34,
  40, 41, 52, 53, 215, 216, 218, 220–8, 233,
  234

Mandarin 191, 192
mapping relations, *see* interface
meaning:
  constructional 60–9
  lexical 56–60, 146
mental lexicon 22, 24, 47, 64, 143–82, 215, 216
mental model (or spatial mental model) 15,
  116, 118, 121, 130, 138, 139
  as conceptual-structure-to-spatial-structure
    interface 94, 112, 115
Minimalist program 14, 17, 21, 23, 26, 27, 30,
  34, 39, 40, 46, 215, 223, 224, 230, 233
modularity:
  Fodor's theory of 4, 79
  representational 3–5, 78–80, 144–7
  see also interface

Name Index